FATE OF THE FLESH

FATE OF THE FLESH

Secularization and Resurrection
in the Seventeenth Century

DANIEL JUAN GIL

Fordham University Press

NEW YORK   2021

Fordham University Press gratefully acknowledges financial assistance and support provided for the publication of this book by Texas Christian University.

Visit us online at www.fordhampress.com.

Library of Congress Cataloging-in-Publication Data available online at https://catalog.loc.gov.

Printed in the United States of America

23 22 21   5 4 3 2 1

First edition

Contents

PREFACE: CHRISTIANITY AS CRITICAL THEORY

When ideas are dead, their ghosts usually walk.

—R. G. COLLINGWOOD

In the background of this book is an understanding of secularization as a complex process of transformation in which key religious ideas and frameworks are not simply cast aside but are repeated in changed forms.[1] I use this framework to trace the fate of the deepest and strangest core of Christianity, namely, its foundational claim that Christ was materially resurrected and that his resurrection is the "first fruits" of a more general process of resurrection of the body and its flesh that will eventually befall all human beings. I argue that in the seventeenth century this idea is placed under more and more pressure from an emerging empirical scientific worldview and a rising Cartesian dualist ontology. In the long run of history, of course, the rise of an empirical scientific worldview paves the way for abandoning the notion of resurrection in favor of the purely metaphorical afterlife of being remembered by the living.[2] But this is not yet in sight in the seventeenth century. Instead, in the seventeenth century the cutting edge of secularization is not in opposition to the notion of resurrection but is coemergent with a historically new form of resurrection belief. At the cutting edge of scientific secularization lies a theory of resurrection in which it is centrally and even exclusively a disembodied soul that lives again (or lives on) after death and where the body is demoted to a mere vehicle for the soul. This view of resurrection reflects and endorses the cardinal ontological distinction upon which early modern empirical science is founded, namely, between a realm of pure matter (including the human body) that is subject to the laws of nature and a realm of pure mind or consciousness or soul that is ruled out of bounds for empirical science. As I shall show, this new (in the seventeenth century) vision of disembodied resurrection as a matter of a soul living on after the death of "its" body makes resurrection safe for science, but it also represents a seismic change to centuries of Christian theology in which the body was central to personhood and therefore central to any hope for an afterlife. As resurrection becomes more and more a matter of the disembodied soul living on after death, the body is demoted to mere flesh and finally abandoned to the grave.

But what is the fate of this abandoned flesh? I argue that seventeenth-century artists, poets, and writers seized upon and strategically deployed the demoted and increasingly outré idea of the resurrection of the body and its flesh. They valued this idea for its deranging power and for its ability to drive a potent dissenting discourse based on a reaffirmation of the body and its role in the life of the social and historical person. Influenced by secularization's focus on the present time, they bend the resurrection of the body and its flesh from an apocalyptic future into the present moment so that they can imagine the resurrection of the body and its flesh to be already underway in the here and now. This starting point enables a theoretical perspective in which a vibrant but strange materiality that transcends human time is understood as the precondition for the social identities and forms of agency that define the social person in historical time even as it also remains deeply alien to all such identities and forms of agency, a fleshly life within the self that both enables and undercuts life as a social person.

I argue that the discursive register in which this notion of the immanent resurrection of the flesh is deployed with the greatest critical payoff is in the seventeenth-century lyric poetry of Donne, Herbert, Vaughan, and Jonson, where it helps define an avant-garde project that combines formal linguistic experimentation with experimentation in the way subjectivity and the world are experienced and conceptualized in light of being flesh in time. Under the pressure of a hypothetical resurrection of the flesh that is already unfolding in the here and now, these poets use poetry, especially formally experimental poetry, to express and take stock of the material strangeness at the heart of the self and therefore to gain a new vision of the person very different from the highly mentalistic and autonomous "buffered self" (to use Charles Taylor's term) increasingly assumed and reinforced within the key discourses of secular modernity including those associated with empirical science.

A key argument I make is that this deployment of the concept of an immanent resurrection of the flesh in seventeenth-century poetry does not represent a return to some presumptively "pure" or even fundamentalist religious commitment unaffected by the advent of science and critical rationality. Rather, I argue that the immanent materialist theory of resurrection and the critical effects it produces are themselves byproducts of secularizing pressures. Thus, the way this poetry uses the (il)logic of the resurrection of the flesh signals not some kind of rearguard resistance to an emerging secular modernity but an alternative way of working through and responding to secularization pressures. This form of oppositional thinking is as much a product of secularization as the dualist thinking that it attacks is. It is for this reason that I term it not "antisecularization" but "countersecularization."

The critical thinking that the notion of the immanent resurrection of the flesh drives anticipates the insights of some of our own contemporary critical theory, most especially that of the so-called new materialists, including Jane Bennett.[3] Indeed, I argue that the project of understanding the historically situated and socialized person as endowed with a body that contains the "signs and seeds" (as Vaughan terms it) of an apocalyptic resurrection of the flesh breaking into time injects Bennett's notion of "vibrant matter" with its own forms of nonsubjective agency into the heart of the human person. At the same time, something like Agamben's "bare life" is obviously also in play in the notion of the vibrant, fleshly life that makes social identities possible and at the same time undermines them.[4] Finally, the critical effects generated by the search for a "resurrection body" within anticipate the specific insights of the critical sociology and phenomenology associated with Pierre Bourdieu and Martin Heidegger. Among these insights is a recognition of the extent and depth of the ways people are conditioned by their social environment in their very bodies and corporeal habita, together with the notion that bringing the conditioned body fully to mind creates an opening for a transformative reconceptualization of selfhood and agency founded on being a body in the world.

Thus, I argue that the early modern poets I examine use the language of resurrection to do "theory work" that is in important ways analogous to the work done by our contemporary critical theorists. But though I am in dialogue with contemporary critical theorists throughout this book, I have tried wherever possible to allow the seventeenth-century discourse of the resurrection of the body and its flesh to function as critical theory in its own right rather than translating it into the vocabulary of modern critical theory. When I describe the resurrection of the flesh as "critical theory" I draw on the understanding developed by the Frankfurt School, namely, a discourse in which knowledge is transformative of the knower (as against positivistic accounts of knowledge as fundamentally not implicating the knower).[5] From this standpoint, psychoanalysis and Marxist analysis are critical theory because their proof, so to speak, is in the praxis that they make possible. Obviously I do not believe that the notion of the resurrection of the flesh is "true," yet as it is deployed by early modern writers it produces indubitable truth effects, namely, a transformative understanding of identity, self, personhood, and how the self in its bodily life is conditioned by yet also capable of transcendence of the social world.

The intuition that under the pressure of the transformative process of secularization religious discourse, including the specifically Christian discourse of the resurrection of the flesh, begins to function as critical theory may be part of the explanation for the "turn to religion" (including the idea of resurrection) in theory work by Giorgio Agamben, Slavoj Žižek, and Jean-Luc Nancy, whose *Noli me tangere: On the Raising of the Body* explores the ways that Christian parables (including that of the resurrection of Christ) have retained their force beyond the sphere of religion.[6] Similarly, in *Saint Paul: The Foundation of Universalism* Alain Badiou recovers and celebrates a Pauline understanding of the resurrection as an "event" that does not affirm the mastery of the subject and therefore does not affirm conventional indices of identity and the modes of politics indexed to them.[7] In a somewhat different register, Eric L. Santner's work on Franz Rosenzweig also suggests the secret paths of secularization that connect explicitly religious discourses (including non-Christian ones) to the discourses of contemporary critical theory.[8] Even in Bennett's writings, some recognition that the ultimate fate of religion is to be transformed into critical theory appears in her decision to close the resolutely secular-sounding *Vibrant Matter* with an updated version of the Nicene Creed: "I will just end with a litany, a kind of Nicene Creed for would-be vital materialists: 'I believe in one matter-energy, the maker of things seen and unseen, [and so forth]'" (122). This conclusion suggests that Bennett's career-spanning project of finding and tracking the implications of vibrant materiality in the world is in some semiacknowledged way animated by an appropriation and transformation of key religious frameworks and structures of thought. In that sense, *Fate of the Flesh* represents an effort to restore to our consciousness the prehistory of seemingly secular theoretical discourses such as Bennett's notion of "vibrant materialism."

By arguing that despite its historical distance and conceptual weirdness, the seventeenth-century discourse of the resurrection of the body and its flesh nevertheless can and should be taken seriously for the critical insights it made possible in seventeenth-century avant-garde poetry, I see myself engaging in a mode of reading championed by Slavoj Žižek when he advocates reinterpreting the world "through the lens of a 'minor' author, text, or conceptual apparatus," where "minor" means "marginalized, disavowed by the hegemonic ideology, or dealing with a 'lower,' less dignified topic."[9] What could be more disavowed by the hegemonic ideology and less dignified today than the "conceptual apparatus" of the ancient Christian hope for the resurrection of the body and its flesh? And yet, what conceptual apparatus could shed a more disrupting light on our deepest assumptions about self, agency, and the world in this increasingly rationalized, digitized, and virtualized age?[10]

The flesh is the hinge of salvation.

—TERTULLIAN, *DE RESURRECTIONE CARNIS* 8.2

Introduction: Secularization and the Resurrection of the Flesh

In this book I argue that in the seventeenth century the ancient hope for the physical resurrection of the body and its flesh began an unexpected second life as a kind of spontaneous, autochthonous "critical theory" and as a driver of literary art. My aim in this introduction is to trace how this development arises within the long intellectual history of ideas about resurrection. When we survey this intellectual history we will find that the first stirrings of secularization and the beginnings of empirical science led to a dematerialization of the ancient hope for the resurrection of the body, so that the person started to be reimagined as essentially a disembodied mind or soul capable of living on after the death of "its" body. This represents a massive change in centuries of Christian theology that had articulated a materialist and monist understanding of the person and had therefore seen resurrection as essentially a matter of the body living again. A fully disembodied account of resurrection is built on—and reinforces—one of the foundations of secular modernity, namely, a canonical dualist distinction between a disenchanted, inanimate, material world, including the human body, that is subject to scientific analysis and technological domination and a world of mind, consciousness, spirit, or soul that is ruled out of bounds of science. Resurrection is made more compatible with an emerging secular modernity by being recast as a matter of a disembodied soul living on separately from its body, while the body itself is reframed as secondary, a mere vehicle for the self, marked by a disenchanted and medicalized materiality that is, at death, abandoned to the grave. I will argue that this disembodied notion of resurrection reflects but also reinforces the intellectual infrastructure of an emerging secular modernity.

But the central claim of this book is that the ancient hope for the resurrection of the body and its flesh is not completely forgotten, either. Rather, in the seventeenth century the view of the body as the substrate of resurrection lives on as an increasingly oppositional, outré idea that can trouble the emerging dualist consensus. This idea becomes especially powerful when, under the pressure of a rising secularization process that foregrounds the present time, it is bent from an imagined apocalyptic future into the here and now so that the body as it exists in time is imagined already to be infused with a "resurrection body," a strange, ineradicable material life that is at odds with the conventional social identity of the historical person. Positing a "resurrection body" within the historical person leads oppositional thinkers in the seventeenth century to develop an awareness of a vital material force within the heart of the self and allows them to reimagine agency, selfhood, and the natural world based on this starting point. By driving people to seek a level of presocialized material life within the socialized identities that define the person in the historical world, the decommissioned notion of the resurrection of the flesh opens a compelling theoretical view of the human person as socialized in the body yet also separated from the social world at the level of the body.[1]

I argue that this oppositional idea drives the highly experimental poetry written by a group of poets in the early seventeenth century—John Donne, George Herbert, Henry Vaughan, and Ben Jonson—and that through their poetry the critical potentials of the idea of the resurrection of the body and its flesh become especially evident. These poets value the notion of the resurrection of the flesh because it provides them with a powerfully oppositional starting point for explorations of self, agency, and language. Under its influence, they turn their poetry into a tool for bringing to light a deranging materiality at the heart of the person. Moreover, they value radical formal experimentation as a way of pushing the language that flows from their pens away from the intentions and calculations of the socially legible persons that they are. Instead, their poetry is characterized by a drive to allow the hypothetical resurrection body itself to become visible and (especially) audible in and through the language games of poetry. Their poetry is also designed to inject this deranging materialism into the lives of their readers, who feel called by the poetry to connect with the bodily life at the core of their own social personhood. Thus, for these poets, the idea of the resurrection of the flesh is valuable for the way it energizes art that is "avant-garde" in the sense that it does not present itself as a representation of the world or as a monumental aesthetic object but as a transpersonal practice that is valued primarily for the effects it creates in readers, including in the communities of readers who assembled themselves around each of these poets. The poetry of Donne and his successors is designed to provoke readers into a new way of life built on a new way of understanding themselves in their bodily life and in their relationship to their historical world, and insofar as this body of poetry joins formal experimentation with a transformative "critical theory" project, it anticipates twentieth-century avant-garde art.[2]

The "theory work" performed by the avant-garde poetry I examine anticipates some strands of contemporary critical theory that address how social identities (including gender, race, sexuality, status, and citizenship) and power (including subjection to sovereign power) are inscribed on the body, for example in work by Alain Badiou, Judith Butler, Pierre Bourdieu, and Giorgio Agamben, whose notion of "bare life" is obviously in play in the notion of the vibrant, fleshly life that makes social identities possible and at the same time undermines them. The thinking performed in the poetry I examine also anticipates critical theory that explores resistance to membership in the social (in work by Jean-Luc Nancy and Roberto Esposito).[3] But the branch of contemporary theory that this seventeenth-century avant-garde poetry anticipates most strongly is the so-called new materialism represented by the work of Bruno Latour, Ian Bogost, Timothy Morton, Graham Harman, and especially Jane Bennett.[4] Bennett's influential book *Vibrant Matter: A Political Ecology of Things* attempts to recover the agency and force of material stuff in the world in the service of cultivating ecological humility. She calls the notion of "vibrant matter" an "onto-story" that conjures a worldview in which stuff, including trash, decaying rodents, plastic gloves, electrical transmission grids, and so forth, are imagined not as passive objects waiting for humans to use them (that is, as a "standing reserve," as Heidegger would call it) but rather as having a kind of agency in their own right with which human agency can cooperate or which it can resist in complex "assemblages" (a term she derives from Deleuze and Guattari).[5] For Bennett, coming to see material things as endowed with an alien agency and vital materiality has the political effect of chastening the self and its fantasies of mastery and domination of the natural world.

The key argument of my book is that under the pressure of secularization in the seventeenth century, the ancient hope for the resurrection of the body and its flesh starts to function as an "onto-story" like Bennett's "vibrant materialism." I argue that this particular onto-story injects some of the qualities of her "vibrant materialism" into the heart of the person him- or herself. Under the pressure of the outré notion of the resurrection of the body and its flesh, in other words, the person comes to be imagined as containing (or simply as being) a material body that pulsates with a strange vibrancy that exceeds the social person's narrow designs and strategies. Thus, the poets I study use the ancient discourse of resurrection of the flesh to locate a recalcitrant materiality and "thing-power" at the heart of persons themselves, and on the basis of this "onto-story" they think about and describe the self and the world in ways that powerfully challenge the emerging notion of the "buffered self" (to use Charles Taylor's term) that stands against the external world as pure subject and as full of agential power.[6] The challenge of their poetry is precisely that, touched and fertilized by the onto-story of the resurrection of the flesh, it has the aesthetic power to induct their seventeenth-century readers and even us today into a stance of critical opposition to the dualist picture of a disenchanted nature, on the one hand, and an autonomous, essentially noncorporeal self that strives for mastery over others and over the natural world, on the other hand. By driving poets to seek a level of unsocialized material life within the socialized identities that define the person in the historical world—and by driving readers of their poetry to do the same— the decommissioned notion of the resurrection of the flesh opens a compelling theoretical view of the human person as socialized in the body yet also separated from sociability and the social world at the level of the body, a view that is worth taking seriously "as theory," so to speak, even today.

The intellectual history of Christian thought about resurrection is long and complex. As major intellectual historians of Christianity, including Caroline Walker Bynum, Fernando Vidal, and N. T. Wright have shown, thought about resurrection is marked by intricate syntheses and discursive reversals, and it has given rise to some of the central philosophical puzzles about agency and identity that have characterized a range of Western philosophical traditions.[7] As we shall see, the earliest roots of Christianity are insistently materialist and monist; from this perspective, the body is the person and the person is the body so that if the person is to live again the body must live again. Late classical and medieval thought about resurrection comes to be marked by a tense fusion of monist-materialist beliefs and a Hellenistic dualism in which a soul is at least to some extent separable from the body and capable of surviving the death of the body. But beginning with the Reformation and intensifying with the advent of empirical science in the seventeenth century, a strong dualist tendency begins to predominate over the monist-materialist elements, and resurrection comes to be seen more and more as an already immortal soul living on separately from the body. But resurrection as something that involves the body "all the way down," as it were, is not simply consigned to the flotsam of an unenlightened premodern past. Instead it persists in various discursive registers in which the body is even endowed with the potential for a new kind of transcendence. I suggest that seventeenth-century poets strategically appropriate precisely this persistent notion of the resurrection of the body and its flesh and use it as a potent lever for critique of an emerging secular order founded on a cardinal dualism. In tracing the intellectual history of ideas about resurrection from classical antiquity to high scholasticism and on to the Reformation and the advent of empirical science, I have two goals. First, I want to show both what a massive transformation of centuries of earlier Christian thought the rise of exclusively dualist and soul-focused resurrection truly was and how this understanding of resurrection is an enabling brick in the intellectual foundation of secular and scientistic modernity. Second, I want to explain how this creates the precondition in which the ancient idea of the resurrection of the body and its flesh could be transformed into a powerful critical lever for oppositional thought and art in the seventeenth century.

Belief that resurrection is centrally about the body living again is built into the foundation of Christianity. For Paul and many of the church fathers, the core of what Christ promises to human beings is that their bodies will be reconstituted and reanimated. Early Christianity disavowed the Greek notion of a detachable soul that lives on after the death of the body. Like the current of Jewish thought from which it sprang, early Christianity assumed the corporeal foundation of identity so that if the person is to live again after death then the body must live again. This antidualist commitment to the body living again after death is what early intellectual opponents of Christianity attacked most vociferously, with Celsus (c. 178, though his words survived only in Origen's refutation) famously calling the Christian hope of fleshly resurrection "the hope of worms" and Porphyry cataloguing the difficulties of reconstituting bodies given what flesh is vulnerable to (noting, among others, the famous problem of cannibalism).[8] But if early Christianity had to confront dualism as an enemy without, it also had to confront dualism as an enemy within, in the form of gnostic heresies that all shared a strong effort to move from materialist monism to body-soul dualism. Such gnostic challenges often included tendentious reinterpretations of the Christian message as being essentially about liberating the soul from the body or, indeed, from all matter recoded as evil.[9]

Christian thought only slowly develops in the direction of positing a soul that is capable of leaving the body behind at death. Augustine's theology synthesizes neo-Platonic notions of an eternal soul and early Christianity's corporeal materialism,[10] but a sustained version of body/soul dualism does not take hold in Christian intellectual history until medieval scholastic accounts that recast resurrection in hylozoic Aristotelian terms. Aquinas posits a soul that is the form of the body, where "form" is understood as the organizing and shaping principle that makes the body what it is, namely, a human body. In a sense, Aquinas's soul is merely the shape of the body, the body insofar as it is a shaped thing and whose shape enables certain functions.[11] Moreover, Aquinas tends to the view that the soul is distinctive and individual only to the extent that it is associated with a particular body and that a truly disembodied soul would be a universally human soul, a view developed by Averroes and ultimately declared heretical by the Catholic Church at the Fifth Lateran Council. Among other things, Aquinas believes that the body is necessary for any concrete knowledge and that without a body the soul could have only abstract knowledge.

When it comes to resurrection, Aquinas does imagine a substantial soul that persists after the death of the body, but this disembodied postmortem existence is a highly imperfect state marked by a yearning for— even a hunger for—reassembly with the body at the general resurrection of bodies at the end of time. The notion of a postmortem soul-life that is temporary is an important driver of the doctrine of purgatory, an idea that already appears with Augustine but is intensified by the Thomist synthesis and eventually becomes a central tenet of Catholic orthodoxy. But the eventual importance of the teaching on purgatory notwithstanding, the early scholastic movement in the direction of a substantial soul that is separable from the body is initially recognized by the Catholic Church as a dangerous innovation, so much so that in 1215 the Fourth Lateran Council reaffirmed the importance of the body in resurrection, decreeing that persons will rise with their own individual bodies which they now "wear" or "bear" ("omnes cum suis propriis resurgent corporibus quae nunc gestant").[12] While this statement certainly contains a dualist metaphor (in the notion that bodies are like clothes), it was, in fact, designed to affirm the ancient and foundational Christian view of the body's centrality in any postmortem life.

Nonetheless, from early Christian concerns with the reassembly of the body (in the face of fire, or cannibalism, or dismemberment), medieval thought moves steadily in the direction of thinking about the conceptually separable soul and its relation to the body. Dante offers the most influential literary version of this nascent dualist account, for while it is true that Dante represents the souls in the afterlife in corporeal terms (that is especially true of the souls in the *Inferno*), he nevertheless imagines that they are already there even though their earthly bodies are still quietly buried on the real historical earth in which the character "Dante" has lost his way.[13] Though Dante's souls still have a yearning for the body, it is nevertheless clear that he has cast his lot with body/soul dualism. This dualism becomes Catholic orthodoxy at the Fifth Lateran Council in 1513, which condemned the Averroeist view that there is only one intellect and Alexander of Aphrodiasias's view that the soul is mortal ("Damnamus et reprobamus omnes assertentes animam intellectivam mortalem esse"). Instead the council claimed that the soul is personal and immortal.[14]

Even as late medieval thought increasingly enshrines a dualist, separable soul, there is nonetheless continuing interest in the importance of the body. Elite and popular religions emphasize a bodily resurrection for different reasons. Elites (including church authorities and theologians) maintained a memory of combating gnostic heresies from the classical era through the Middle Ages, for example in the Albigensian Crusade in the thirteenth century. But at the popular level, there is resistance to a detachable soul because, as Philippe Ariès argues, the lived beliefs and worldviews of people change much more slowly than the trends of intellectuals, and this is especially the case when it comes to death and the possibility of an afterlife. Ariès shows persistent popular pushback throughout the Middle Ages against any theological tendencies that devalue bodily life on earth.[15]

Nonetheless, by the early modern period there is a strong tendency toward body-soul dualism within Catholicism. With the Reformation, Protestant thought undergoes a parallel development in the direction of dualism. Martin Luther (1483–1546) was broadly dualist in his thinking, but his abiding concern with the centrality of the body to human life leads to discomfort with any notion of the soul as capable of activity without a body. As Gergely M. Juhász notes, Luther's discomfort about the soul as capable of acting separately from a body is intensified in the context of his hostility to the notion of purgatory, which leads him to posit "soul sleep," the theory that though the soul is separable from the body and survives the death of the body it is nevertheless not conscious or active without its body.[16] This has the effect of emphasizing the body's life as central to the life of the person. Similarly, Philip Melanchthon (1497–1560) emphasizes the importance of the body, which he saw (at a minimum) as an expression of the soul, and his understanding of emotional phenomena from this perspective leads him to advocate something like embodied anthropology.[17] Thus, although in principle Luther and Melanchthon did accept the separability of the soul and the body, they nonetheless emphasized the resurrection of the body as central to the Christian promise of a future life.

But as the Reformation unfolded, Luther's notion of a soul sleep, and the concomitant emphasis on the importance of the body for any true life, migrated from the mainstream of Reformation thought into the radical and Anabaptist fringe, where it becomes the basis for doubts about any kind of postmortem judgment or punishment until the apocalyptic second coming, a point of view that had an antinomian force in the here and now. Radical antinomianism on the fringes of the Reformation, in turn, led the leaders of the mainstream or magisterial Reformation to attack the soul-sleep concept as dangerous to social order. Thus, motivated by his opposition to Anabaptist radicalism, Huldrych Zwingli (1484–1531) attacked soul sleep as a dangerous heresy just as Andreas Karlstadt (1486–1541) doubled down on dualism by teaching that once the soul has left the body, the soul immediately entered either heaven or hell.

Partly because of the continuing pressure of materialism on the radical fringe of the Reformation, the kind of hard dualism championed by Karlstadt and Zwingli gradually becomes orthodoxy in Reformation circles. Jean Calvin (1509–1564) in his 1534 treatise *Psychopannychia* utterly rejects the notion of soul sleep. Via Calvin, this hard dualism becomes orthodoxy within the mainstream of the Reformation, which comes to imagine a two-step resurrection in which the detachable soul's immediate entry into heaven (or hell) is followed only at the last day by the reanimation of the body and the recombination of body and soul (though what the body would add to a completely separable soul already enjoying the bliss of heaven is unclear).

Calvin and his theological successors within the intellectual tradition of the magisterial Reformation commit themselves to an increasingly thoroughgoing version of body/soul dualism, and this view becomes the default for early modern English Puritan writers such as William Perkins (1558–1602), who assumed that the soul is wholly detachable from the body and that it goes somewhere immediately upon death to wait to be reunited at the end of time with a body that is reduced to the soul's mere receptacle. This position is enshrined in the 1553 English Articles of Religion.[18] In England, this strong dualism also appears increasingly in elite university circles, including the Cambridge Platonists such as Benjamin Whichcote (1609–1683), Ralph Cudworth (1617–1688), and Henry More (1614–1687).

One reason that mind/body dualism becomes predominant in abstract theological debates is that dualism is increasingly aligned with the most rationalizing, secularizing tendencies within early modern culture as a whole and, most especially, with the rise of an empiricist scientific worldview. It may seem surprising to say that dualism is on the side of an emerging secular modernity but in fact strong soul/body dualism becomes a way of affirming the power of science to analyze and make sense of a nonsoul material realm, including the human body increasingly imagined as a physical machine (explicitly so with the rise of Cartesian thought), while preserving a separate realm—the realm of the disembodied soul and its dramas—that is not in conflict with scientific inquiry but simply separate from it.[19] Indeed, the logical endpoint of what emerges in the seventeenth century as strong dualism is eighteenth-century deism committed to the clockwork operations of the natural order and the absolute irreducibility of the soul, and this becomes the very ideology of the Age of Reason.

The dominant trend of an emerging rationalized and scientistic worldview endorsing and emphasizing dualist views of the person notwithstanding, there is evidence of some interesting transitional thinking in which early modern scientists (including hermeticists like Athanasius Kircher)[20] try to square the resurrection of the physical body with the emerging principles of empirical science, for example by positing physical structures such as a "universal sperm" or a "balsam" capable of regenerating a whole person around itself.[21] Justin E. H. Smith argues that even so important a member of the natural philosophy community as Leibniz was troubled by the difficulty of making resurrection of the flesh compatible with the new empirical science, and that Leibniz spent considerable energy trying to identify some physical analogue of soul, a quasi-physical element capable of powering the regeneration of the body after death.[22] He termed this hypothetical protoembryonic power the "stamen" or the "flower of substance," which he imagined as a hard kernel that could survive all change, even fire. Smith argues that Leibniz eventually rejected this view in favor of the idea that what gives a body personal identity and continuity is that it is constantly changing the environment into more of itself via nutrition (*Stoffwechsel* in German). This points forward to a solution in which the essence of the self is posited to be pure information written in DNA, which represents a kind of double dualism: disembodied information for creating a physical mechanism (a body or a brain) that will itself create the disembodied mental life that is the essence of the person.[23]

This dualist understanding of humans sponsors a vision of the self as essentially and categorically different from the body and therefore as inhabiting a sphere separate from the material world, so that it is ideally free from being shaped or defined by its environment. This point of view is eventually codified by Descartes in his 1641 *Meditationes de prima philosophia, in qua Dei existentia et animæ immortalitas demonstrator,* or, in English, *Meditations on First Philosophy in Which the Existence of God and the Immortality of the Soul Are Demonstrated.* Gary Hatfield tracks the ways Descartes redistributes the three Aristotelian souls into disembodied mind on the one hand and mindless automaton-body on the other.[24] George Makari traces how the Aristotelian soul (or souls) became the disembodied mind, eventually casting aside such deviant views as Gassendi's notion that matter itself is imbued with the power to think.[25] And Raymond Martin and John Barresi argue that the ensuing dualist vision of resurrection confirms an emerging individualism by imagining the person as essentially a soul and only accidentally embodied and therefore as highly "buffered" from social life and endowed with a high degree of autonomy and agency separate from social conditioning. Thus, the hard body/soul dualism that first emerges in the magisterial Reformation culminates with a vision of the natural world, including the human body, that is purely mechanistic and that can be studied as a pure mechanism.[26] The exact counterpoint is a mind that seems to be utterly different in kind from the body or matter and that is simply ruled outside of scientific inquiry. For Thomas Nagel, this division between natural matter, including the body (as the proper object of scientific inquiry), and mind or consciousness (as outside of science's purview) is precisely what granted early modern science its power but also laced it with irresolvable antinomies.[27]

My key argument in this book is that in the seventeenth century, as a consolidated and purified version of dualist resurrection belief is assimilated by an emerging secular modernity, the deep materialist-monist currents of resurrectionist thought do not wither away. Instead, they are concentrated to become an internally coherent and self-consciously oppositional discourse founded on a concentrated and transformed experience of the body. Under the pressure of the insistent here-and-now perspective of secularism, the eventual resurrection of the body is bent from an apocalyptic future into the here-and-now, leading to the notion that a future resurrection is also "immanent" or already unfolding in human bodies as they exist here and now, so that it might be possible to see "matter as pregnant with potential for otherness," as Bynum puts it of an earlier generation of theorists of material resurrection. In seventeenth-century England, such a counterdiscourse of material and immanent resurrection appears in several registers—in elite theology and sermons (including Donne's sermons, which I examine in Chapter 1), in protoscientific discourse such as the early modern vitalism explored by Diane Kelsey Mc-Colley[28] and in Paracelsian hermeticism (which I address in Chapters 3 and 4), in treatises on what we would now (in a dualist framework) term mental life (some of which I discuss in Chapters 2 and 4), and in religious self-help and devotional treatises (some of which I examine in Chapter 4).[29] It is not the dominant discourse in any of these registers; it is precisely a dissenting discourse in all of these registers.

But this dissenting discourse of immanent materialist resurrectionism appears most explicitly—comes closest, in other words, to becoming dominant—in the most formally experimental poetry of the seventeenth century, including work by Donne, Herbert, Vaughan, and Jonson. In the context of the emergence of a hard-dualist view of the person associated with a hard-dualist view of resurrection, these poets value the materialist and immanent theory of resurrection for its ability to power art that calls into question a purely mentalistic and highly autonomous selfhood. From this perspective, the life of the body as it exists here and now comes to be valued as the sign or seed of a future, apocalyptic resurrection, an experience in the here and now of the strange "material vibrancy" that will be gloriously present on the hypothetical final day. As such, the theory of immanent materialist resurrection leads to a vision of the self here and now as essentially bound up with a bodily life that cannot be fully mastered.[30] For these poets, a commitment to immanent, materialist resurrection drives a poetic project of seeing the material body as the precondition for any social markers of identity (including gender, race, age, health, and status) but at the same time as something that is strange and resistant to any ultimate human meaning being imposed on it.[31] Under the pressure of this perspective, seventeenth-century poetry becomes an art form that seeks to find and bring to consciousness a deranging materialism inside persons as well as things.

The poets I examine seek an art that will do the work of resurrection not by immortalizing the self and its worldly achievements and identities (as with the poetry of praise, epideictic poetry, the classical ideal) but by allowing the poet and then also the reader to touch the strange material core in the self that subtends all worldly achievements and identities. Looking for the signs and seeds of resurrection within the self and in others (and even in the natural world) leads poets away from what can be named or said in any conventional way within a historical language community. And the challenge of (paradoxically) saying what is resistant to systems of human meaning in history is precisely what accounts for the distinctive formal power of the major poets of the century.

That immanent corporeal resurrectionism drives the most distinctive literary art of the seventeenth century has not been noticed because immanent corporeal resurrectionism has not been identified as a coherent, unified, oppositional discourse that emerges out of early modern secularization as the twin of rationalizing dualism and its privileging of a disembodied soul. The efforts by these poets to find ways to capture the vibrant material force of the human body (and the rest of the natural world) beyond human meaning is part of what drives the verbal and formal experimentation of their best poetry, starting with Donne. I therefore uncover a link between the materialism of the démodé idea of resurrection of the flesh and the insistent formal experimentalism of seventeenth-century poetry. These poets use the language games of poetry to seek the signs and seeds of a material resurrection in the vibrancy of material life as it is experienced here and now. This poetry pushes and twists language in ways designed to distance it from straightforward representation or reference in order to reveal a being or ontology that is at once deeper yet also more elusive than the ontology of objects and persons that are conventionally meaningful within a historical language community. In so doing, this poetry may reveal a truth about language in general, suggesting that even as language brings a world into the human space of meaning it also creates the opportunity to see that there is a remainder, as it were, something ontologically strange in the objects and persons that language names. Thus, making things and persons meaningful by bringing them into language inevitably also creates an awareness of how these things and persons have a primary reality that remains outside of the naming (and taming) power of language. In the poetry I examine, this insight is conveyed through the impulse to use poetry to seek the signs and seeds of a resurrection body that is already straining to break into eternity in its material life in the here and now.

This impulse appears in Donne's drive to capture and present a body in the extreme states created by desire or loss, and in Herbert's wish to make audible the emotions of pain and joy and the "groaning" of what he imagines as the other person inside the conventional self, and in Vaughan's pointing to the self and the natural world as pregnant with a new creation. In their best moments, these poems make audible an alien voice rooted in the body and make visible an alien materiality in the world. Moreover, this poetry is designed to provoke readers into a parallel awareness of themselves and the world as strange matter, for the cultural phenomena of Donne, Herbert, Vaughan, and Jonson all suggest that readers feel that the strangely materialized voice of this poetry gets under their own skins, infects their own voices, and provokes answers and responses in alien voices of their own, including in responsive poetry. Thus, the poetry of Donne and Herbert and their followers is experienced as a call to "conversion" (as Vaughan says explicitly in relation to Herbert), conversion not only or not primarily to Christianity but to a form of life centered on poetry with the strange, extrapersonal voices it unleashes into the world and the materiality it brings to light. This effect is very much bound up with the role of these poems as a kind of "critical theory" that makes possible new conceptions of the self, agency and the world. Rather than seeking to represent the world in a closed, beautiful object, these poems push outward to effect transformation in both the poet and the reader, in how the body is felt and understood within the social self.

This provides a basis for one of the strong claims I make in this book, namely, that seventeenth-century poetry is in a meaningful sense "avant-garde" in a way that is bound up with the transformative "critical theory" project built on seeking the signs and seeds of an immanent resurrection of the body and its flesh. Indeed, I propose "seventeenth-century avant-garde poetry" as a more fitting nomenclature for the still common term "metaphysical poetry." This label was introduced by Samuel Johnson, who understood it as a term of abuse, but its modern use is indebted primarily to T. S. Eliot's famous 1921 essay "The Metaphysical Poets," in which he championed the poetry of Donne and his contemporaries. I address this essay in more detail in the chapter on Donne, but I believe it is telling that Eliot recognizes in these seventeenth-century poems something very similar to the fragmented, formally innovative, and even self-consciously difficult art that Eliot himself engages in.

There have been several prominent efforts to define the notion of avant-garde art as it emerges in the early twentieth century. Among the most important theorists is Renato Poggioli, for whom the essence of avant-garde art is self-conscious opposition or antagonism to social conventions, expressed even at the level of language. For Poggioli, the driver of avant-garde art is a quest for a kind of extreme form of freedom, including in language use. Theodore W. Adorno also argues that formally challenging avant-garde art forms can grant readers an experience of genuine free-dom, an experience of a subjectivity that stands in an undominated and undominating relationship with objects (including words as material manifestations). Influencing both Poggioli and Adorno is the earlier work of Russian formalists such as Roman Jakobson and Victor Shklovsky, who argue that avant-garde poetry has the social utility of renovating the ref-erential power of language, which is always threatening to descend into cliché. From this perspective, when poets push language beyond the lim-its of conventional usage in acts of "defamiliarization" they reinvigorate language, thus preserving the possibility of genuine communication.[32]

But what I see as definitive of seventeenth-century poetry is not a quest for freedom (as Poggioli and Adorno understand avant-garde art) or a desire to renovate language to maintain its power to communicate (as the Russian formalists understand it) but the impulse to use lan-guage in such a way as to allow the self and its voice to appear strange to itself, to use language in such a way as to allow an "other" self that is fundamentally associated with the body and its energies to appear in the poetry. And at the same time, by using poetry to allow this other self to appear, this poetry also interpolates readers to relate to this other strange self in the poet and also in themselves. Rather than offering it-self as a closed representational art object, the poetry I examine offers itself as a form of social praxis founded on a transformative relationship to the material thing that is the self and the way that thing appears in language.

Precisely for these reasons, I argue, Peter Bürger's account of the avant-garde is a powerful model for understanding the art of Donne, Herbert, Vaughan, and Jonson. For Bürger, early twentieth-century avant-garde art is the culmination and also the critique of a historical development in which art is defined as an autonomous domain and is characterized by closed, beautiful, and representational works of art that stand apart from social life and therefore have no implications for social praxis or how people live. Bürger argues that the avant-garde artists both recognize this development and actively turn against it, using violent techniques to wrench art out of its autonomous apartness and return it to social life. Bürger argues that avant-garde art is driven by the impulse to break down the wall between art and everyday life and to see art as an alternative kind of social praxis, an opportunity to engage in new forms of social experi-ence and connection. Thus, for Bürger, avant-gardism challenges the sa-cred apartness of art, forcing art back into the world by creating visceral, sometimes deranging experiences in readers and creating communities around such experiences even (or especially) when they are hostile to traditional canons of beauty and to the traditional artistic function of representation.[33] Bürger writes:

> The avant-garde not only negates the category of individual production but also that of individual *reception.* . . . Given the avant-gardist intention to do away with art as a sphere that is separate from the praxis of life, it is logical to eliminate the antithesis between producer and recipient. . . . Producers and recipients no longer exist. All that remains is the individual who uses poetry as an instrument for living one's life as best one can.
>
> (53)

Thus, for Bürger, avant-garde art is essentially a cultural happening, an experience that breaks down the divide between art and social life insofar as art becomes "an instrument for living one's life."

I address the issue of whether or to what extent there is a category of autonomous art in the seventeenth century in later chapters, especially in the chapter on Herbert, in which I consider Bürger's arguments at length. But the notion that the essence of avant-garde art is to spring past the borders of classical and representational art that can be decoded and contemplated and "to reintegrate art into the praxis of life" (22) is quite applicable to the poetry I consider in this book. I see this poetry as driven by the desire to create a "happening" in the culture that is built on novel experiences of self by the artist and that also provokes answering experiences of self in the auditors or readers. In the grip of the decommissioned idea of the resurrection of the flesh, seventeenth-century poetry is pitted against the conventional social identity and the conventional forms of the self in the poet and the reader alike and against the forms of social bonding and affiliation based on social status and calculated interests. In place of these, seventeenth-century poetry from Donne to Jonson creates shared experiences around the impulse to alienate the self from itself, to grasp the body as suffused with an alien life, to allow a different voice to appear, and the impulse to have that voice elicit alien voices from others is at the heart of the early modern avant-garde project. Something like a recognition of this lies at the heart of Eliot's claim that "Donne looked into a good deal more than the heart. One must look into the cerebral cortex, the nervous system, and the digestive tracts."[34] The "critical theory" power of the decommissioned idea of the resurrection of the flesh is at the heart of poetry that actively seeks to establish itself as "an instrument for living" by reopening the question of how the conventionally social self (with its recognizable social identities) inheres in, captures, and is also unsettled by the life of the flesh beneath. This theoretical project and the effects it generates by means of challenging linguistic and poetic experiments is what is at the heart of my claim that the poetry of Donne, Herbert, Vaughan, and Jonson should be understood as "avant-garde."

I want to end this introduction by situating the development I have described here within a theoretically informed understanding of secularization as a broad process. Recent years have seen an explosion of interdisciplinary work on secularity and modernity.[35] By and large this work has moved in the direction of complicating what Charles Taylor calls a "subtraction" model, which describes the rise of a secular, modern world as the result of a simple reduction of religion in both personal and public life. In its place, theorists have developed understandings of secularization as a process of transformation in which there are continuities between religious structures of thought and key institutions and assumptions of secularity. Thus, Taylor and others, including Marcel Gauchet, argue that the intellectual construction of a "disenchanted" natural world, purged of occult forces, that can, therefore, be grasped in terms of abstract laws of nature is indebted to a systematic Protestant program of iconoclasm and suspicion about any claims to the sacred being immanent in creation.[36]

More generally, as prominent historians of science like Stephen Gaukroger and prominent intellectual historians of Christianity like Hans Küng have argued, all the major early modern scientists (including Pascal, Copernicus, Kepler, Galileo, Leibniz, Newton, and Boyle) were profoundly indebted to a theistic framework for some of their major methodological and substantive breakthroughs.[37] In politics, the Reformation's reactivation of Augustine's distinction between the City of God and the City of Man paved the way to a religion/politics divide and to rational, bureaucratic approaches to managing society, something evident, for example, in Calvin's own concern to create social welfare agencies in Geneva.[38] Moreover, seeing humans made in the image of God laid the groundwork for the discovery (or invention) of individual rights that even sovereign political orders cannot infringe upon. And perhaps most obviously, the Protestant emphasis on faith, individual scripture reading, and the priesthood of all believers was a powerful incitement to new, deeper experiences of "interiority," individualism, individual freedom, and the emphasis on individual conscience in moral life.

But if secularization is marked by important continuities with its supposed religious other, it is obviously also marked by profound discontinuities, as emphasized by theorists (from Max Weber to Talal Asad) who highlight the disorienting effects of disenchantment and rationalization and the new forms of political and cultural control it brings. In fact, secularization is a dialectical process in which contradictions and tensions within religious systems of meaning give rise to new, distinctively secular formations. As such, secular formations sometimes echo or repeat (in a transformed form) the religious structures of meaning from which they sprang. But what I want to highlight is that, as with any dialectical process, the back and forth between thesis and antithesis is not always smooth but sometimes produces glitches or hang-ups, and these glitches or hang-ups can sometimes be valuable for the thinking they make possible.[39]

It is just such a dialectic between religion and an emerging secularism giving rise to counterdialectical glitches that I see playing out in the history of ideas about resurrection. In articulating my project this way, I am echoing the pattern that emerges in Jane Bennett's book, *Unthinking Faith and Enlightenment*. Bennett posits an era of "Robust Faith" that brings with it a view of nature as saturated with God's purposes and meaning. But she argues that the polyvalence and ambiguity of the natural world gradually leads to self-critique of this perspective, so that where once people had been happily absorbed in a meaning-saturated natural world they eventually come to experience a theoretical detachment and distance from it, a stance that she identifies as the basis for Enlightenment rationalism and ultimately the impulse toward technological mastery of the natural world. Thus, for Bennett, the rationalistic Enlightenment is rooted in the way the "Robust Faith" perspective turns critical of itself in a properly dialectical fashion.[40] Bennett's discussion suggests a view of secularization as a dialectic in which "robust faith" and "Enlightenment" enter into a mutually transformative encounter between different ways of structuring thought, so that the persistence of an originally faith-based view (what she terms "natural holism") within a regime of modern "Enlightenment" (marked by the impulse toward technological domination) is the inevitable result of a dialectical development in which the original terms of the dialectic ("robust faith" and its spontaneous autocritique) are preserved in a sublated form (as "natural holism" and the will to technological mastery).

But in Bennett's account, the dialectic between robust faith and Enlightenment also creates a kind of glitch that generates what she sees as a radically critical discourse. For her, the dialectic between a faith-based view of the natural world and the Enlightenment view of nature as subject to human power gives rise to the particular, radically oppositional discourse she terms "fractious holism" (to differentiate it from the unproblematic holism she associates with a successfully secularized faith). Fractious holism represents an awareness of nature not as mystically holistic (or "enchanted") or as inert matter available for human use but as something essentially recalcitrant and resistant to human purposes. Bennett values this "fractious holism" precisely because it produces a vision of nature as essentially resistant to people and their concerns and as fracturing or interrupting human purposes, a view that anticipates the notion of "vibrant materialism" she subsequently developed.

Similarly, in looking at the fate of ideas about resurrection, we can see a double process in which some strains of resurrectionist thinking—namely, the most dualist strains—are preserved and elevated (or "sublated," to use the Hegelian term) into core institutions and discourses of secular modernity, leaving behind an increasingly outré materialist resurrection in intensified form. Moreover, this outré idea is not only left behind but also transformed by being bent back into secular time to become critical theory, a powerful tool for critique and an aid for imagining other paths for modernity than the dominant, dualist form of secularization. As such, I do not see the commitment of the poets I examine to the resurrection of the body as a recalcitrant religious fundamentalism or fideism that simply refuses an emergent secular modernity. Indeed, Olivier Roy powerfully demonstrates that fideistic fundamentalism is utterly bound up with and even an expression of a relatively recent form of neoliberal globalization, and, as such, it was unavailable in the early modern world.[41]

I therefore term this oppositional discourse not "antisecularization" (or "fundamentalism") but "countersecularization," since it does not reject a rising secularization so much as it accompanies it and seeks to transform it from within.[42] Indeed, the ultimate claim of the book is that by looking at the fate of ideas about resurrection in their dualist and immanent materialist forms we can see that early modern culture oscillates between a dominant secularization impulse (built, in part, around dualist discourses of the soul and of the soul's persistence after the death of the body) and an internal critique spawned by the dialectical process itself, a form of countersecularization built on an immanent materialist notion of resurrection that is identified as outré within mainstream seventeenth-century thought and for that very reason invested with the power to call into question some of the key institutions of an emerging secular modernity, including the forms of subjectivity, identity, and agency it assumes and privileges. "Countersecularization" seeks to capture the way these poets do not pit some putative fundamentalism against an emerging secular modernity but rather take up dialectical transformations within resurrection discourse itself as a lever for critiquing key elements of an emerging secular modernity.

But do these poets believe in an immanent materialist resurrection, or do they merely deploy this idea tactically in order to generate formally and thematically interesting poems? And do we, as readers, have to believe it in order to engage in the thought this poetry makes possible? In some ways, the question of belief is a red herring. The discourse of immanent materialist resurrection that the poets I examine deploy can and should be valued for the thinking it makes possible. I see the discourse of materialist-immanent resurrection in seventeenth-century poetry as similar to Simon During's account of William Thomas Beckford's transgressive, aesthetic atheist Catholicism as "a true untruth around which a practice of life can form."[43] This notion of a "true untruth" is like Bennet's claim that vibrant materialism is an "onto-story." Both are in some obvious way connected to the special status of imaginative literature, including, in Piero Boitani's account, Shakespeare's plays, when he suggests that only the suspension of disbelief demanded by a play allows us to "believe in resurrection of the dead, the mystery and miracle preached by Christianity."[44] Indeed, the kind of relationship to religious beliefs that literature makes possible for Boitani characterizes Wittgenstein's understanding of religious claims in general, as he argues that religious claims cannot be untrue in the way that scientific claims can be untrue.[45]

And it is precisely as a "true fiction" that resurrection persists even in our apparently terminally disenchanted world today. Indeed, the fantasies of self that we live by today can almost be said to be structured by the dualist vision of a purely mentalistic afterlife. Today, the way people think about the nature of the self is often marked by the assumption that the body is contingent and that the essence of the self lies in a disembodied mind. Moreover, in view of the genetics and cybernetics revolutions, this disembodied understanding of the self often morphs into imagining that the essence of the self is information that could, in principle, be coded or uploaded onto other biological or nonbiological systems and in that way achieve a kind of cybernetic immortality.[46] Bernard E. Harcourt connects the "digital self" with the political theology of the "king's two bodies." He writes that the "liberal democratic citizen" creates the "now permanent digital self, which we are etching into the virtual cloud with every click and tap, and our mortal analog selves seem by contrast to be fading like the color on a polaroid instant photo."[47]

But instead of being rooted in the political theology of "the king's two bodies," are such ideas not more likely rooted in the persistence of a transformed but still recognizable, fully dualist notion of the Resurrection? That is suggested by Sheila Briggs, who argues that in contemporary modernity, unacknowledged dualist resurrectionist assumptions create a situation in which the discursive body has so devoured the fleshly body that the sensuality of the body is endlessly invoked only to be embalmed in a digital world.[48] These phenomena are symptoms of the victory of the most dualist version of resurrection thought as a historical driver of secular modernity and, moreover, as continuing to drive the core ways many people have of understanding themselves as persons and agents in the world and in time.

But if dualist resurrection continues secretly to structure our contemporary culture, what of the counterdiscourse of immanent materialist resurrection that I uncover in this book? Has it disappeared altogether? My methodological approach of framing the immanent materialist variant of resurrection belief as critical theory makes it possible to see how bodily resurrection is still with us today even in the redoubts of the culture seemingly most thoroughly stripped of religion. For on reflection it does seem that the undead or postdead body is everywhere in our culture today, especially in the realms of art and entertainment in the form of characters coming back to life and zombie bodies with a strange, ineradicable life, from the films of George Romero to *Game of Thrones*. Seeing all of this as the ghostly afterglow of centuries of "official" theological engagement with the bizarre and even deranging idea of resurrection forces us to reevaluate what we thought we knew about secular modernity and the place (or nonplace) of religious ideas—including the idea of resurrection—within it. Given our secular worldview, how are we to understand this continuing fascination with the body as able to survive death? I think it is to be understood as a culture-wide protest to the increasingly hard dualism that sees the essence of the person as information that can exist separate from any bodily life, as it does in the virtual world.

The presence of a complex of ideas and thoughts related to the theology of resurrection in the world of art and entertainment today reflects material resurrection's curious contemporary status as theory. It is not an explicit object of belief (at least for many people), but it is an idea that engages our interest, an idea that we use to think about the world we inhabit, the kinds of selves we are, what future we can expect. In the age of ecological disaster and denationalized bodies of refugees traversing the globe, the resurrection of the flesh provides pop culture with an especially engaging way of imaginatively grasping and thinking through the world. Zombie culture emphasizes the centrality of the body, the importance of bodily life together, and the way the body subtends all identity even while showing the strangeness and ultimate unmasterability of the body. Here the body again reminds us of the contingency of all sense of self and of all human institutions. And when we find ourselves engaged in this kind of thinking, we are fundamentally engaged in a project of early modern countersecularization.

Strange and even embarrassing as the belief in the resurrection of the flesh may seem to modern, scientifically minded readers, it represents a complex set of tools for thinking about the body, the material world, the social life of the person, and the limits of language. It is precisely because of its leverage as a theoretical complex that it forms the basis for the countersecularization I chart in this book and flowers again in contemporary zombie culture. Immanent corporeal resurrectionism leads to a quest not for identity. Instead it leads to a quest to see through all identities and meanings to something deeply strange inside the self, other persons, and even the whole material world. In that sense it cuts against the basic, most fundamental assumption of modernity—the bifurcation of the world into, on the one hand, a disenchanted realm of mechanical matter that is subject to the knowledge procedures of empirical science and, on the other hand, a magical realm of totemic consciousness.

The five chapters that follow are each organized around a major figure. Each chapter reconstructs a particular set of intellectual commitments with respect to the issue of resurrection and then traces how those commitments energize and play out in the poet's distinctive art; the Epilogue examines the afterlife of the oppositional discourse of immanent materialist resurrection in contemporary zombie culture.

In Chapter 1 I argue that when we look at Donne from the vantage of the history of secularization, we must understand him as playing a double game, advancing the dominant path of secularization by endorsing body/soul dualism (including in his thoughts about resurrection) while simultaneously resisting this dualism by emphasizing the centrality of the body to any experience of personhood. To bring this project into focus I start with the important early deist work by Donne's friend Edward Herbert (brother of the poet who is the focus of the next chapter). Edward Herbert is often seen as the father of deism, and in his magnum opus *De veritate* he articulates a reasonable, rationalized version of Christianity founded on dualist assumptions. As I have suggested, the dominant path of secularization is built on foregrounding dualist tendencies within Christianity, thereby creating a division between a natural world (including the human body), which is divested of supernatural or transcendental elements and can therefore be studied by means of the new empirical sciences, and a highly buffered, highly autonomous inner life that becomes the scene of a privatized experience of God. But whereas Edward Herbert fits perfectly within this rationalizing movement toward dualism, Donne illustrates the tension between this form of secularization and a countersecularization built on embracing the "rump" elements of Christianity, including its materialism. Thus, on the one hand, in his sermons and prose writings Donne embraces the dominant path of secularization, acknowledging the explanatory (if also disillusioning) power of science and foregrounding a strong, highly buffered religious subjectivity. This secularizing trend pushes toward a reasonable and moderated form of Christianity in which dualism, including in thinking about resurrection, comes to seem increasingly like "common sense." On the other hand, however, in all the genres he works in, Donne undermines this form of secularization by returning again and again to the body as irreducible to the self but also as alien to any conventionally socialized sense of agency or identity.

I examine Donne's sermons for evidence of the interplay of secularizing and countersecularizing tendencies. For example, in the sermon over King James's dead body and in his famous sermon "Death's Duel," Donne uses the decaying body as an object of contemplation to feel the self and its conventional social coordinates and identities scrambled and to touch a strangely vibrant material core within the self. Similarly, in the *Devotions upon Emergent Occasions* Donne presents his own sick, feverish body as something akin to a Baroque crucifix, and as he contemplates himself in light of his body he engages in a theoretical project of deranging the self and its conventional coordinates within the social and historical world. I argue that this particular use of the body is also what energizes Donne's formally experimental erotic verse. Donne's erotic poems suggest an understanding of sexuality in which interruption, deferral, and blockage are valued as a way of intensifying and increasing the experience of being a body with a life of its own separate from the conscious and reasoning life of the soul. I argue that in his poetry Donne uses techniques of formal estranging to investigate forms of subjectivity, embodiment, and social relationship resolutely conditioned by a hypothetical future in which the body will live again. The formal experimentalism generated by Donne's commitment to resurrection is precisely what T. S. Eliot recognized as modernism *avant la lettre*, and I argue that Donne's writings should, in fact, be termed not "metaphysical" but "avant-garde."

In Chapter 2 I argue that George Herbert adopts and expands Donne's project of treating the body in the light of an eventual resurrection as a way of deranging any conventional sense of self or identity. For Herbert this project is essentially bound up with his avant-garde project of using language in ways that push against the limits of communication within a historical language community. Herbert is interested in the hypothesis that beneath the ambitions, emotions, and personal history of his socially conditioned self there is another self that inheres in the body and that is in some sense "truer" than his social self. Herbert thus uses his poetry to seek a self (and a voice) different from the highly acculturated social person "George Herbert." For Herbert, formally experimental poetry is a way of articulating the voice of this other self. I track the trope of the "body speaking" (for example in snapped sinews, broken bones, and onomatopoetic "groans"), and I argue that Herbert tries to drive his poetry to the point where his "own" voice is drowned out by a voice associated with the body. By seeking to hear his body, Herbert is seeking the seed of a future resurrection body. As against aiming to "represent" himself Herbert sees poetry as a way of touching the self that cannot be represented because it is alien to the social categories of personhood. Moreover, for Herbert's readers, the sound of his poetry has typically had an emotional impact well in excess of the religious and ethical content of his poems, often effecting spectacular "conversions" to a life of Christianity but also to a life of poetry, as evidenced by his many imitators. By moving from a vision of poetry as representation or as a beautiful object to a vision of poetry as a form of social praxis, a way of creating new selves and communities, I see Herbert as anticipating the avant-garde art of the early twentieth century as theorized by Peter Bürger. I conclude the chapter by looking at what Herbert's poetic theory of identity implies about an understanding of the emotions, which are a key focus of many of Herbert's poems. I argue that Herbert's poems implicitly (and sometimes explicitly) cut through the debate between a mechanistic humoral understanding of emotions and an emerging cognitivist judgment-based understanding of the emotions. Instead his poems posit the importance of "mood" as a presubjective way of being in the world through which the historical world and the persons in it are disclosed. I see this interest in "mood" as anticipating key elements of twentieth-century phenomenological psychology. Thus Herbert's search for the "resurrection body" within himself leads him to anticipate two of the most important intellectual developments of the twentieth century: avant-gardism and phenomenology (including twenty-first-century affect theory).

In Chapter 3 I turn to one of the most important of the many poets who explicitly claimed to be "converted" by Herbert (both religiously and poetically), Henry Vaughan. Vaughan explicitly asserts an understanding of resurrection as essentially and fundamentally about the body, and he understands resurrection to be "immanent" in the sense that signs of resurrection are breaking into the here and now. This theory leads Vaughan to use his poetry to search within himself for the material reality of a resurrection body that displaces him from his conventional sociological coordinates. Vaughan's goal in his poetry, in other words, is to uncover "Traces, and sounds of a strange kind," as he puts it in "Vanity of Spirit." Bypassing any soul/body distinction, Vaughan's searching analysis of himself splits his bodily life into two: on the one hand, a socialized and historicized life and, on the other hand, a life that, in its material strangeness, is alien to his time and place and therefore the substrate of resurrection. At the same time, Vaughan is also interested in investigating the material stuff of the natural world separate from the meanings that human language imposes upon it. By mystical attention to material stuff, including feathers, rocks, rainbows, and trees, Vaughan believes he can discover a perspective that transcends historical time. In that sense, Vaughan anticipates the Romantic poets, and my argument shows how that poetic perspective is rooted in a distinctively early modern transformation of the Christian idea of resurrection. I argue that in its approach to the sublime otherness of nature, Vaughan's poetry is designed to detach readers from the mindset of being inside a language community, a mindset defined by the assumption that everything has (human) meaning, and I contrast this poetic project to the accounts of poetry offered by Roman Jakobson and Susan Stewart. By becoming aware of the way a language imposes historically contingent meanings on the world of things (including human bodies), Vaughan's poetry is designed to produce a mindset oriented toward seeing the seeds or signs of an immanent physical resurrection in the stuff of the self and in the stuff of the world.

In Chapter 4 I articulate more explicitly than in the previous chapter the way resurrection beliefs in Vaughan's poetry function as "critical theory" about selfhood, identity, and the social world. To do so I look at some of Vaughan's devotional and religious "self-help" literature and at Vaughan's translation and expansion of a hermetic medical treatise. (Vaughan worked as a physician for much of his life and thus had an interest in medical literature.) Vaughan's immanent corporeal resurrectionist commitment to finding the "seeds" of resurrection in the socialized body is transposed in his devotional and medical writings into positing an essential core of bodily life—the radical balsam—that seeks eternal life but that is sickened when it is penetrated and rewired by the social and historical world. The goal of Vaughan's devotional writings and medicine alike is to rewire the self so that it reduces its investment in the historical and social world by having its life directed by the essential core, a move that I see as analogous to his poetic search for the seeds and signs of resurrection within himself that I examined in Chapter 3. In that sense I argue that when resurrection thought is translated into medical and therapeutic terms, it becomes the site for a kind of organic theory work that attains insights into the self's habituated relationship to the social world in a way that anticipates Bourdieu's theory of habitus.

I also examine how Vaughan's commitment to a corporeal and immanent understanding of resurrection leads him to a way of thinking about emotional life that departs sharply from the predominant humoralism of his day. In place of positing that emotions are the effects of mechanical humors sloshing around the body, Vaughan sees emotional life as giving information about the way and the degree to which the self inhabits the historical world. Thus, he adds to his translation of a hermetic medical treatise the story of a man who died in the act of sex, and he posits that it was not the sex that killed him but the "excess of joy" that accompanied the sex. The notion that joy can kill is strange to us, but in the context of Vaughan's notion that the emotions are a bridge between an essentially bodily core life and an external social world that imposes its values and claims upon the body, joy can seem like an excessive and therefore enervating investment of the core bodily self into the social world that leaves the core bodily life dissipated and spent. Leo Bersani has taught us to see sexuality as a beneficent crisis of selfhood, and killing joy would seem to qualify as such a crisis.[49] But Vaughan's vision also seems to depart from Bersani's account insofar as Vaughan sees killing joy not as a beneficent death of the person but as a kind of explosive screwing of the self into the world. The field of sexuality that Vaughan opens up with his discussion of sex and joy is thus marked by the notion of the body as socialized yet also as potentially unhinged from that social connectedness, a vision that ultimately derives from his interest in corporeal resurrection.

Finally, in Chapter 5, I argue that Ben Jonson's popular play *Volpone* charts a massive cultural shift in which, within a rising capitalist order, a fully disembodied understanding of resurrection is transformed into a legal personhood that allows the individual's will to survive past the limit of death. In other words, *Volpone* is a kind of elegiac death knell for the specific form of countersecularization that I chart in the rest of the book, in which a materialist understanding of resurrection is celebrated for its critical power. *Volpone* glances at such ideas only to mark their ultimate impotence to stem the tide of a now legally institutionalized disembodied personhood. However, I argue for a bifurcation within Jonson's own corpus of work between *Volpone* and his poetry, and most especially his poetry of praise and memorialization, which participates in the same project of Donne, Herbert, and Vaughan, but in a new way. Jonson is quite committed to a dualist notion of resurrection in which a disembodied soul ascends directly to heaven, leaving behind its body until the final resurrection at the end of time. But in his poetry Jonson imagines that the separation of soul and body creates a gap in the ontological fabric of the world, and he wants his poetry to fill this gap. His poetry evokes the symbolic achievements of the person who has died, but he wants to combine this informational evocation of who the person was in the world with a kind of ersatz body in the form of the poem itself. Jonson emphasizes the weightiness of his poetic text as a memorial, especially in its intertextual density, its indebtedness to classical texts, its formal and grammatical complexity, and its metrical shapedness. For Jonson the formal patterning in poetry is a way of transcending the fleetingness of everyday speech and thus allowing his poems to "do the work of resurrection" in the gap between death and the final resurrection. For Jonson, poetry supplements dualist resurrection by creating a material presence that exists not fully on the timescale of eternity (Jonson still looks forward to eventual literal resurrection) but at least on a much longer timescale than the fleeting lives of human persons. By continuing to think about agency, personhood, and identity in relation to a body, whether biological or textual, Jonson's most formally weighty poetry reveals a countersecularization impulse even in the midst of a fairly consistent dualist model. I compare Jonson's fantasy about poetry's ability to make people present as textual bodies to our modern fantasies about the special incantatory power of "code," whether genetic code or computer-based code, as a kind of language that does not represent but enacts presence in the world.

But in the balance of the chapter I look at the different future for residual resurrection beliefs that is suggested by *Volpone*, a play in which several characters vie with one other to be named heirs in Volpone's last will and testament. I argue that in this play Jonson reveals his culture's increasing fascination with the idea that the essence of the person exists in a network of legal institutions and legally entitled wealth (or "substance") that enables the person as agent to survive the death of the person as body. And if this fantasy is to some extent ridiculed in the play, its prominent role within an emerging capitalist order is nonetheless shown. In *Volpone* I see the conversion of the complex, contested notion of resurrection into the completely disembodied fantasy of the legal person who exists as a nexus of legal documents and legal institutional frameworks and that comes, in secular modernity, to displace the old body-based countersecularization discourses I have been studying.

Finally, in the epilogue I examine the current pop culture fascination with the undead body visible in the explosion of TV shows and films about zombies. I begin by considering Emmanuel Carrère's *The Kingdom*, in which the well-known French writer tells the story of his brief but intense conversion to Christianity, in the grip of which he was involved in developing the French TV series *Les revenants*, which was the model for A&E's *The Returned*. I argue that Carrère's account of the power of the Christian theology of resurrection as an inspiration for *Les revenants* reveals the truth of the "undead" genres more generally, namely, as a culture-wide return of the repressed, a protest against the increasingly disembodied, virtualized way we live today. Implicitly, the undead character (including the zombie) attacks the modern fantasy that the self is, in its essence, disembodied and therefore reducible to information, data, and code, a fantasy in which people yearn for a cybernetic resurrection that will take the form of entering into the disembodied life of the digital world. In the midst of this disembodied virtualized world, zombie pop culture, like the poetry I have studied in this book, is a reminder of the body's abiding vulnerabilities, limitations, and also potentials for transcendence.

1 / Secularization, Countersecularization, and the Fate of the Flesh in Donne

John Donne's writings are driven by an idiosyncratic theory of resurrection that is informed by a distinctive relationship to secularizing pressures. Donne's search for a "resurrection body" that is already now stirring in the conventionally social self pushes him toward emphasizing the body and its life in all their deranging energy and vibrancy, especially in experiences of sex, passion, sickness, and dying, and he values the body and bodily life precisely for their ability to make him question and rethink the nature of selfhood or personhood and the connection between the self or the person and the material and social world. Recovering this perspective will allow for a new understanding of Donne's overall intellectual project. Somewhat surprisingly, it will also allow for a new way of understanding Donne's peculiar appeal to early twentieth-century avant-garde poets including, most famously, T. S. Eliot.

I call Donne's distinctive way of appropriating and deploying the idea of the resurrection of the flesh "countersecularization," and to explain it I want to start by contrasting Donne's ideas with those of his friend Edward Herbert, first Baron of Cherbury (1582–1648), the older brother of the poet George Herbert, who is the subject of the next chapter. Donne was a close friend of Edward and George Herbert's mother, Magdalene, whom he relied upon for patronage and whose funeral sermon he preached. Through Magdalene Herbert, Donne also became quite friendly with Edward Herbert, whom he visited several times in his life and to whom he wrote several poems, including one of his best and most famous, "Goodfriday 1613. Riding westward," ostensibly written while on horseback on his way to Lord Herbert's estate in Wales.

Lord Herbert is a unique character in seventeenth-century England, notable for his international adventures as a soldier and ambassador and for his proneness to violence. He is also noteworthy for his philosophical work in epistemology in which he advocates a rationalizing and comparatist procedure for truth-testing. Herbert wrote poetry (in both English and Latin) but is more famous today for his philosophical treatises about the nature of knowledge and truth including in religious matters. In his treatment of religious claims, Herbert is at the vanguard of secularization. But what "secularization" means in the seventeenth century is not attacking or debunking or seeking to reduce the importance of Christianity. Rather, what it means is a transformation of how people practice and think about Christianity to make it more compatible with an emerging rational and empirical worldview. For Herbert this means reconceiving of the role of reason in ascertaining religious truth and managing religious disagreement. In many ways, he recasts Christianity into a more reasonable and universal form. Indeed, Herbert is sometimes described as the first "deist." Though it is an exaggeration to equate his views with the rationalized version of Christianity that became the religious ideology of the Enlightenment, it is nevertheless true that Herbert represented an early impulse toward rationalizing Christianity. Examining his work before turning to Donne has the advantage of making clear how different Donne's relationship to this dominant path of secularization is by contrast.

While serving as an ambassador in Paris in 1624 Lord Herbert wrote and published in Latin his most famous work, *De veritate*. This text is notable for the philosophical rigor with which it explores issues of epistemology and the question of what can be known with any certainty. In it Edward Herbert rejects an appeal to authorities, whether ancient or recent, and instead proposes the use of comparative reason as the only test of truth. Anticipating Kant, he argues that the space for disagreement is ultimately limited because God has implanted in people basic modes of thought that also give rise (through experience) to basic common ideas that are universally shared. These "common ideas" flow from the basic modes of thought that all humans share. As such, Herbert argues that finding universally shared ideas is the best guarantee of absolute truth, and he writes that truth is "what all men of normal mind believe."[1] Edward Herbert applies this epistemological approach to all areas of human knowledge, and he develops a methodology in which individuals apply their own individual reason and then check their conclusions against the reasoned conclusions of others; for Herbert, only where there is universal agreement can we be sure that we have arrived at truth. As though to enact its appeal to universal judgment, the original 1624 edition of *De veritate* was dedicated to "the whole of humanity"; the second and third editions (published in 1633 and 1645) were dedicated to "all readers of sound and fair judgement."

The most controversial element of *De veritate* is that Herbert applies his comparatist epistemology to religious questions. Predictably, Herbert rejects the authority of revelation, whether personal or scriptural. Instead, he argues that people should apply their own reason and then compare their conclusions to the reasoned conclusions of others. This epistemological starting point leads Herbert to a "comparative religions" approach in which he compares different religious systems to identify shared principles common not only to all the variants of Christianity available in his own day but also common to historically different religious systems, including that of the ancients. If the comparatist approach aims for truth it begins by first suspending any convictions about any specific religious system in order to then seek commonalities among them all. This comparatist approach is more fully developed in another of Herbert's works, the posthumously published *De religione gentilium*, which systematically compares a variety of religious systems, but already in *De veritate* he writes that "I firmly maintain, however, that it is and always has been possible for all men to reach the truths I have described. . . . For by no other method could the existence of Divine Universal Providence, the highest attribute of God, be proved by the principles of common reason" (41).

The rise of a comparative-religions perspective associated with Herbert is itself one of the markers of secularization. Charles Taylor argues that under the regime of secularity, religious life is conditioned by "optionality," the knowledge even on the part of committed religious believers and practitioners that not everyone believes and practices as they do, that there are other religions and even the possibility of no religion. From this perspective, believers oscillate between a mindset of commitment or engagement and a mindset of detachment or even self-criticism founded in the knowledge that the principles of any one religion are "optional" rather than a universally accepted starting point, as they would have been in a presecular context.[2] For Taylor the new experiences of religious faith defined by "optionality" can be marked by an authenticity and an intensity that might have been out of reach to most or even all believers in a premodern context, in which some particular religion was nonoptional. For other scholars, such as William T. Cavanaugh, the very notion of "religion" as a comparative quasi-universal category brings with it political struggle about what properly counts as "religion."[3] Because it assumes the optionality of any one religious system, Herbert's interest in developing a rational comparative perspective places him unambiguously at the cutting edge of secularizing pressures in the early modern period.

From his comparatist approach Lord Herbert concludes that there are five religious principles that are (according to Herbert) universally shared not only within the world of Christianity but across all religions and that are therefore true. Herbert's five religious "common ideas" are: that there is a God, that people should worship God, that God demands moral virtue, that one must ask forgiveness for moral error, and that there is an afterlife in which people are either punished or rewarded for their behavior on earth. Turning to the question of revelation, Herbert concludes that though there may be revelation within particular religious traditions, including Christianity, any possible revelation must be checked against these five common notions and only if it is found compatible with them can it be accepted.[4] Herbert implies that the warrant for belief is not revelation but reasoned assent, and he proposes to revise Christianity to align it with the rational core of all religions. Thus, one of the notable features of *De veritate* is Herbert's elucidation of the rational principles from which the Ten Commandments can be derived, in essence treating these laws as Kantian categorical imperatives.[5] So reduced, belief in the Commandments, or in any other elements of Christianity, no longer derives from the authority of scripture or revelation at all. Indeed, Herbert's willingness to sanitize Christianity in light of reason and comparative truth-testing is part of why he is sometimes seen as the father of eighteenth-century deism, in which a completely rationalized theism emerges as an alternative for the historical beliefs and practices of Christianity.

Herbert's project is certainly not hostile to religion or Christianity but seeks to recast religion into a form compatible with reason and universal truth as he sees it. In Herbert's work, Christian thought is preserved and becomes the basis for a new, highly rationalized form of religious belief in the form of the five common principles. But inevitably major elements of Christianity are cast aside in the process insofar as they are not confirmed by reasoned comparison with other religions. And for many seventeenth-century Christians, the "losing" elements cast aside by Edward Herbert would no doubt be precisely the most cherished, most centrally valued parts of the religion, which they would be loathe to give up.

What are the implications of Herbert's project for the central concern of this book, namely, the fate of the ancient Christian commitment to resurrection in the face of secularization? Here it is the fifth of Herbert's common principles that is decisive, the notion that there is an afterlife of reward and punishment. Herbert posits this to be a reasonable because universally shared principle, but only insofar as it is aligned with radical body/soul dualism, for in writing about the afterlife what Herbert finds commonsensical and universally shared is not that the body will live again but only that a disembodied soul, imagined as the essence of the person, will live again (or just continue to live) separately from the body. Thus in *De veritate* he writes that any doctrines "which express doubts about the eternal state of the soul, cannot be considered either Common Notions or truths" because "that the soul could be immortal if God willed it is clearly a Common Notion in that among the most distant peoples, holding every type of superstition." For Herbert, nature itself points toward an eventual separation of soul from body:

> Since nature unceasingly labors to deliver the soul from its physical burden, so Nature itself instills with its secret conviction that virtue constitutes the most effective means by which our mind may be gradually separated and released from the body and enter into its lawful realm. And though many arguments could be cited to the same purpose, I know no more convincing proof than the fact that it is only virtue that has the power to draw our soul from the delights which engulf it, and even restore it to its native regions, so that freed from the foul embrace of vice, and finally from the fear of death itself, it can apply itself to its proper function and attain inward everlasting joy.
>
> (36–37)

Herbert suggests that virtuous action (that is, action not governed by physical appetites) allows a preexperience of a disembodied afterlife in which the soul has been freed from its body. Herbert proposes that this understanding is, in fact, universally shared among all religions and therefore calls it a "common idea" and one of the five universal principles. In addressing the afterlife, therefore, Herbert posits a vision of resurrection founded on a strong body/soul dualism that imagines that the soul is the essence of the person and is capable of independent postmortem existence separate from its body.[6]

What Edward Herbert's project shows is that under the pressure of a rising dominant form of secularization, an implicit dualism becomes a kind of common sense and the basis for a "reasonable" form of Christianity including in questions about the ultimate fate of the self. Entering into a self-reinforcing circle, body/soul dualism with an emphasis on the soul as the primary scene of selfhood energizes an emerging secular modernity and is, in turn, "blessed" by this emerging secular modernity as embodying a reasonable and rational version of Christianity.

But if resurrection is retained in Herbert's writing by being transformed into a reasonable body/soul dualism that prioritizes the soul, what of the body and the monist-materialist theory of the person that Herbert sets aside? If Herbert's writings are unconcerned with the fate of the body in the face of rationalizing dualism, then it is precisely here that Donne departs Herbert's company. Donne was a friend of Edward Herbert and was throughout his lifetime a collector of intellectual provocations, and he was certainly aware of Herbert's search for shared and reasonable principles to base his religious life upon. Indeed, half of Donne's mind is traveling the same path as Edward Herbert, namely, the path of rationalizing Christianity, including by reconceptualizing it as a religion of body/soul dualism. But the other half of Donne's mind travels in a very different direction, by seizing upon and celebrating precisely those elements of Christianity, including the idea of material resurrection, that are least reasonable, rational, commonsensical, or universally shared. For Donne, the body and its fate become the basis for a critique of the reasonable and rational discourse of Christianity that represents the cutting edge of secularization. In doing so, Donne simultaneously critiques the autonomous and rational self that the dominant path of secularization represented by Herbert endorses.

I call this particular "use" of the least reasonable and least rational elements of Christianity, including the commitment to the resurrection of the body and its flesh, "countersecularization." What I mean by that term is that Donne is not engaging in anything like a fundamentalist return to some kind of archaic orthodoxy in religious matters. Rather, Donne seizes on the notion of the resurrection of the body as that idea is itself transformed by secularizing pressures as a basis for rethinking and reimagining some of the key elements of an emerging secularized vision of religion and of selfhood. Donne uses a heightened emphasis on the body in its strangeness and vulnerability to undermine any stable, role-based identity but also any notion of the person as an autonomous reasoning subject capable of arriving at truth, the sort of reasoning subject that Herbert of Cherbury assumes. Thus, I see Donne's interest in the "resurrection body" as a critical theory that attacks the founding assumptions of an emerging secular order visible in Lord Herbert's work.

I have suggested that Donne plays a two-handed game in relation to secularization and therefore to resurrection. Donne oscillates between something very close to Herbert's rationalizing dualist vision and a return to those elements of Christianity that are least amenable to this vision. Thus, in Donne's work a commitment to a dualist understanding of the person and of resurrection is haunted by a discourse in which the body is centrally valued as the essence of the person and in which this perspective is valued for its ability to undercut or even transform the basic building blocks of an emerging dominant secularization built on dualism. Donne's writing is marked by an inability to turn away from the body, and Donne values the body for its ability to make him question and rethink the nature of selfhood or personhood and the connection between the self or the person and the material and social world.

The best critical scholarship on Donne has sought to do justice to the complexity and contradictoriness of Donne's thought and writing, the way his texts hold conflicting ideas together, including conflicting ideas about the nature of the soul, the body, and resurrection. This is certainly true of the most important book on Donne in the past twenty-five years, Ramie Targoff's *John Donne, Body and Soul.*[7] In practice, Donne's dualist and monist-materialist views of self and body are completely intertwined. Insofar as I split them apart and treat them separately I do some (I hope temporary) violence to the complex reality of Donne's writing. But I hope this approach will show the high intellectual stakes of the oscillation between, on the one hand, driving forward a form of secularization that appears first and foremost as a systematic preference for dualism and, on the other hand, a critical project built on what is most resistant or oppositional to that form of secularization.

I will therefore begin with the half of Donne's mind that is traveling the same secularizing path as Lord Herbert. Donne certainly does evince the same comparatist and rationalizing spirit that we see in Herbert's work. By temperament, Donne seemed to value debate or at least discussion and reasoning about religion and religious ideas. He valued the process of building up a tested set of convictions by means of reasoned discussion with others who hold personally tested convictions of their own. In "Satire III" he attacks the "fires of Spain"—meaning the Inquisition's attempts to impose a shared vision of truth—and advocates that his reader "seeke true religion." He writes that "in strange way / To stand, inquiring right, is not to stray; / To sleepe, or runne wrong, is" (24, 43, 77–79).[8] Being in a state of seeking is valuable from Donne's perspective, more so than accepting someone else's orthodoxy at face value or on authority—that is, accepting religious ideas simply because "a Philip, or a Gregory, / A Harry, or a Martin taught thee this" (96–97). This vision of freedom is connected to a celebration of individual reason because "though truth and falshood bee / Neare twins, yet truth a little elder is; / Be busie to seeke her, beleeve mee this, / Hee's not of none, nor worst, that seekes the best" (72–76). As Donne puts it in a sermon preached at Whitehall in 1616, "we forbid no man the use of Reason in matters of Religion," and "Mysteries of Religion are not the less believ'd and embrac'd by Faith, because they are presented, and induc'd, and apprehended by Reason."[9] When Donne writes, in a letter to his friend Henry Goodyear, "that religion is certainly best which is reasonablest" he means "reasonable" as the outcome of comparison and reasoned debate.[10]

Donne's *Essays in Divinity* (published posthumously by Donne's son in 1651) attest to his spirit of reasonable inquiry into the basics of Christian theology. Though it was Donne's son who gave them the title "essays," and it is not clear whether Donne used this word in relation to the text, the word nevertheless captures the spirit of these inquiries—they are nonsystematic stabs at ideas, and they are undertaken in the spirit of inquiry rather than dogmatism. In that sense they are reminiscent of another important text in the history of secularization, Francis Bacon's *Essayes Religious meditations. Places of perswasion and disswasion* (1597). Bacon's is only the second book published in England with the word "essays" in the title, the first having been James I's *The essayes of a prentise, in the diuine art of poesie.*

Many of Donne's sermons are equally infused with the nondogmatic "essayistic" spirit of secularization that seeks a rational and reasonable version of Christianity where differences can be debated without sparking violence.[11] Katrin Ettenhuber argues that Donne's theological reasoning is characterized by the humility of knowing that fragmented and incomplete knowledge was inevitable in a fallen world. She writes that "paradoxically, Donne's commitment to this model is clearest when he imagines himself outside of time, as in a late sermon on Matthew 6:21, which envisages the resurrection as a grand reunion of theologians through the ages. In 'Heaven,' Donne says expectantly, 'I shall finde the Fathers of the first Age, dead five thousand years before me; and they shall not be able to say they were a minute before me.'"[12] Here Donne imagines the afterlife as a debating society where his own distinctive views will not be corrected so much as they will be entered into the conversation with the greatest of theologians. Alison Shell and Arnold Hunt attempt to reconstruct the main points of Donne's reasoned theology and argue that Donne's toleration for differences in religion came from his acute consciousness of the shaping power of the environment each individual encounters in the world.[13] For this reason, Donne often "argues" for Christianity in ways that define disagreements as (merely) rhetorical.[14]

Donne's distinctively secular spirit is visible in the way his sermons address what is surely one of the most controversial theological issues in early modern England, namely, the Eucharist. Literary critics have been interested in the issue because the Eucharist—by foregrounding how one thing can point to or embody another thing—seems to enact the structure of (depending on the precise theology) either metaphor or symbol.[15] What is most striking about Donne's sermons that address this specific issue is how they seek to defer conflict. In the Christmas sermon of 1626, for example, Donne attempts to thread the needle between seeing the Eucharist as mere memorialization and seeing it as literal transubstantiation:

> That bread which thou seest after the Consecration, is not the same bread, which was presented before; not that it is Transubstantiated to another substance, for it is bread still, (which is the heretical Riddle of the Roman Church and Satans sophistry . . .) but that it is severed, and appropriated by God, in that Ordinance to another use.
>
> (7:294)

Donne goes on to explain what he means by "appropriated to another use," by comparing it to the difference between a judge who is seated on the bench and that same judge at home as a private man. This is a remarkable metaphor for its effort to defuse a potential source of conflict (a potential that appears, as though to remind us of the stakes of avoiding conflict, in the reference to the "heretical Riddle of the Roman Church and Satans sophistry"). Donne's emphasis on irenic modesty in argument is as prominent a theme in this sermon as his actual, specific theory regarding the Eucharist. Thus, Donne writes:

> A peremptory prejudice upon other mens opinions, that no opinion but thine can be true, in the doctrine of the Sacrament, and an uncharitable condemning of other men, or other Churches that may be of another perswasion than thou art, in the matter of the Sacrament, may frustrate and disappoint thee of all that benefit, which thou mightst have, by an humble receiving thereof, if thou wouldest exercise thy faith onely, here, and leave thy passion at home, and refer thy reason, and disputation to the Schoole.
>
> (7:291)

But despite the concluding admonition to confine "thy reason, and disputation to the Schoole," the majority of the sermon is devoted to the issue of how to engage in debate or disputes in religious matters broadly speaking and the attack on the "peremptory prejudice upon other mens opinions, that no opinion but thine can be true." One distinctive feature of Donne's sermons is reasoned engagement with a whole spectrum of other authorities in the intellectual history of Christianity; in this one sermon, Donne's interlocutors include Origen, Augustine, Tertullian, Irenaeus, and Jerome. Donne concludes the sermon with the tag, "As thou wouldest be well interpreted by others, interpret others well" (7:291).

In moving toward a secularism defined, at least in part, through the irenic principle of "As thou wouldest be well interpreted by others, interpret others well," Donne is very emphatically serving the interests of the early modern state. It is true that the early modern state is still in the business of using religion to bolster its power, especially the religious authority of the institutional church; "no bishop, no king," as King James famously put it, a position intensified by Charles I's claim to rule by divine right. But on the other hand, the irenic approach to religious questions by monarchs as different temperamentally as Elizabeth, James, and Charles points to a shared interest in reducing religiously based disagreement and disputes. As Jonathan Goldberg has shown, Donne wanted to understand his writing and his art as being in the service of the absolutist state, and the flipside of Donne's celebration of the power, mystery, and authority of the monarch is his project of defining religious disagreements down to debating quibbles.[16] A religious domain so domesticated is deprived of any power to undermine the sovereign or the sovereign's domestic peace. Donne's consciousness and awareness of the way domesticated religion serves the interests of the state is most explicit in *Pseudo-Martyr*, his effort to persuade Catholics to take the oath of allegiance.

There is a virtuous circularity between Donne's commitment to reasonableness in religious matters and his commitment to body/soul dualism. In the "Seed-Pearl" sermon Donne—echoing Edward Herbert's protodeism—begins by saying that body/soul dualism is so obviously reasonable that it did not even need to be stated in the early creeds. "There are so many evidences of the immortality of the soule, even to a naturall mans reason, that it required not an Article of the Creed, to fix this notion of the Immortality of the soule" (8:97). Part of why body/soul dualism seems so commonsensical to Donne is that it is an important premise of the natural philosophy that was an increasingly exciting part of intellectual life in his day. Metaphysically speaking, dualism is foundational for early modern science in the sense that it separates a purely material realm subject to the laws of nature and therefore open to empirical study in terms of efficient causes from a spiritual and value-based realm that increasingly becomes the domain of a privatized religious life.[17] And while Donne does notice (and bemoans) the way empirical science has the power to strip the world of meaning (a tendency especially marked in "A Funeral

Elegy" and the two "Anniversaries"), generally Donne's fascination with the emerging, empirically based modes of knowing and the new technologies that are associated with them are quite evident.[18]

But dualism is an important part of a rising secular order not only because it makes a science focused on a purely material realm possible but also because dualism endorses a new conception of the faculty of reason itself. Donne sees the soul as the home of the particular mode of reasoning he champions. Indeed, the equation of a disembodied soul and the capacity to reason is so foundational a concept for Donne that the very capacity to reason becomes a proof for the existence of the separable soul, as he suggests in a sermon he delivered on January 25, 1628/9 at St. Paul's Cathedral on the subject of St. Paul's conversion. He writes:

> The Platonique philosophers did not only acknowledge Animam in homine, a soule in man, but Mentem in anima, a minde in the soul of man. They meant by the minde, the superior faculties of the soule, and we never come to exercise them. . . . Poore intricated soule! Riddling, perplexed, labyrinthicall soule! Thou couldest not say, that thou beleevest not in God, if there were no God; Thou couldest not believe in God, if there were not God; If there were no God, thou couldest not speake, thou couldest not thinke, not a word.
>
> (8.327)

Here Donne posits that the very capacity to think at all, the real existence of the soul, and the real existence of God all establish one another in a logical circle. The same argument appears in the *Devotions*, where the ultimate proof of the real existence of a separable soul is Donne's mentalistic capacity to reflect consciously upon himself:

> If I will ask mere philosophers what the soul is, I shall find amongst them that will tell me, it is nothing but the temperament and harmony, and just and equal composition of the elements in the body, which produces all those faculties which we ascribe to the soul; and so in itself is nothing, no separable substance that overlives the body. They see the soul is nothing else in other creatures, and they affect an impious humility to think as low of man. But if my soul were no more than the soul of a beast, I could not think so; that soul that can reflect upon itself, consider itself, is more than so.
>
> (*Devotions*, "Meditation 18," 91)[19]

Here the issue of the soul is demoted to a philosophical quibble that can be treated reasonably. And the most distinctive feature of the soul and, for Donne, the ultimate proof for its real existence separate from the body is the mentalistic capacity for critical self-reflection that Donne cannot imagine as a material phenomenon, that is, as an emergent property of organized matter. For Donne the mentalistic capacity is itself enough to refute the idea of the philosophers that the soul is only the "composition of the elements in the body," for "if my soul were no more than the soul of a beast, I could not think so; that soul that can reflect upon itself, consider itself, is more than so." Thus, soul is mind and mind is reasoning power, so that the power to reason is itself proof of the separable soul's reality.

This strong body/soul distinction creates a buffered, reasoning self that is ideally free from all social determinants and that is the proper home of religious belief. The appeal to Donne should be obvious, but this perspective also has a dark side visible in Donne's own early anxieties about finding employment as a way of stabilizing his identity in the world. Throughout Donne's early life one can see a paradoxical combination of Donne asserting a very strong degree of autonomy and freedom anchored in an essentially mentalistic and therefore highly "buffered" sense of self and of Donne expressing persistent anxiety about his own self's ungroundedness, which leads him to seek some way to anchor or stabilize the self by attaching himself to something larger than himself, whether another person or an institution such as the court or, ultimately, the Anglican church. This sense of exaggerated separateness from the social and historical world and the ways in which it can determine or shape the self and give it a distinctive purpose but also constrain its freedom is certainly one of the features of the rising dominant form of secularism that Donne is pushing, and the point I am making here is that it is strongly indexed to body/soul dualism because that dualism is what creates the appearance of a self that is ideally unconstrained by the social environment it happens (contingently, so to speak) to find itself in. Donne's own quest for "employment" that would lend him a stable sense of self is connected to the Protestant sense of a vocation that might stabilize and center the human person, and it is, at the same time, a sign of how very strong Donne's own sense of autonomy and separateness of his self are.[20]

We can summarize this first phase of my argument by saying that, as much as Edward Herbert, Donne is at the forefront of a secularizing trend in England. The ways in which Donne is an agent of secularization include three elements that all reinforce one another in a circular pattern:

1. Donne develops a discourse of Christianity that emphasizes a personal set of convictions rather than acceptance of authority, and he sees reasonable discussion and debate as the path to a set of

convictions that can be held precisely because they are deemed reasonable.

2. Donne represents the self that can reason about religion as a mental phenomenon inhering in a soul; the real existence of a soul is what enables abstract reasoning in the first place. This move also preserves a distinction between a material world subject to scientific knowledge-making procedures and a subjective world rooted in a disembodied self that is ideally free.

3. Donne sees the self-as-soul as radically separate from the social or historical world, therefore as marked by a very high degree of freedom and autonomy (it is what Taylor calls the "buffered self"), and that, when it suffers the consequences of "too much" freedom, seeks voluntaristically to regain a sense of anchored coherence by seeking a calling in both the religious and the secular realms; the noncorporeal self must choose projects in the world in order to impose coherence on itself.

As should be obvious to anyone familiar with Donne, so far I have told only one side of the story, for the important point about Donne is that there is everywhere a countermovement to the path of reasonable and dualist Christianity. This countermovement is centered on the body in all of its insistent here-and-now strangeness, the very subject of the ancient Christian hope for the resurrection of the flesh, a hope that seems increasingly incompatible with the rising tide of a reasonable, science-friendly dualist version of Christianity. In the face of Donne's dualism, his body has the force of the return of the repressed, flooding his otherwise highly autonomous self with a tide of strange, vibrant, material life. For Donne, his body is essential to his sense of self, and while he does believe that the soul is capable of separate existence in the interim between death and the general resurrection, he thinks that the life of the soul separate from its body will be diminished and thus eagerly welcomes and embraces the eventual reunion of the soul and the body. As he writes in his 1625 Easter sermon:

> That God, all Spirit, served with Spirits, associated to Spirits, should have such an affection, such a love to this body, this earthly body, this deserves wonder. . . . Man cannot deliberately wish himself an angel, because he should lose by that wish, and lack that glory, which he shall have in his body. *We shall be like the angels* (Mark 12:25) . . . in the exalting and refining of the faculties of our souls; But they shall never attain to be like us in our glorified bodies.[21]

Here Donne says that resurrected humans will be superior to the angels insofar as they will have bodies. That this state makes resurrected humans like the resurrected Jesus, who also has a body, is the point Donne makes in one of the *Devotions*:

> We upon earth do know what thy saints in heaven lack yet for the consummation of their happiness, and therefore thou hast afforded us the dignity that we may pray for them. That therefore this soul, now newly departed to thy kingdom, may quickly return to a joyful reunion to that body which it hath left, and that we with it may soon enjoy the full consummation of all in body and soul, I humbly beg at thy hand, O our most merciful God, for thy Son Christ Jesus' sake. That that blessed Son of thine may have the consummation of his dignity, by entering into his last office, the office of a judge, and may have society of human bodies in heaven, as well as he hath had ever of souls.
>
> (*Devotions*, "Prayer 18," 96)

The importance and value of the body is obvious here and, indeed, throughout Donne's writings, as a check on any mystical wish to transcend the body into some purely spiritual realm.

Moreover, even the limited dualism of imagining a temporary separation of soul and body is at odds with Donne's tendency to see the soul and its capacity for reason as entwined with and shaped by the body. Kimberley Anne Coles describes the way Donne understands reason—as the power of the intellectual soul—to be susceptible to the organic body's effects, just as David A. Hirsch notes the many instances in Donne's thinking where reason is made possible and shaped by the body, notably in his juvenilia, though the idea runs beneath the surface of even Donne's most dualist moments.[22] Similarly, Douglas Trevor has noted the ways Donne understands his body, especially its physical tendency to produce spleen or melancholy, to shape his experience of mind.[23] In general, as Nancy Gail Selleck argues, Donne imagines that reason is only possible within the constraints imagined by a humoral imaginary.[24]

I have suggested that Donne's sermons point to his secularizing tendency, where he reduces religious questions (such as the question of the Eucharist) to matters of reasonable difference and asserts a "common-sense" or "self-evident" body/soul dualism. But that is only one face of the sermons. The other face of Donne's sermons is his efforts to force his audience to engage with the strangeness of the body, often in ways that are rhetorically *in excess* of whatever pastoral or theological point Donne might be trying to make. This is a countercurrent in the sermons that is often very much at odds with the announced Bible text or occasion of the sermon.

One example is the sermon preached for the wedding of the Earl of Bridgewater's daughter on November 19, 1627. As many commentators have noted, this sermon is striking for the irreducible weirdness of making people attending a wedding pay careful attention to the body in its gruesome postmortem putrefaction. The point I want to highlight is that Donne begins the sermon by noting that the idea of a separable soul is eminently rational and easy to accept; the part that he thinks is hard to accept (because ultimately at odds with an emerging secular modernity and its "common sense") is the resurrection of the body (I have already quoted the first line of the sermon but will quote it again here):

> There are so many evidences of the immortality of the soule, even to a naturall mans reason, that it required not an Article of the Creed, to fix this notion of the Immortality of the soule. But the Resurrection of the Body is discernible by no other light, but that of Faith, nor could be fixed by any lesse assurance then an Article of the Creed. Where be all the splinters of that Bone, which a shot hath shivered and scattered in the Ayre? Where be all the Atoms of that flesh, which a Corrasive hath eat away, or a Consumption hath breath'd, and exhal'd away from our arms, and other Limbs? In what wrinkle, in what furrow, in what bowel of the earth, ly all the graines of the ashes of a body burnt a thousand years since? In what corner, in what ventricle of the sea, lies all the jelly of a Body drowned in the generall Flood? What coherence, what sympathy, what dependence maintaines any relation, any corresspondence, between that arm that was lost in Europe, and that legge that was lost in Afrique or Asia, scores of yeers between? One humour of our dead body produces worms, and those worms suck and exhaust all other humour, and then all dies, and all dries, and molders into dust, and that dust is blowen into the River, & that puddled water tumbled into the sea, and that ebs and flows in infinite revolutions, and still, still God knows in what Cabinet every seed-Pearle lies, in what part of the world every graine of every mans dust lies.
>
> (8:97)

Donne is quite wrong to say that the reason the resurrection of the soul does not appear in the Apostle's Creed is only that it was so obvious. In fact, as I noted in the Introduction, the most ancient form of Christianity is defined by its rejection of the Hellenistic idea of the soul as separable from the body; early Christianity insists on the notion that the self is the body and the body is the self, so that if the self is to have any life after death then it must be a matter of the whole body living again (this is what made early Christianity seem so absurd to competent Hellenistic philosophers and rhetoricians). But in the context of the early modern English emergence of modernity, I think Donne is quite right that the separability and persistence of the soul is almost common sense whereas the reconstitution and reanimation of the flesh is what increasingly seems strange and deranging, especially under the pressure of a rising empirical science. The point of this sermon delivered on the supposedly happy occasion of a marriage is to posit attention to the body and its potential resurrection as a potent antidote to the dualism of body and soul. As the phrase "seed-pearle" suggests, there is something transformative about the flesh in its luminous and strange otherness, and maybe for Donne the sexuality that he thinks of on the occasion of a marriage is about touching that luminous fleshly otherness, and perhaps that is how he gets, in his mind, from the marriage occasion to the gruesome content of the sermon, a connection we will encounter again when we turn to his erotic poems.[25]

Donne invites his listeners to see themselves as bodies and therefore as being at once vulnerable to radical dispersal and at the same time as containing the seeds of an unimaginable future resurrection, as "seed-pearl." This theoretical shift in focus has a deranging effect upon how listeners see themselves, an effect worked out in the sermon Donne preached on April 26, 1625, shortly after the death of King James. This sermon was delivered in Denmark House, before the king's body was removed for burial. Donne tells the audience that they do not essentially consist in worldly indices of identity, including (as Suzanne Smith summarizes them in her discussion of this sermon) honors, offices, pedigree, posterity, and alliances.[26] In the sermon, Donne says that the lesson of contemplating the dead body is that we can find true knowledge of the self (or knowledge of the true self) only by going beyond the externals of social classification. "Get beyond thine own circle," he exhorts his auditory, "consider thy selfe at thine end, thy own death, and then Egredare, Goe further than that, Go forth and see what thou shalt be after thy death" (6:285). Seeing the self as it exists only in the context of its life in the social and historical world, Donne suggests, is not really self-knowledge at all. Only by looking at ourselves as we will be at or in death can we know ourselves: "Still that which we are to look upon, is especially our selves, but it is our selves, enlarg'd and extended into the next world; for till we see, what we shall be then, we are but short-sighted" (6:285). Donne does not propose the abandonment of the project of acquiring self-knowledge but rather proposes a more expansive understanding of its object in which we struggle to see the self in the light of resurrection, and the contemplation of the dead body of James lying in front of Donne's listeners on this occasion is central to the project of gaining a new perspective on the self outside of time.[27]

Something very similar happens in Donne's most widely read sermon, "Death's Duel." This sermon is often taken as Donne's final statement on himself, yet Donne presenting himself or memorializing himself means memorializing his body as it looks as it enters the zone of physical resurrection. The emphasis throughout the sermon is on a deranging materiality that haunts all of life, beginning with the "winding sheet" that is our mother's womb and culminating in the shocking and scandalous catalog of putrefaction and decay to which mortal bodies are subject and that Donne implicitly invites his audience to contemplate in contemplating Donne's own sick, indeed dying, body: "yet it is an entrance into the death of corruption and putrefaction, and vermiculation, and incineration, and dispersion in and from the grave, in which every dead man dies over again" (10:235).[28] The "image" of Donne presented here is quite different from the conventional indices of social identity that one might expect referred to in a conventional eulogy. Donne is offering his own body as an object of contemplation for himself and his audience, in exactly the same way as James's body is implicitly an object of deranging contemplation in the sermon delivered at his death.

If in the sermon over James's dead body and in "Death's Duel" Donne is advocating a meditative process of using the body as an object of contemplation to feel the self and its conventional coordinates scrambled, to touch a strangely vibrant material core within the self that anticipates heavenly life, then in the *Devotions upon Emergent Occasions* Donne uses his own sickness to accomplish the same goal. In the *Devotions*, Donne presents his own sick, feverish body as something akin to a Baroque crucifix, and as he contemplates himself in light of his body, and invites readers to contemplate themselves in light of his and their own bodies, he engages in a theoretical project of deranging the self and its conventional coordinates within the world. Achsah Guibbory argues that in the *Devotions* "it is not enough for Donne to feel God within him, spiritually, like Milton whose God prefers 'the upright heart and pure' before 'all Temples.' . . . And Donne is no kin to the later seventeenth-century Quakers who treasured only the 'light within' the conscience. Donne, always, wants to feel God—and find evidence of God—in his bodily experiences, and even in the most unpleasant ones. We find this in the *Devotions* no less than in his poetry."[29] Guibbory's observation is the starting point for grasping the distinctive way that Donne's text bends a future of physical resurrection into the here and now so that in his sick body he can already feel the beginnings of an ultimately triumphal process of resurrection, what Vaughan will call the "seeds" or "bright shoots of everlastingness."

Announcing the basic gambit of the entire work at the outset, Donne begins with the observation that under pressure of sickness he must now consider himself as "dust and ashes," the very emblems of the resurrectable material stuff of the body, for "the *Lordes* hand is the *Vrne*, in which these *ashes* shall be preseru'd" (*Devotions*, "Expostulation I," 8). In "Prayer XIII" Donne reflects on the spots that his illness creates on his body and the fevers that go with them and interprets them as written signs of God's claim upon him, almost like signatures on a legal deed: "These heats, O Lord, which thou hast brought upon this body, are but thy chafing of the wax, that thou mightst seal me to thee: these spots are but the letters in which thou hast written thine own name and conveyed thyself to me" (*Devotions*, "Prayer XIII," 70). In "Expostulation II" Donne worries that his sickness is a sign that God has abandoned him, but ultimately he decides that the sickness is actually a sign that God is already now preparing resurrection, such that in sickness Donne can feel the beginning of a process that is apocalyptic but also breaking into his experience of himself in the here and now:

> I consider in my present state, not the haste, & the dispatch of the disease, in dissoluing this body so much, as the much more hast, & dispatch, which my God shal vse, in recollecting and reuniting this dust againe at the Resurrection. Then I shall heare his Angels proclaime the Surgite Mortui, Rise yee dead. Though I be dead I shall heare the voice; the sounding of the voice, and the working of the voice shall be all one; and all shall rise there in a lesse Minute, then any one dies here.
>
> (*Devotions*, "Expostulation II," 13)

What begins with the theory that God only punishes what he intends to save quickly morphs into the claim that dissolution is the necessary first step in the ultimate process of resurrection, and it is this ultimate process already now breaking into time that Donne is feeling and touching in his own sickness. The dissolution of the body into its parts, becoming aware of all the parts of his body, puts Donne's mind on the Resurrection, and by trying to see dissolution from God's perspective Donne touches the reality of himself as resurrected. Whereas the social self sees sickness as dissolution and divorce, the other point of view that Donne struggles to achieve here sees it as a sign of a strange, inextinguishable, material life that will continue on after the socially recognized person who is horrified at the advent of sickness has disappeared.

At times in the *Devotions* Donne says that he comes to feel the corporeal reality of the dead but resurrected body of Christ within himself, as in "Expostulation VII," where he hopes that his sickness will make him "the ark, and the monument, and the tomb of thy most blessed Son, that he, and all the merits of his death, may, by that receiving, be buried in me, to my quickening in this world, and my immortal establishing in the next" (*Devotions*, "Expostulation VII," 39). The important point here is that resurrection becomes immanent in the world (and the body) as it exists now. Under the pressure of sickness, Donne comes to see within or under his conventional social identity a vibrant, material "quickening" that militates against the conventional social axes of identity that he tends to associate with the soul.

In "Meditation XIII" Donne says explicitly that contemplating the sick body, including from the inside, takes you out of the conventional social roles and conventional social experiences and concerns and instead makes the self seem a body that is suffused with the potential for quickening into another life after death:

> O death, how bitter is the remembrance of thee, to a man that lives at rest in his possessions, the man that hath nothing to vex him, yea unto him that is able to receive meat! Therefore hast thou, O my God, made this sickness, in which I am not able to receive meat, my fasting day, my eve to this great festival, my dissolution. And this day of death shall deliver me over to my fifth day, the day of my resurrection; for how long a day soever thou make that day in the grave, yet there is no day between that and the resurrection. Then we shall all be invested, reapparelled in our own bodies.
> (*Devotions*, "Expostulation XIV," 75–76)

Here sickness is understood as a process of bracketing the normal social concerns of "a man that lives at rest in his possessions," which makes it possible, instead, to focus on a future of resurrection when "we shall all be invested, reapparelled in our own bodies," but this future is, paradoxically, here now, since the point is that (at least phenomenologically) there will be no gap between the dissolution Donne is already experiencing now and the experience of resurrection ("how long a day soever thou make that day in the grave, yet there is no day between that and the resurrection"). The note of seeking a beneficently deranging materiality within the self has been struck at the outset, and as his sickness progresses it becomes ever more the object of his attention as he uses the occasion of his sickness to investigate the body and its capacity to transcend time.

The *Devotions* are applied critical theory centered on taking seriously the material force of the body. To feel the self as dust and ashes, potentially dispersed to the four corners of the earth, the subject of an eventual but already now immanent material resurrection, is a beneficent, positive development that Donne thanks his illness for giving him. He uses his meditations, written in the present tense almost immediately after his recovery, to transfer that experience to readers, for, in the most famous words of the *Devotions*, "never send to know for whom the bell tolls; it tolls for thee "(*Devotions*, "Meditation XVII," 86). Donne foregrounds his own body as a kind of crucifix, the object of a meditative practice designed to make strange the disembodied and socialized self that we conventionally take for granted in favor of a new self, one fundamentally material, one that does not posit itself as a mind separate from others, separate from society in its agency and autonomy. In articulating this perspective in the *Devotions* but also in his sermons, Donne uses the increasingly démodé idea of corporeal resurrection as critical theory, as a way of gaining a transformative perspective on the self and the world.

The notion that the payoff of the most material and monist notions of resurrection is to make strange the conventionally social, decorporealized, highly buffered self in favor of a new self, one fundamentally rooted in the body and its experiences, is also key for understanding Donne's verse, especially his erotic verse. For Donne, the essential experience of sexuality is to feel like a body that is in some important sense a stranger and that has the ability to connect with other bodies in ways that bypass the conventional modes of social affiliation. And paradoxically, the desire to be reduced to a body will be most completely fulfilled when he is reduced to a body by death. This explains why so many of his erotic poems include references to death, corruption of the body, and the possibility of eventual physical reanimation. In many of his erotic poems, death and resurrection define the hypercorporeal state that love aims at, and as such many of Donne's erotic poems bend an imagined future of resurrection into the here and now to capture the reality of the body in the grip of desire. This happens, for example, in the famous image in "The Relique" in which Donne imagines himself buried with a lock of his beloved's hair wrapped around his arm so that at the resurrection the beloved will have to return to Donne to get her hair back.

When my grave is broke up againe
    Some second ghest to entertaine,
    (For graves have learn'd that woman-head,
    To be to more than one a Bed)
      And he that digs it, spies
A bracelet of bright haire about the bone,
      Will he not let'us alone,
And thinke that there a loving couple lies,
Who thought that this device might be some way
To make their soules at the last busie day,
Meet at this grave, and make a little stay?
                     ("The Relique," 1–11)

Evidently, for Donne, love in the here and now points forward to the general resurrection, when the lovers, having become weirdly vibrant, zombie-like bodies, will seek each other out in the grave. The image of the bone with the bright hair twined around it achieves a luminous intensity that only a few of Donne's lyric images do. It points to a physical interconnection that the lovers failed to achieve in life:

Difference of sex no more wee knew,
    Than our guardian Angells doe;
      Coming and going, wee
Perchance might kisse, but not between those meales;
    Our hands ne'r touchd the seales,
Which nature, injur'd by late law, sets free:
                     ("The Relique," 25–30)

If this poem nominally looks forward to a future of actual resurrection when the lovers will be reunited, then the experience of two zombie-like quasi-dead bodies seeking each other or at least experiencing proximity to each other is also bent into the here and now and becomes the essence of the erotic experience that the poem documents and represents. It seems that what Donne most values in love is that it forces him back into his body, forces him to become a body in the way that he will be fully and amazingly a body when the body is reanimated at the last day.

In many of Donne's erotic poems, love becomes a heightened experience of being a body among other bodies, and the kinds of connections between lovers that the body allows often take place in the absence (or even the blockage) of any conventionally social connection or even conventional physical consummation. The equation of love as the heightened experience of being a body with the decommissioned theology of the resurrection of the flesh is especially characteristic of the poems of heterosexual eroticism (as compared to the same-sex eroticism I will examine below). As Rebecca Ann Cach reminds us, Donne lived in a time long before the ideology of intimacy, *especially* heterosexual intimacy between men and women. In fact, for Donne, all relationships with women are built on the absence of the possibility of an emotional union based on equality. The latter is something that Donne can imagine only in relation to men, as with his sometimes erotic letters to his lifelong friend Henry Goodyear.[30] In "Love's Alchemy," Donne concludes with the nasty lines: "Hope not for mind in women; at their best, / Sweetness and wit they are, but mummy, possess'd." "Mummy" is a reference to putative Egyptian carcasses that were valued for their supposed medical properties. Mummy is dead bodies, and as always in Donne, death foregrounds the body so that the misogynistic point he is making— women are mindless body—is especially intensified by comparing them to *dead* bodies. The point of mummy is to be cannibalistically ingested as a supposed therapy, to make the self-body digest and incorporate the body of the other, and this is (somewhat oddly) the experience that Donne has in "The Dissolution," in which grief at the death of the beloved is fantasmatically experienced as making her (now) dead flesh part of his flesh so that he experiences himself as bloated with dead (nonnourishing) meat:

> Shee'is dead; and all which die
>   To their first Elements resolve;
> And wee were mutuall Elements to us,
>   And made of one another.
> My body then doth hers involve,
> And those things whereof I consist, hereby
> In me abundant grow, and burdenous,
>   And nourish not, but smother.
>
> ("The Dissolution," 1–8).

The value of women (for Donne) is that they are bodies who, through their touch, have the zombie-like power to make Donne, also, into a body. Similarly, in "A Nocturnall upon S. Lucies Day" love is celebrated for its power to render Donne as a (paradoxically) living dead body. The actual experience of love that he remembers seems defined by an anticipation of death, as the speaker and his beloved are repeatedly forced into dissolution caused by tears and other powerful emotions; they then decay, culminating with the (happy?) preemptive experience of feeling like "carcasses":

> Oft a flood
> Have wee two wept, and so
> Drownd the whole world, us two; oft did we grow
> To be two Chaosses, when we did show
> Care to ought else; and often absences
> Withdrew our soules, and made us carcasses.
>
> ("A Nocturnall," 22–27)

As with the mummy reference, the carcass, by being a dead body, emphasizes the bodyness of the body, but this time it is both Donne and his
beloved who are like dead bodies. It seems strange to imagine remem-
bering being a carcass as a happy memory, but that is how it functions
in this poem, where it is a compensatory memory. In general for Donne,
being made into a body, often a dead body, appears to be essential to the
experience of love.

The same idea of love transforming the self and the beloved into carcasses appears again in "The Ecstasy," whose opening conceit is that
the souls of Donne and his beloved have left their respective bodies to
commune in some disembodied space, leaving their bodies literally inanimate, a condition he likens to being funerary statues covering the
grave:

> And whil'st our soules negotiate there,
>   We like sepulchrall statues lay;
> All day, the same our postures were,
>   And wee said nothing, all the day.
>
> ("The Ecstasy," 17–20)

On the one hand, this poem invokes body/soul dualism and imagines that
the souls of the lovers alone are somehow capable of communing with
each other. On the other hand, this supposed communing is offstage, as
it were, and the center of the poem, the "payoff" of love, is to feel unalive,
in this instance, to feel like funeral statues pointing down, as it were, to
dead and moldering bodies below. The situation of being made a corpse
is tied to the *unconsummated* nature of their relationship. Near the beginning of the poem Donne notes that as of yet the only consummation
these lovers know is holding hands:

> So to'entergraft our hands, as yet
>   Was all the meanes to make us one,
> And pictures in our eyes to get
>   Was all our propagation.
>
> ("The Ecstasy," 9–12)

And he winds around to asking, "But O alas, so long, so farre / Our bodies why doe wee forbeare?" and ends with the decisive proposition "To our bodies turne we then" (49–50, 69). Yet the experience of being a frozen body next to another frozen body occurs so frequently in Donne's poems that one comes to wonder whether he thinks of it less as a problem to be overcome through erotic conquest and more as the essential experience of love itself, an experience without which love is not love.

It is wrong to say that the speaker of Donne's poems seeks but fails to find intimacy; rather, it seems that Donne's poems *value* nonmutuality, nonconsummation, and nonsuccess and that they do so because they value erotic blockage as a way of being forced to be—and to linger in the state of being—a body next to another body. Indeed, we might well say that Donne's poems deploy an erotics of denial and interruption of the sex drive as a way of creating an intensified experience of having or being a body. After all, precious few of Donne's love poems contemplate any kind of consummation, and even the ones that do admit of consummation are written in the face of interruption ("The Sun Rising") or a new reality of forced chastity in the here and now (perhaps because of separation, as in "A Valediction: Forbidding Mourning," and, indeed, all the Valediction poems). Physical nonconsummation is the essence of an experience that makes Donne intensely aware of his own body. And that seems to be what his poems value; they value the delay, the deferral of physical consummation as a way of intensifying and increasing the experience of a body as strange, as having a life of its own, separate from the conscious and reasoning life of the soul.

Love makes it possible to touch that other life, the life of the body, and never more so than when physical desire is insistently not gratified, a situation that Donne routinely engineers and intensifies in his imagination. Again and again in Donne's poetry this experience of an eroticism built on heightening and intensifying being a body is associated with the resurrection of the body. We have already noted that in "The Ecstasy" Donne and his beloved are sepulchral (that is, funerary) statues marking the tombs where, on the last day, their bodies will be reanimated. In "The Anniversarie" Donne notes that "two graves must hide thine and mine coarse" (11). In "A Valediction: Of My Name, in the Window" Donne imagines the name that he has scratched into his beloved's windows as a death's head: "It, as a given deaths head keepe, / Lovers mortalitie to preach, / Or thinke this ragged bony name to bee / My ruinous Anatomie" (21–24). In "Loves Exchange" he ends by warning a personified Love not to torture him, for "Rack't carcasses make ill Anatomies" (42). In "A Nocturnall upon S. Lucies Day" Donne says that "I am every dead thing, / In whom love wrought new Alchimie" (12–13). The premise of "The Will" is that Donne will bequeath his qualities to the world at death, for "I'll un-doe / The world by dying; because love dies too. / Then all your beauties will be no more worth / Than gold in Mines, where none doth draw it forth" (46–49). "The Funeral" (like "The Relic") imagines Donne's dead arm enwreathed with a bracelet of his beloved's hair. In "The Expiration" Donne asks his beloved to "Ease mee with death, by bidding mee goe too" (8). "The Paradox" culminates with "Once I lov'd and dy'd; and am now become / Mine Epitaph and Tombe. / Here dead men speake their last, and so do I; / Love-slaine, loe, here I lye" (17–20). To some extent these poems traffic in the pun of death/orgasm, but at the same time I want to high-light how frequently Donne equates love with becoming a body, especially the body at its most bodily, as it were, in death.

There is a virtuous circle in Donne between thinking of himself as a body (made a body by love, as it were), thinking of his body at the point of death or beyond death, and then also imagining his body at the point of resurrection. The common link is the interest in seeing the body as pro-foundly endowed with a surplus of vibrant life in excess of any conventional social identity. To some extent, this view connects to the "vibrant material-ism" that concerns Jane Bennett and the other new materialists and that attempts to extend agency to things. Indeed, discussing the "Funeral Ser-mon" Drew Daniel argues that "if Bennett wants us to see even the dead rat as suffused with a vibrancy, Donne wants us to see even a live rat as already preparing for its certain material annihilation even while still embryoni-cally 'buried' in its mother's womb."[31] The point I am making here is that the erotic poems are engineered to foreground the material vibrancy in the self and the beloved as they encounter each other in the here and now.

Donne cherished resurrection imagery precisely because it foregrounds the notion that what is valuable about love is that it makes you aware of having, of being, a body. Thus, when in "A Valediction: Of My Name, in the Window" Donne imagines that the letters of his name he has carved in the beloved's window are the "rafters of my body, bone," he imagines that the beloved—endowed with the power of resurrection—can make them into flesh again:

> Then, as all my soules bee,
> Emparadis'd in you, (in whom alone
>   I understand, and grow, and see)
>   The rafters of my body, bone
> Being still with you, the Muscle, Sinew, and Veine,
>   Which tile this house, will come againe.

> Till my returne repaire
> And recompact my scattered body so.
> As all the virtuous powers which are
> Fix'd in the stares, are said to flow
> Into such characters, as graved bee
> When these starres have supremacie.
> ("A Valediction: Of My Name, in the Window," 25–36)

Here a future of reunion (and final consummation) with the beloved is cast as the final day in which bodies will be joyfully refleshed. In life, love heightens the body and its desires, makes lovers aware of having or being bodies, makes lovers aware of the intensity of life encoded into the sinews and flesh, a life that will only be liberated at the final resurrection and perfection of the flesh. Feeling desire in and for a body is associated by Donne with looking forward to that incomprehensible moment when bodies will be reassembled. In the light of resurrection, the central fact of love—having a body or, better, being a body—is rendered "mysterious," as "The Canonization" puts it. The mystery of love is having or being a body, and that is increasingly a mystery to the kind of buffered, mentalistic self that Donne champions to the extent that he is a proponent of the secularization process and the highly buffered, mentalistic self that goes along with it.

The eroticism of blockage and delay that we see in the erotic poems culminates with moments of full-blown masochism whose goal is precisely to intensify the experience of being a body. To call Donne a masochist is somewhat strange, for he is famously full of a hyperaggressive masculinity ("masculine persuasive force," as Fish called it), but this hypermasculinity is shadowed by a kind of vulnerability (diagnosed by Fish as a tendency toward "bulimia").[32] The moments of self-assertion in Donne's poetry are typically only the means to the moment when the self is revealed as (nothing but?) a body, and this wish to be a body, to be treated as a body, to write poems that represent the self as a body, is fundamentally masochistic. Thus, in "Elegy XIX: To His Mistris Going to Bed," the driving, authoritative male voice who is confident that he will indeed have his desires satisfied is surprisingly undercut by the concluding revelation that "To teach thee, I am naked first; why then, / What needst thou have more covering than a man?" (47–48). Given the Western literary and visual tradition's emphasis on the female nude and deemphasis of the male nude, this is quite a surprising development. The poem's "payoff," as it were, comes with the sudden awareness by Donne of being very insistently and visibly a body. The conclusion interrupts the narrative of a successful consummation by reintroducing the reality of the body as Donne is reduced to a body desperate for the consummation of its desires.

The desire to be reduced to a body and its connection to an ideology of monist-materialist and immanent resurrection is most fully on display in poems in which the cross-gender dynamic of the poems I have examined thus far is transposed into a male-male dynamic, often with God as the lover and Donne as the beloved, as happens in the *Holy Sonnets*. In a sense, the problem in the (heterosexual) erotic poems is that Donne has a hard time imagining women being as effectively dominating as he has an easy time imagining a putatively masculine God to be; the practice of suspended or interrupted consummation is a stopgap that allows a woman to dominate him (nearly) as effectively as God, but in the explicitly same-sex religious poems this stopgap is set aside in favor of a more direct encounter with what, for Donne, is the quintessentially erotic experience, namely, the experience of being reduced to a body.[33]

For the Donne of the *Holy Sonnets*, a masculine God is better than the feminine beloved evoked by the Petrarchan sonnet tradition because more capable of dominating him.[34] The most obvious example is "Holy Sonnet XIV: Batter my heart, three person'd God," in which Donne ends up in a masochistic position, begging to be ravaged. But if God has the power to make Donne into an honorary woman even as he is still a man, then what is equally or even more important is that he also has the power to make Donne into a (mere) body (and this, in turn, may be what feminizes Donne most effectively).[35] The physical quality of the body appears here because it is subject to divine punishment and dispersal; Donne wants God to "breake, blowe, burn" him (4), thereby evoking the very concerns of materialist resurrectionist thought that he cites in a Christmas sermon: "Every puff of wind within these walls, may blow the father into the sons eyes, or the wife into her husbands, or his into hers, or both into their childrens, or their childrens into both. Every grain of dust that flies here, is a piece of a Christian" (6:365). In this sonnet, the future of postmortem physical dispersal is bent into the here and now, for it is through a wished-for dissolution of the body that Donne feels transcendence. In the *Holy Sonnets*, the body is no longer a house for the soul or an instrument of the will; rather the body becomes a tool for deranging the self, as Donne asks God to use physical punishment to "make me new." This divine punishment is not a means to inculcating some "holier" habitus or mode of being; the punishment is itself the thing in which this new experience of selfhood inheres and consists, and I think the sense that divine punishment is its own immanent payoff is what accounts for the erotic quality of the poem. Masculine masochism is on display here, in which feeling the self's body denigrated and desecrated is itself redeeming (by pointing in the direction of fantasmatic union with the abused body of Christ, as in "Holy Sonnet XI").

A similar dynamic appears in "Goodfriday, 1613. Riding Westward." This poem begins with a categorical dualism, separating out the soul from the body. In its pursuit of worldly "pleasure or businesse," the soul determines the movement of the body toward the West and away from the East, where the crucifixion and resurrection happened: "Pleasure or businesse, so, our Soules admit / For their first mover, and are whirld by it. / Hence is't, that I am carryed towards the West / This day, when my Soules forme bends towards the East" (7–10). Here the soul "admits" pleasure and business as its prime movers—in other words, the soul is captured by the historical social world that gives to Donne the identity and the calling that lead him to travel West on this Easter Day. But the point of the poem is surely that if there is something deep inside Donne's socialized person that yearns toward the East, it is only his body that can touch the East, and only in a very perverse way. While at first Donne interprets his body's physical orientation facing the West as a sign of sin or worldliness in him, he ultimately determines that this posture contains the seeds of its own correction, for by turning his back to the dying Jesus on the cross he opens his body to what is again an erotics of physical abuse:

> and thou look'st towards mee,
> O Saviour, as thou hang'st upon the tree;
> I turne my backe to thee, but to receive
> Corrections, till thy mercies bid thee leave.
> O thinke mee worth thine anger, punish mee,
> Burne off my rusts, and my deformity,
> Restore thine Image, so much, by thy grace,
> That Thou may'st know mee, and I'll turne my face.
> ("Goodfriday," 35–42)

Here "corrections" and punishment are a means to an end (that is, to be made new so that he will turn his face toward Christ) but are also an end in itself, the very thing that Donne wishes for. To be restored to "thy image" is, after all, to be the object of physical punishment, represented by the image of the "Savior, as thou hang'st upon the tree." It is almost as if Donne were discovering a Freudian unconscious in which his conscious will to pursue pleasure and business is shadowed by a secret will to turn his back to the East, a move equated with the desire to secure physical humiliation and punishment.

Resurrection, automatically invoked by the Easter occasion of this poem, makes the body insistently present as something other than a tool of the soul, and that is what makes resurrection such a useful topos in the poetry, erotic and religious alike. The ultimate value of punishment for Donne is to make the body into a body, to bring the body to the fore, and not as a tool for obtaining the pleasures and business that the soul is moved by but because the body is strange and recalcitrant as opposed to the worldliness of the soul. In that sense, the punishment in the context of his relationship with God is analogous in its effects with the enforced blockage and nonconsummation that he experiences in relation to the beloved in the heterosexual poems: Both open the body as a scene of vibrant life at odds with the conventional indices of social identity.

I want to conclude my discussion of Donne by describing how his commitment to immanent monist-materialist resurrection, his brand of eroticism, and his yearning to *be* a body all lead to Donne's distinctive aesthetic formal practice, both in his poetry and in his prose. Kimberly Johnson argues that the formal patterns in Donne's poems make "presence present" in a metaphysical way.[36] But in Donne's writing, including "The Canonization," the formal and metrical density of his text foregrounds a presence that is counter to any worldly indices of identity or even human meaning. As practiced by Donne (and, I will argue in subsequent chapters, also by Herbert and Vaughan), poetry is a discourse that uses language to posit a world but that at the same time reminds the reader of its constructedness, its artificiality, its tenuousness, its contingency in time; this allows readers to glimpse the strangely vibrant materiality of the world in the instant before it is made meaningful within the terms of a particular historical language. Donne's writing is therefore an engine for "making strange" the world, people, and things, and this is achieved via the insistent strangeness of the language that comes out of Donne's mouth or that flows from his fingers. We can therefore say that a project of estranging readers from themselves and their world and how they and the world are meaningful is reflected in the strangeness of the voice and the language that we hear in Donne's writing.

Many of the best readers of Donne's prose and poetry have described those elements of the poems and prose that seem to resist meaning-making. Judith Scherer writes that Donne's poems "baffle provocatively and usefully any attempt to fix their meanings, directing our attention to the words, their figuration, shape, and patterns, often more than to the ideas."[37] C. A. Patrides notes that Donne establishes metrical patterns and rhythms only to subvert them, noting the disturbed rhythms and stresses displaced from an expected pattern.[38] He notes the tension between the many moments in which individual lines seem to lift away from the larger poem they are a part of. Elaine Scarry connects the formal challenge of making sense of both the poems and the prose with a deep background interest in foregrounding matter and materiality. Scarry writes that there is "a broader continuity between language and the material realm it seeks to represent," especially when the language becomes fragmented and hard to unify. She notes examples such as "The Dampe," in which a doctor cuts up the body and surveys its parts, and "The Funeral," in which we see the body reduced to the sinewy threads that normally hold it together. For Scarry, the refusal of these poems to become an organic or coherent linguistic whole is related to their interest in representing the body in its heterogeneity and vulnerability.

Building on these accounts, I want to argue that Donne's goal in writing about the world and about the experience of having or being a body—including the experience of love—is not to make that experience make sense within the canons of coherence provided by language categories but the opposite, namely, to preserve the body and the material world in its strangeness. It is not the conventional social Donne as a speaker and his understanding of the world as meaningful whom we hear in these poems but "another person" rooted in the body and its life. This way of understanding Donne is counterintuitive because on our usual way of thinking, rendering something in language is a way of making it meaningful and therefore of making it less strange. Not so for Donne. Thus, in the *Devotions* and in his sermons, Donne writes about bodily experience in such a way as to *make that experience more strange*. As such, Donne sets up a virtuous circle between formally wrought language and the bodily life it brings to light, each intensifying the strangeness of the other.

Looking at Donne's project in this way, it is possible to extract an implicit theory of literary language from his work, and in some ways, this implicit theory anticipates some of the ideas articulated in the early twentieth century by the Russian formalists, especially Viktor Shklovsky. Shklovsky was not interested in seeing literature as a message, a story, or a moral; rather he views the point of literary art to "make strange" or "defamiliarize" the world through what he calls formal "devices." In his famous essay "Art as Device," he writes that "the purpose of art is to impart the sensation of things as they are perceived and not as they are known. The technique of art is to make objects 'unfamiliar,' to make forms difficult, to increase the difficulty and length of perception because the process of perception is an aesthetic end in itself and must be prolonged."[39] In one of Shklovsky's best-known essays—entitled "The Resurrection of the Word"—he argues that all words are originally tropes but that, over time, they become conventional and therefore deadened, and he argues that as a medium, literature is designed to make words alive again.[40] Another of Shklovsky's essays describes a short story by Tolstoy in which the device is that the narrator is a horse and, therefore, does not understand private property. For Shklovsky, what is important is that this device allows Tolstoy to describe things as though he were seeing them for the first time rather than simply naming them.

But one important contrast between Shklovsky and Donne has to do with the purpose or payoff of this literary defamiliarization. For Shklovsky, the purpose of literary defamiliarization is to reinvigorate language and its ability to deliver the world anew. For Donne, by contrast, the purpose of literary defamiliarization seems to be to make us aware of the way that the world only ever appears to us through the conceptual categories of language and by becoming aware of this fact to at least begin to listen for a "real" that exists beyond the confines of language even if—by definition—it cannot be discussed or described without losing its strangeness. And for that very reason, Donne's poetics move in the direction of seeing the world itself as infused with a strange animated power that seems to transcend the conceptual and linguistic apparatus we use to make sense of it. There is a fine line between reinvigorating language and thereby making the world look fresh (Shklovsky) and revealing the limits of language and thereby infusing the world with a potentially transcendental strangeness that is, in some sense, the excess that goes beyond language (Donne). But there is a distinction nevertheless, and it is decidedly the second project to which Donne is committed.

The experience of fully undergoing Donne's writing is to suggest that if language in its proper functioning discloses a world then it also covers up that world.[41] When one reads a lot of Donne's prose and poetry one comes to feel that under normal circumstances (certainly not the circumstance of reading a lot of Donne) language gives a world that is humanly meaningful but that by giving the world that "makes sense" language also represents a loss or an occlusion of something primally "there" ("Being," perhaps). Thus, for Donne, the function of art—and especially of poetry—is not merely to revitalize a particular language and (therefore) to make that language able to grasp the world anew. Rather, Donne aims to make us aware of the fact that we can only see the world through our language, that the world given by our language is, in fact, irreducibly contingent, and, therefore, that there is also something that always lies beyond that language (the hypothesis of the "really real," as it were).

Donne's poetry and prose are a school that teaches that the "natural" meaningfulness of the world is not *ultimately* meaningful but only contingently so, from within the horizon of conventional uses of a particular language. Moreover, Donne's writing suggests that by becoming aware of language it is possible to become aware of a tiny gap between the stuff of language and the meanings it conveys, and in the hiatus or pause between when language appears and it snaps (as it were) into meaningfulness it is possible to catch sight of the self and the world in a new way before or beyond language. If, for Shklovsky, poetry functions to refresh language and to rescue it from becoming clichéd, thereby allowing us to see the world afresh, then Donne's writing is designed to make us aware of the fact that we inhabit, as an inescapable horizon, a language community and thereby to make us aware that the only world we know is a historically defined world delivered by a particular, contingent language. And the point or payoff of this awareness of language is to push us to imagine or grasp the world (including the part of the world that is the self) as infused with the vital strangeness that is in excess of the meanings and categories of a historical language.

The mindset of being inside a language community is profoundly human; language is how we make sense of the world, how we make the world meaningful, and assuming that the world is meaningful is an important feature of being inside a language community. But Donne's writings detach readers from that mindset; there is no native speaker of Donne's language, as it were. Donne's prose style and poems make the experience of being inside a language community strange (in a way that is echoed, as we shall see in the next chapter, by George Herbert's poetics). That this project is in some deep way linked to Donne's commitments to the resurrection of the body as something that always troubles any conventional understanding of the human person and human identity is suggested by many of his poems, including one of his most literarily self-conscious, "The Canonization":

> Wee can dye by it [i.e., love], if not live by love,
>> And if unfit for tombes or hearse
>> Our legend bee, it will be fit for verse;
> And if no peece of Chronicle wee prove,
>> We'll build in sonnets pretty roomes;
>> As well a well wrought urn becomes
> The greatest ashes, as halfe-acre tombes,
>> And by these hymnes, all shall approve
>> Us *Canoniz'd* for love;
>
>> ("The Canonization," 28–36).

Here Donne says that what is most important about the lovers cannot be conveyed on a "tomb" or in a "chronicle." What can be conveyed or communicated on a tomb or in a chronicle is an account of the achievements of the lovers in the world. But the achievement of love is precisely to leave behind the social persons who can succeed in the world, and, as such, to communicate their erotic achievement they must turn to the formal games of poetry and "build in sonnets pretty roomes"—but only insofar as these sonnets are now conceived of not as a worldly résumé but as receptacles for their ashes, for "As well a well wrought urn becomes / The greatest ashes, as half-acre tombes" (32–34). Indeed, the whole conceit of the poem—invoking the Catholic ideal of canonization of saints and the notion that Donne and his beloved will be "canonized for love"— strongly foregrounds the body, the remains of the body, in the form of the veneration of the bodily remains of saints, which is one of the Catholic practices most insistently attacked by Protestant reformers. Donne and his beloved will be lost to the world, as it were, but by means of poetry the bodies that turned to each other in love will be preserved in the experience of reading these verses. The distinctive achievement of "The Canonization" is the tight association he proposes here between the experience of touching the body that is other to any social indices of meaning, reputation, or identity and the artfulness and strangeness and insistence on the materiality of language itself of a poetics that sets aside representation in favor of using words almost as stones, to build "pretty rooms" in ways Herbert will go on to explore in his "shape poems."[42]

Thinking about the connection between the lost and found idea of the resurrection of the body and its flesh and the formal complexity of these poems suggests a new way to understand the work of Donne and his imitators in the seventeenth century, namely, as strongly anticipating the avant-garde art of the early twentieth century. I believe that we should term the work of Donne and his successors "seventeenth-century avant-garde poetry," and in making this claim I am especially drawing on Peter Bürger's work. As I noted in the Introduction, Bürger understands the avant-garde as defined by a drive toward art that is not meant to be contemplated as a sealed packet of representational meaning but rather as an event that transforms the reader. I have suggested that the theory of the resurrection of the body drives Donne's poetry away from the closed perfected beauty of a work of art and to enter into the mind of the reader, where the aesthetic experience is at one and the same time the experience of transformation in the essence of the self and how it dwells in the world.[43] It is this impulse to treat art as a kind of social praxis that explains Donne's distinctive drive to use formal experimentation in language to get under the skin, as it were, of his readers.

Though it was Dr. Johnson who introduced the term "metaphysical" for the poetry of Donne and his successors, the contemporary use of the label "metaphysical" is indebted to T. S. Eliot's 1921 essay on "The

Metaphysical Poets." Eliot summarizes (and disagrees with) Dr. Johnson's famous claim that what characterizes metaphysical poetry is the conceit in which "the most heterogeneous ideas are yoked by violence together."[44] But if Eliot disagrees that the characteristic effect of "metaphysical poetry" is the "violent" conceit, then Eliot nevertheless says that "Johnson has hit, perhaps by accident, on one of their peculiarities, when he observed that 'their attempts were always analytic'" (245). Eliot argues that what distinguishes the metaphysical poets is the way they combine thought, including analytical thought, and feeling. As such, they represent a moment before a putative "dissociation of sensibility" in which thinking and feeling separate, making subsequent poetry, from Eliot's perspective, one-dimensional, either filled with feeling or analytical but not both.

Eliot's intuition that the work of the metaphysical poets represents a fusion of analytical thinking and feeling, such that the analytical thought is the feeling and the feeling is the analytical thought, is important. In this context, Eliot notes that what matters about ideas is less their truth than the effect they generate. He writes that "a philosophical theory which has entered into poetry is established, for its truth or falsity in one sense ceases to matter, and its truth in another sense is proved" (248). This notion of a "philosophical theory" whose "truth or falsity in one sense ceases to matter" is very like the way the resurrection of the flesh operates in Donne's writing. To echo Jane Bennett's formulation, I see the resurrection of the body and its flesh as a powerful "onto-story" and maybe even a "fable" that becomes a critical lever for Donne as he confronts a rising secularization founded on a cardinal dualism.[45] Indeed, I claim that it is precisely the "philosophical theory" of the resurrection of the body and its flesh that drives the combination of analytical thinking and feeling that Eliot recognizes and values in Donne's poems.

Eliot is certainly not aware of the general importance of the theory of material resurrection in Donne's work as I have argued for it here, yet he seems instinctively drawn to the role of the dead or dying body as essential to the distinctive literary experience he prizes in Jacobean and Elizabethan literature. Thus, one of his main examples of Donne's capacity to create powerful thought-feeling experiences is the famous phrase from Donne's "The Relic," in which a future reader is invited to imagine Donne's body being raised from the grave with "A bracelet of bright hair about the bone." Eliot appreciates the same thing in John Webster in "Whispers of Immortality" where he writes:

Webster was much possessed by death
And saw the skull beneath the skin;

And breastless creatures under ground
Leaned backward with a lipless grin.
("Whispers of Immortality," 1–4)[46]

With the notion that seventeenth-century poetry is defined by seeing "the skull beneath the skin" Eliot suggests that in metaphysical poetry the dead or dying body provokes (or even *becomes*) thought. Here Eliot comes close to intuiting the driving idea of this book: that under conditions of secularization the idea of the dead or dying body inside the living, socialized self triggers a powerful experience of analytical thought about the nature of the self and of subjectivity and that this particular experience of analytical thought is the essential subject matter of seventeenth-century "metaphysical" poetry. Thus, my concern in this book with the persistence and animating power of the ancient notion of the resurrection of the flesh as a way of directing seventeenth-century poets back to the alien power of their bodily life would seem finally to converge in some fashion with Eliot's claim that "Racine or Donne looked into a good deal more than the heart. One must look into the cerebral cortex, the nervous system, and the digestive tracts" (250). The poetry of Donne and his successors is driven by the impulse to use poetry to push a new analytical experience of the body, and the poetry (in its formal estranging) is designed to provoke a parallel kind of thinking in readers (as opposed to simply contemplating aesthetic beauty). The distinctive formal effects of Donne's poetry (and the poetry of other seventeenth-century poets) are not fireworks or displays of virtuoso power but are efforts to force thought about the connection between self, the body, the world, and meaning. It is this interest in using poetry as praxis, as equipment for living a new life, that is at the heart of Eliot's recognition of kinship with Donne and that I see as the basis for my claim that this poetry anticipates the avant-garde art of the early twentieth century as theorized by Bürger. Donne's verse was received in his culture not as an outpouring of beautiful objects or as simple representation of the world but as a kind of "happening" that crystallized around it new groupings of readers with a new experience of self and the world, the "subculture" of Donne lovers who appeared first around the Inns of Court and then later in other cultural circuits.[47] In Donne's poetry, the outré idea of the resurrection of the body and its flesh drives formally estranging poetry designed to trigger readers to renegotiate selfhood in relation to the social world. It is this complex of ideas and practices that Donne bequeaths to his most important successor poet, George Herbert, to whose poetry we now turn.

2 / Wanting to Be Another Person: Resurrection and Avant-Garde Poetics in George Herbert

In this chapter and the next I will look at two of Donne's most important successor poets, George Herbert and Henry Vaughan. I will argue that they are inheritors not only of Donne's distinctive poetic techniques but also of Donne's project of using the resurrection of the flesh as a critical lever to rethink and reimagine the nature of subjectivity and agency. I will start here with George Herbert (1593–1633). Donne was a close friend of Herbert's mother, Magdalen Herbert, and Herbert knew and spent time with Donne (who was twenty years older than Herbert). Herbert would have heard and read Donne's poetry and would have been interested in Donne's move into the Anglican ministry, and he followed Donne's path from secular poetry to the Anglican ministry and sacred verse. In a deeper sense, Herbert follows Donne in using verse, and especially formally experimental verse, to chart the fate of the body within the increasingly dualist path of the dominant form of secularization.

I wish to start with some poems from Herbert's posthumous collection *The Temple* (first published in 1633), in which death and resurrection are Herbert's explicit focus. My goal is to persuade readers that the apocalyptic convictions that power these poems are founded on an immanent understanding of the resurrection of the flesh and that this theory foregrounds the essentially strange, nonsocialized material substrate of personhood.[1] Herbert's poems are designed to catch the sight and (especially) the sound of a body that is him but that is also not his conventionally social self and that will be the substrate of an eventual resurrection of the flesh already now breaking into time. I will connect this theoretical vision to a poetics designed to bring to light and emphasize a material strangeness within any person, the poet as much as the reader, and I will ascertain the role that language plays in bringing to light and working with this transhistorical material substrate of personhood.

As I have argued in the Introduction and in the chapter on Donne, in early modern England a rising scientific tide puts pressure on the old, hybrid body-and-soul conception of resurrection and increasingly replaces it with a dualist vision in which the soul is more or less identical to the socialized person, the person accommodated to the historical world, and the body is merely its passive vehicle. From a dualist perspective, resurrection is a matter of a disembodied soul-essence living again separate from its body. But emerging alongside this new canonical dualism—as its equal and opposite reaction—is an exclusively materialist account of resurrection. And moreover, because of the increasing focus on the here and now associated with secularization pressures, this materialist account of resurrection is increasingly bent into the here and now, so that writers begin to imagine that they might find evidence in themselves or in other material elements in the world of a transformative process on the one hand apocalyptic and on the other hand immanent in the world as it exists.

Herbert does sometimes operate with a somewhat conventional dualism, and he does write poems in which he figures the body as a prison or as clothing that the soul wants to escape, and therefore he does sometimes write as though death might be immediately followed by the ascension of a detachable soul to a disembodied state of being. But what is more characteristic of Herbert is a desperate effort to hang onto the body in all of its strangeness. Thus even Herbert's most conventionally dualist poems are often internally undercut by a creeping emphasis on the body as the thing that will live again after the death of the social person. In "Death" Herbert imagines that Christianity has changed the experience of death and the dead body away from seeing the body as nothing but the shell of the soul with no inherent importance and toward seeing the body as the scene of a wished-for but only incompletely realized transcendence:

> Death, thou wast once an uncouth hideous thing,
>   Nothing but bones,
>   The sad effect of sadder grones;
> Thy mouth was open, but thou couldst not sing.
>
> For we consider'd thee as at some six
>   Or ten yeares hence,
>   After the losse of life and sense,
> Flesh being turn't to dust, and bones to sticks.

We lookt on this side of thee, shooting short;
    Where we did finde
        The shells of fledge souls left behinde,
Dry dust, which sheds no tears, but may extort.

But since our Saviours death did put some bloud
    Into thy face;
        Thou art grown fair and full of grace,
Much in request, mucht sought for as a good.

For we do now behold thee gay and glad,
    As at dooms-day;
        When souls shall wear their new aray,
And all thy bones with beautie shall be clad.

Therefore we can go die as sleep, and trust
    Half that we have
        Unto an honest faithfull grave;
Making our pillows either down, or dust.

("Death")[2]

Reversing the actual chronology of secularization, this poem claims that people used to have an incorrect understanding of death, by seeing death through a dualist lens in which the dead body is nothing more than the shell of a soul that has ascended to heaven. But according to the poem, with the advent of Christianity, in place of the ugliness of the dead and decaying body (ugly precisely because abandoned, left behind, because it is no longer the scene of personhood), "we" are now (quite paradoxically) able to see death as life; that is, in the light of resurrection, we see death as though it showed us not a dead body but a body that is on the point of being reanimated to a radically new life. That's what it means to behold death "as at doomsday," at the moment of reanimation. Seeing the dead body as beautiful rather than ugly is valued because it deranges the more conventionally dualist perception by which the self is somehow separate from the body, whose life is merely the precondition but not the essence of the person. Seeing the body that is subject to death and decay as the scene of life imbues the self with a life very different from the conscious egoistic life of the socialized subject. By foregrounding the body at death, that is, at its most hostile to the socialized ego, this poem tries to effect a disorientation, a limited detachment from the conventional self, to find a point of view on the still living self that homes in on an essentially bodily life that already now anticipates the strangeness of what will live at the general resurrection.

The poem "Longing" reveals the same impulse to see the self in a new and deranging light by focusing on the material substrate of the person, which is at once the precondition of socialized identity and other to socialized identity:

> Behold, thy dust doth stirre,
> It moves, it creeps, it aims at thee:
> Wilt thou deferre
> To succour me,
> Thy pile of dust, wherein each crumme
> Sayes, Come?
>
> ("Longing," 37–42)

According to the perspective articulated by this poem, the life of the person as it exists here and now is not an unsteady amalgam of body and soul but is all one thing, a body animated with a strangely impersonal vitality, like the zombies that populate contemporary television and film. The future reality of the resurrection of the flesh is immanent in the body as it exists now (the reader is instructed to "Behold, thy dust"), which is therefore opened to a search (via poetry) for what is strange and potentially transcendent in the body as it exists now.

Herbert's invitation to himself (or to his readers) to see himself (or themselves) as dust is an invitation to see past the normal or conventionally social person to a mysteriously animated substrate that points beyond itself, out of history and time. The decaying or already decayed thing Herbert imagines himself to be is the thing that is infused with the desire to join with God, as it will do on the day of the final resurrection, which the speaker wants to hurry along with the persistent appeal of "Come."

This lesson is also what Herbert learns in the "school of dust" he imagines attending in "Church-Monuments." Here Herbert begins with nominal dualism—he imagines that his "soul" has detached itself from the body through fervent prayer—before getting down to materialist business in the bulk of the poem, which is focused on contemplating the rotting bodies that lie beneath the stones of the church floor:

> While that my soul repairs to her devotion,
> Here I intombe my flesh, that it betimes
> May take acquaintance of this heap of dust;
> To which the blast of deaths incessant motion,
> Fed with the exhalation of our crimes,
> Drives all at last. Therefore I gladly trust

> My bodie to this school, that it may learn
> To spell his elements, and finde his birth
> Written in dustie heraldrie and lines;
> Which dissolution sure doth best discern,
> Comparing dust with dust, and earth with earth.
> These laugh at Jeat and Marble put for signes,
>
> To sever the good fellowship of dust,
> And spoil the meeting.
>
> ("Church-Monuments," 1–14)

Here contemplating death (even experiencing it imaginatively, for Herbert will "intombe" his flesh even as he contemplates the already entombed flesh of those who have gone before him) changes the nature of Herbert's self-experience and self-understanding here and now. In place of all individuality and distinction between persons—represented by the plaques and monuments that demarcate discrete burial sites—the self experiences itself in the "good fellowship of dust."

It is certainly true that Herbert—like Donne—imagines that all of his *own dust* will be tracked down and reassembled at the final resurrection. As he puts it in "Faith":

> What though my bodie runne to dust?
> Faith cleaves unto it, counting evr'y grain
> With an exact and most particular trust,
> Reserving all for flesh again.
>
> ("Faith," 41–44)

But having his "own" flesh detoured through the fellowship of dust changes the nature of what his own flesh feels like or what it means that it is his own in the first place. In this poem and the others I have been discussing, contemplating death and resurrection as a somewhat gruesome physical process is valued for its effects in the here and now, which are to make the self feel like a different self, as in the cemetery that is a "school" for making the self into a new and different self fundamentally built on renewed attention to the body—not as clothing or a vehicle or a tool for the soul but as the very scene of a mysterious, scarcely comprehensible animated force that *is* the self. The poem begins by positing a soul/body distinction, but the point of the poem is to effect a radical identification with the body at its most alien to the socialized self, that is, the self conventionally associated with the soul.

Similarly, in "Dooms-day" Herbert yearns for the day of resurrection, which means imagining himself as noxious decayed material that threatens to poison others and then imagining himself even further in time, at the moment where God reanimates precisely that decayed material:

> Come away,
> Make no delay.
> Summon all the dust to rise,
> Till it stirre, and rubbe the eyes;
> While this member jogs the other,
> Each one whispring, *Live you brother?*
>
> ("Dooms-day," 1–6)

Here the postdeath body is imagined to have a strange kind of decentralized agency—each limb whispers to the other limbs as it is reassembled. Moreover, the effect of the poem is to transport the apocalyptic future experience into the here and now, since the poem invites Herbert (and his readers) to identify with the body as the scene of the alien, almost zombie-like life that it will have exclusively at doomsday. And if this poem reports an experience that the speaker has himself, then it is nonetheless true that his poems are designed to allow or even to force readers to imagine and identify with their own body at its most hostile to socialized personhood.

The point of the experimental poetics that Herbert develops throughout his poetry is precisely to allow the strangely animated substrate that is-and-is-not him to speak, to sing. Indeed, a surprisingly oft-repeated topos in Herbert's poems is the notion of the dead body singing, speaking, or making sounds that inspire or can even be heard in Herbert's poetry. The poem "Death" begins with the claim that the distinctive contribution of Christianity is to allow death to sing: "Death, thou wast once an uncouth hideous thing, / Nothing but bones, / The sad effect of sadder grones; / Thy mouth was open, but thou couldst not sing" (1–4). If, with the advent of Christianity, death *can* sing, then implicitly it is in the poem itself that we can hear this song. In "Repentance" Herbert again imagines that death—here specifically his own dead and broken bones—will sing: "But thou wilt sinne and grief destroy; / That so the broken bones may joy, / And tune together in a well-set song, / Full of his praises, / Who dead men raises. / Fractures well cur'd make us more strong" (31–36).

Sometimes it is Herbert's (dead) body that sings in his poems, but in "Easter" it is the sound of Jesus's tortured body that is captured by the poem:

> Rise heart; thy Lord is risen. Sing his praise
> Without delayes,

Who takes thee by the hand, that thou likewise
       With him mayst rise:
That, as his death calcined thee to dust,
His life may make thee gold, and much more, just.

Awake, my lute, and struggle for thy part
       With all thy art.
The crosse taught all wood to resound his name,
       Who bore the same.
His stretched sinews taught all strings, what key
Is best to celebrate this most high day.

("Easter," 1–12)

The poem imagines itself as infused with death made vocal or audible, notably in the shocking image of the poem as lute, whose wood has been taught to sing by the cross and whose own stretched sinews (the lute strings) echo the stretched sinews of Christ's racked body: "His stretched sinews taught all strings, what key / Is best to celebrate this most high day." This is the sound of Herbert's own poems; he opens his mouth, as it were, expecting to hear his own voice, and instead what come out of his mouth are the sounds of Christ's body snapping. The point is that he discovers that Christ is in him (a conventionally reassuring claim in Christianity), but he discovers this only when a body and voice that Herbert thinks of as his "own" is replaced by the sound of the dying of Christ's body. In "Easter," finding Christ's body and voice within himself morphs into Herbert seeing his own body within him as the scene of resurrection.

Thus Herbert's fundamental goal for his poetry is to seek a stranger's body and its voice within the self, and the way he finds this stranger's body is to imagine what his own body will look and sound like at the moment of his death and reanimation. This approach to the issue of resurrection has the effect of transforming resurrection ideas into a tool to recast the essence of the person, of any person, away from socially legible attributes and toward a strange, material thing. Herbert's poetic project is one of trying to see around the corners of the conditioned body to catch sight of some kind of living, pulsating core separable from (though always, in this life, coassembled with) a socialized person. And the trope for this is finding a way to allow the body (which is mysteriously also Christ's body) to sing.

In his classic study of Herbert, Richard Strier casts the poet as a proto-pietist, as someone who believes that God values sincerity and genuine emotion more than elaborate ritual, and in that sense Strier sees Herbert as having much more in common with Protestant sectarians in the run-up to the English Civil War than with the Anglicans with whom Herbert is often classed.[3] There is something deeply right about Strier's point of view—more right than the countervailing new historicist reading that sees Herbert as socially ambitious, never bound by the call of sincerity, always willing to say whatever it takes to get ahead—but sincerity is a complex notion for Herbert, as it was for Augustine. For in a Christian context defined by the premise of universal sinfulness, the first and most heartfelt thing that comes out of Herbert is not necessarily genuine or sincere. Or rather, it is sincerity from the "wrong person," as it were, a point that Herbert makes in many poems, including "Grace," where "Sinne is still hammering my heart / Unto a hardnesse, void of love," which leads him to petition for a new self: "Let suppling grace, to crosse his art, / Drop from above" (17–20). What is most Herbert, his heart, is the part that has been most infected by sin, and therefore asking *this* Herbert to speak sincerely is to ask for sin to speak. In contrast, what Herbert wishes is to hear a different "Herbert," a Herbert who is the object of redemptive grace, but what I am arguing is that in these poems, the signs of being the object of redemptive grace are to be found in the body, that strange presocial thing that will live again at doomsday. And this other Herbert, who is fundamentally and essentially inseparable from the living body, is precisely the Herbert who "speaks" in the poetry, or, perhaps, to put it in a more correct way by putting it in a more passive voice, this other Herbert is the voice we come to hear through the poetry.

Thus, when in "Sion" Herbert says that what God really wants is not a formally elaborate poem but an honest groan ("one good grone"), the emphasis is not on the fact that this is a sincere moment as compared to all the elaborately staged hokum of the other poems (they are all sincere and formally contrived in equal measure) but that this groan is the sign of a different person rousing and revealing himself (herself? itself?) in a poem that has suddenly "quickened," to use an important Herbert word, into an alien voice. In place of the elaborate building of Solomon's Temple (and, implicitly, the ritual religious life at home there), God prefers the good groan that testifies to the emergence of a new person out of the cocoon, as it were, of socialized existence:

There thou art struggling with a peevish heart,
Which sometimes crosseth thee, thou sometimes it:
     The fight is hard on either part.
     Great God doth fight, he doth submit.
All Solomons sea of brasse and world of stone
Is not so deare to thee as one good grone.

And truly brasse and stones are heavie things,
Tombes for the dead, not temples fit for thee:
  But grones are quick, and full of wings,
  And all their motions upward be;
And ever as they mount, like larks they sing;
The note is sad, yet musick for a king.

("Sion," 13–24)

The point is that now that God has taken up residence in the human heart, he is at war with another part of the heart, the sinful or "peevish" part, which means, for Herbert, the part that is conventionally at home in the social world. In contrast to this sinful and peevish heart, the groan is a sign of another life, one that seems to escape from the world—it is "quick, and full of wings, / And all their motions upward be; / And ever as they mount, like larks they sing" (21–23). In place of the silence of a putatively disembodied soul, what this new life gives rise to is an insistent celebration of emphatically bodily groaning.[4] In "Affliction I" Herbert wishes that that he could "tune my breath to grones" (27), and in the poem whose very title is "Sighs and Grones" Herbert posits the whole poem as nothing but sighing and groaning. This idea is taken up again in "Home," as "gasps" and "sighs" (11, 43) but especially in that repeated cry ("O") at the end of each one of the thirteen stanzas: "O Show thyself to me, / Or take me up to thee!" (5–6 and final couplet of all subsequent stanzas).[5] In "Businesse" Herbert rhetorically asks himself, "Hast thou sighs, or hast thou not?" and links the capacity to groan with the mysterious and strange fact of having a body that will live again: "If thou hast no sighs or grones, / Would thou hadst no flesh and bones!" (11–13). In "The Search" Herbert imagines shooting groans at God in order to secure his transformative concern for Herbert just as in "Praise (III)" Herbert associates groans with tribute to God:

  Lord, I will mean and speak thy praise,
    Thy praise alone.
My busie heart shall spin it all my dayes:
    And when it stops for want of store,
Then will I wring it with a sigh or grone,
    That thou mayst yet have more.

("Praise [III]," 1–6)

In "Superliminare," Herbert associates groans with a yearning to be different, indeed to give birth to a different self, one "holy, pure, and cleare":

Avoid profanenesse; come not here:
Nothing but holy, pure, and cleare,
Or that which groneth to be so,
May at his perill further go.

("Superliminare," 5–8)

Here the groan is probably associated (as in Romans 8:22–24) with the notion of pregnancy; it is almost as if Herbert imagines his social person to be pregnant with another person and the groans are the sound of this other person's birth. In "Longing" the groan is again associated with a new awareness of the body itself, perhaps the scene of the rebirth that "Superliminaire" wishes for:

With sick and famisht eyes,
With doubling knees and weary bones,
To thee my cries,
To thee my grones,
To thee my sighs, my tears ascend:
No end?

("Longing," 1–6)

In "The Sinner" Herbert associates the groan with the "quintessence" of his true self beyond all the "dregs" of his conventionally socialized self:

In so much dregs the quintessence is small:
The spirit and good extract of my heart
Comes to about the many hundredth part.
Yet Lord restore thine image, heare my call:
And though my hard heart scarce to thee can grone
Remember that thou once didst write in stone.

("The Sinner," 9–14)

In "Gratefulness" Herbert says to God that "thou hast made a sigh and grone / Thy joyes" (19–20). In "Ephes. 4.30. Grieve not the Holy Spirit, &c." Herbert notes that in his incarnation, God also "doth grone," and Herbert goes on to associate his own groans with the sound of music and, in particular, the music of his own poem:

Oh take thy lute, and tune it to a strain,
Which may with thee
All day complain.
There can no discord but in ceasing be.
Marbles can weep; and surely strings
More bowels have, then such hard things.

("Ephes. 4.30. Grieve not the Holy Spirit, &c" 17, 18–23)

Similarly in "The Crosse" Herbert wishes that "once my grones / Could be allow'd for harmonie" (15–16).

To understand Herbert's poetics it is important that the word "groan" is more than an arbitrary signifier that carries a signified within the system of differences of a language. On the one hand, the word "groan" is indeed a word like any other, with a defined meaning inside a conventional language community. But on the other hand, the word "groan" has an onomatopoetic quality and, as such, it strains against being a word within a temporally and spatially delimited language community and pushes into the realm of sounds that signify by themselves. It picks up some of the spontaneous sounds of human embodiment, and this is emphasized in the many poems where Herbert associates groans with the pure (as it were) sound of music, including the music of praise, as in the final line of "Sion," in which Herbert notes that though the groan is sad it is yet fit music for a king. The groan is a word trying to cease to be a word, trying to be a mere sound, perhaps a musical sound, and the struggle to cease to be a word within a language (English) and to become instead tonal is centrally important to Herbert's poetics.

Poems that are written in words that come around to celebrating a partly onomatopoetic groan (or a repeated cry of "O," as in "Home" and several other poems) are poems that are fighting themselves, poems that are trying to move from the realm of representational language that carries meaning within a particular historical language community to the realm of nonlanguage or shaped and sculpted sound. And that move is also a move out of the conventional social world where the man named George Herbert has a mouth that produces language that has meaning to others within his language community. This conventional Herbert (and his conventional uses of language) is always already in the business of calculating what the other thinks, what effects the words will have on the other, is always already engaged in a game of pretense, something that Herbert is happy to lay claim to, indeed to celebrate, in *The Country Parson*, especially the sections on preaching. By contrast, if the celebration of the groan is a celebration of sincerity, then the sincerity at work here is so radical as to move in the direction of dislodging the speaker and his poem out of the conventional social world and the language community altogether, the only place where the language game of sincerity is even an option (and the fact that this dislodgement does not ever work all the way—since the word "groan" is always still a word—is simply a sign of the human predicament as Herbert sees it). The groan therefore represents a beneficent crisis in personhood and language in which a sound appears from beyond defined, codified, representational language and where the body that issues the sound appears from beyond the social person. It is another self, a different self than the conventionally social (sinful) self that speaks here, and it "speaks" only by speaking a word that is barely a word in the conventional sense. Instead, this other self speaks by making a sound, a sound that allows the body, the inevitable but inevitably strange substrate of the social person, to appear even as the poems allow the inevitable but inevitably strange substrate of any use of language, namely, sound itself, to appear. This sense of using poetry to push the "other" person that is the bodied self to speak is connected to the theology that values the body as animated dust, the very thing that will be resurrected on the last day, when all the social games and postures of history will be blown away.

I have been suggesting that the impulse to see and to hear the body as it exists separate from the historically conditioned, social person that is Herbert drives the interest in onomatopoeic groans and other efforts to make the body itself "sound" in poetry. I want to suggest that this impulse is theorized by Herbert as a break from the "courtly" poetry that is used to advance and articulate the worldly ambitions and agendas of the poet. In contrast to the social game of pretention and self-presentation that poetry represents at court, Herbert uses poetry as a way of deforming and estranging language in an effort to catch a glimpse of himself and the world outside of the conventional social categories that language automatically projects.[6] In this regard, it is noteworthy that Herbert frequently contrasts his poetry with the courtly love poetry that shows off the poet as a refined and articulate lover. In the two "Jordan" poems, Herbert emphasizes the distinction between his own poetry and the conventional courtly poetry of love and flattery that shows off the poet as a refined and elegant lover. "Who says," he asks, "that fictions onely and false hair / Become a verse? / Is there in truth no beauty / Is all good structure in a winding stair? / May no lines passe, except they do their dutie / Not to a true, but painted chair?" ("Jordan [I]," 1–5).

In Herbert criticism, the distinction is often understood in terms of secular love poetry on the one hand and sacred poetry on the other, though this distinction is in some ways a false one, as the eroticized and witty religious poetry of Donne, for example, illustrates. I want to argue that what differentiates Herbert from the world of competitive courtly poetry has less to do with the content of poetry (erotic versus religious) and more to do with the social effects of the poems, for what Herbert truly breaks with are the distinctive social effects of courtly poetry that aims to show off the poet to the best possible effect, placing a marker, as it were, for a genteel, elegant, verbally witty, and highly refined status, claiming, in short, cultural capital. I want to argue that Herbert really does want to break with the conventional social voice and the conventional social effects of courtly poetry in favor of a poetry that is not different because religious but in declining to use poetry to celebrate and advance the interests of the socially legible person and agent that is George Herbert.

In this regard, "The Forerunners" is a powerful poem for understanding Herbert's poetic project and the way it emerges in dialectical tension with the distinctive social stance of courtly poetry. In the first two stanzas, Herbert compares signs of old age in himself (white hairs) with the "harbingers" or "forerunners" who enter a town in advance of a visit by the king to identify houses to be used to lodge the king and his retinue by painting the door frames with a white mark:

> The harbingers are come. See, see their mark;
> White is their colour, and behold my head.
> But must they have my brain? must they dispark
> Those sparkling notions, which therein were bred?
>   Must dulnesse turn me to a clod?
> Yet have they left me, Thou art still my God.
>
> Good men ye be, to leave me my best room,
> Ev'n all my heart, and what is lodged there:
> I passe not, I, what of the rest become,
> So Thou art still my God, be out of fear.
>   He will be pleased with that dittie;
> And if I please him, I write fine and wittie.
>
> ("The Forerunners," 1–12)

This is a poem about accepting a change to old age and imbecility. But given Herbert's youthful age at the time of writing, it is not right to say that Herbert uses the poem to come to terms with the real fact of advancing age. Rather, Herbert uses the poem as a vehicle for triggering this feeling by transporting Herbert out of his own relatively young (if tubercular) body/self and into the body/self of a very old man whose hair is turning white. Strangely enough, Herbert *wants* to feel senile, and he wants to feel senile because he sees senility as a beneficent opportunity to become a new person, and that new person is experienced first and foremost in a new kind of poetry, a new relationship to poetry, a new voice in poetry. Herbert wants to stop being the kind of man who wants or even needs his poetry to be witty, sparkling, inventive (the way courtly poetry, whether religious or secular, always must be), and instead he wants to be the sort of person who can lay claim to the "bad" poetry (bad because uninventive, unwitty, predictable, average) of the line "Thou art still my God" as his ownmost speech.

This point is worth thinking over: The kind of transformation that Herbert wishes is one where language that is not "his" comes out of his mouth (the "bad" line is a quotation, in a sense, from someone else; it is language different from anything Herbert, with all his wit, would utter) but also forces him to accept that language as truly his own.[7] It is not unlike being forced to give a speech that isn't your own—for example at a show trial where you read a confession that has been written for you. It's easy to dismiss this poem as an instance of false humility, where Herbert writes a witty poem that attempts to disavow itself even as it shows off. It is certainly a poem that any poet would be proud to lay claim to, to call his own. Any poet could rightly expect credit for this poem, even (or especially?) insofar as the poem (wittily) claims that it is disavowing the kind of thing it is. But I think it is worth taking seriously that basic wish of the poem—shared by many other Herbert poems—which is the wish to be a different person, which, insofar as Herbert is a poet, means, first and foremost, the wish to use different language, to imagine language that is not his own coming out of his own mouth.

As the poem engineers a new kind of personhood for Herbert, it revisits a kind of primal scene of Herbert's poetic selfhood. As the poem presents him, Herbert is a man who has been to the brothels (perhaps only in his mind, by reading love poetry, but he treats that as a virtual visit to the brothels and stews, maybe like pornography) and who has wrestled the seductive and erotic language appropriate for brothels into his own mouth so that the language of the brothels has come to feel like his own, has come, indeed, to seem like the essence of his own personal voice.

> Farewell sweet phrases, lovely metaphors.
> But will ye leave me thus? when ye before
> Of stews and brothels onely knew the doores,
> Then did I wash you with my tears, and more,
> > Brought you to Church well drest and clad:
> My God must have my best, ev'n all I had.
>
> Louely enchanting language, sugar-cane,
> Hony of roses, whither wilt thou flie?
> Hath some fond lover tic'd thee to thy bane?
> And wilt thou leave the Church, and love a stie?
> > Fie, thou wilt soil thy broider's coat,
> And hurt thyself, and him that sings the note.
> > ("The Forerunners," 13–24)

The erotic language Herbert has been using in his poetry—once alien and then domesticated for holiness—must now be left behind for a new kind of language that again feels strange in his mouth—the aggressive plainness of "Thou art still my God," which he must now take into his mouth even though it is not his "own" language (just like the sugary language that was once not his own, having properly belonged to the stews).

> Let foolish lovers, if they will love dung,
> And canvas, not with arras, clothe their shame:
> Let follie speak in her own native tongue.
> True beautie dwells on high: ours is a flame
>   But borrow'd thence to light us thither.
> Beautie and beauteous words should go together.
>
> Yet if you go, I passe not; take your way:
> For, *Thou art still my God*, is all that ye
> Perhaps with more embellishment can say,
> Go birds of spring: let winter have his fee,
>   Let a bleak palenesse chalk the doore,
> So all within be livelier then before.
>
>   ("The Forerunners," 25–36)

The chalk that the forerunners use to mark rooms that they will take over for the king, which is equated here with white hair as a sign of senility and age, alienates Herbert from his old poetic self, but it is now reinterpreted as (at least potentially) a sign of a paradoxical "liveliness"—"Let a bleak palenesse chalk the doore, / So all within be livelier then before." Here the principle of life is intensified in a situation where the self has been stripped of its old sense of selfhood and social identity and therefore its old voice, in a scenario reminiscent of the way many of Herbert's poems about death frame the moment of death as a moment of heightened vitality (rather than the end of all vitality).

How are we supposed to understand this poem in relation to Herbert's poetry in general? In his classic study Stanley Fish argues that Herbert should be understood as in the grip of a Calvinist insistence on radical dependency on God and that the poems therefore enact a "self-canceling" quality, seeking to erase all claims of human-earned merit in favor of pointing back to a radical dependency on God.[8] A good illustration of this dynamic is "The Pearl," in which each of three stanzas enacts a pattern in which a whole paragraph of witty, smart, perfectly iambic assertions of what the speaker knows (each stanza begins "I know . . .") is counterbalanced (in the first three stanzas) by the assertion that the only thing that really counts is that "Yet I love thee" (10, 20, 30), a claim that itself (in the fourth stanza) turns out to be something the speaker can claim no responsibility for, since that feeling of love was initiated by God, who a "silk twist let down from heav'n to me" to enable the speaker "to climbe to thee" (38). This does indeed appear to be a Calvinist negation of agency, and as such it is at least compatible with the wish to write "self-canceling" poetry that Fish sees as being the very essence of Herbert's project.[9]

But what Fish sees as a Protestant theology of radical grace might be seen, instead, as an expression of a more general wish on the part of Herbert to use his poetry to transcend himself, to be a new kind of person who speaks a new kind of language and relates to readers in a new way. Thus, while it seems implausible that Herbert genuinely wishes to disavow his poetry, as Fish claims, it does seem plausible to see him as wanting to use poetry to disavow his social persona, first and foremost by finding a language that feels strange in his own mouth. Seeing that impulse as central to Herbert's poetry allows us to see that he is not aiming for a super-wittiness but rather that he is aiming for a super-strangeness that always raises the question of whether it is truly *Herbert's* language at all. What is at stake, truly at stake, for Herbert in his poetry is not that he look witty and smart and get credit for his work—something that he might indeed disavow, as Fish thinks he disavows it—but rather the issue is whether he gets to the point in a poem where the poem does not feel like his own anymore. And that can come about by radical complication (as in "Home," when his formal ingenuity leads the poem to have a life of its own) or by radical simplification (as in "The Forerunners," where he tries to talk himself into seeing a line that is somehow not his as being his). This poses the question of whether the most successful seventeenth-century poetry is not always the product of another self, a dimly recognized self that only shows itself in poetry and/or in moments of crisis, such as whatever supposed sign of senescence triggers "The Forerunners."[10]

Herbert certainly has poems where he thinks he has had a breakthrough as a poet only to see that his apparent breakthrough is now the very problem—as in "Jordan (II)," where early victory in poetry is undercut by a friend who whispers: "*How wide is all this long pretence! / There is in love a sweetnesse readie penn'd; / Copie out only that, and save expense*" (16–18, italics in original). Poetry that is too strong, too original, too witty, and for which he might get too much credit is genuinely at odds with a poetics designed to bring to life a strange, alien thing within the socially conventional persona.

This way of seeing Herbert's project suggests a novel perspective on some biographical cruxes that have troubled Herbert criticism. Herbert's relationship to the world of witty, competitive poetry among social elites in and around court, including in Herbert's family's circle, is an important question, and answers to this question might even be said to define the major fault lines separating Herbert critics. Thus, contra Fish, Michael Schoenfeldt and Christina Malcolmson argue that Herbert's poems are forthrightly participating in the courtly game of poetry, never more so than when they ostentatiously deny that they are doing so. For her part, Malcolmson believes that Herbert's poems were likely shown to (and even sung for) members of Herbert's powerful family circle, and she explains (away) the fact that they rarely appear in manuscript collections as the effect of Herbert's insistence that they be restricted to a very small and very elite circle. Malcolmson argues that even parody and critique of the conventions of courtly love poetry are recognizable moves within the game of courtly love poetry, and she notes that several of Herbert's poems are framed as explicit, witty responses to other well-known poems and that as such he is often participating in the literary game of satirical response that was quite popular and especially enjoyed by William Herbert, Earl of Pembroke. Thus Herbert's "Parodie" is an answer to Pembroke's "Soul's joy" (in just the way that Donne's "Ecstasy" is a response to Sidney's "Eighth Song" in *Astrophel and Stella*).[11]

Malcolmson reminds us that in the seventeenth-century context, poetry is a social game with rules and that breaking the rules is a move in the game. She sees Herbert as playing a game and that his goal is to draw attention to himself and build his reputation in the (few) eyes of those who matter to him. The claim that what "really" (so to speak) animates Herbert's poetry is social ambition, the desire to get ahead, to be recognized, to gain cultural capital was foundational to New Historicism (it is at the heart of Michael Schoenfeldt's important work on Herbert). For his part, perhaps more in line with Fish, Richard Strier departs from this view when he takes seriously the religious and even theological motivations that animate Herbert and that cannot always be "decoded" into extratheological social agendas.

I am suggesting a third way, where Herbert neither is using poetry to climb the slippery social pole nor simply a religious or theological poet genuinely disavowing the social effects of poetry. Rather I see Herbert, infused with the corporeal resurrectionism that I have explored at the outset of the chapter, trying to use poetry to touch, to make visible, to make audible a different self, a different voice than the conventionally socialized voice of the social persona that is Herbert. In that sense, the alien, nonself voice that Herbert wants to hear coming out of his mouth by means of his poetry is an analogue of the "groan" he thinks would be evidence of the other self that is the living animate body that subtends all social identity but is also different from any social identity.

The notion that Herbert wants to hear a strange voice coming out of his mouth (and also, not incidentally, out of the mouth of anyone who reads one of his poems out loud) is a strong framework for understanding Herbert's formal experimentation. Herbert uses inventive formal technique to push language out of its conventional, stereotypical functioning, which is also to say he uses formal experiment to push language away from the conventional language he uses in normal everyday social environments when he is "himself," as it were. Herbert uses formal inventiveness as a way of forcing a different voice and a different sound to emerge in his poetry as opposed to his utterances as a social persona. And as I have tried to show, that project is inseparable from his resurrectionist commitment to seeing his poetry as a way of allowing that bodily substrate to appear and be heard.

Herbert uses formal patterns as a way of creating a life in the poem that is not under the conscious control of George Herbert the social person, who uses language to communicate within his language community. As T. S. Eliot notes in his famous 1921 essay "The Metaphysical Poets," Herbert mostly uses a humble vocabulary and builds his poems from everyday words. But in its formal inventiveness, Herbert's poetry is like a rack designed to stretch and contort the language that spontaneously comes out of Herbert's mouth, not in quest of pain or self-punishment but in quest of a new, quite unexpected voice. I have already discussed instances where Herbert pushes in the direction of onomatopoeia. Similarly, Herbert sometimes creates verse forms that rely on repetition of individual words to such an extent that the words come to seem either hypnotically incantatory or meaningless but certainly not communicative in any straightforward sense of the word. Sometimes Herbert's poems turn on making words strange by revealing them to have other words hiding inside them, such as the poem "Paradise," which mines larger words to reveal smaller words: Grow/row/ow, Charm/harm/arm, Start/tart/art, Spare/pare/are, Frend/rend/end, or the poem "Jesu," in which Herbert describes a "great affliction" that carves up the name Jesus to reveal it to contain the phrase "I ease you" (3, 9). At other times, formal estranging happens when the formal pattern of a poem becomes so dominant that the content or meaning of the poem is forced to adjust to it, as though the sound and rhythm of the poem were its essence and the meaning of the poem only important as a way of creating that sound and rhythm. But the opposite also happens, when a formal pattern is suddenly or unexpectedly forced aside, as in "Home," in which Herbert engineers a situation in which the rhyme scheme pushes in one direction while the logic of the poem pushes in a different direction:

> Come dearest Lord, passe not this holy season,
>   My flesh and bones and joynts do pray:
> And ev'n my verse, when by the ryme and reason
>   The word is, Stay, sayes ever, Come.
>   O show thy self to me,
>   Or take me up to thee!

> ("Home," 73–78)

In this final stanza Herbert breaks with the rhyme scheme established by the previous twelve stanzas by ending a line with "come" when (as he explicitly points out) the rhyme scheme would call for "stay." In contrast to poems where the formal pattern is framed as the part of the poem outside of Herbert's intentions, here Herbert presents the formal scheme as preeminently the thing that he controls and the logic of the poem as having a life of its own and as leading him to violate the rhyme scheme, even if it means breaking the beautifully crafted poem that Herbert the poet has created.[12]

As I have said, the important point throughout all the formal estranging is that what Herbert wants is for an alien language to come out of his mouth, for words that do not feel like his to come out of his mouth.[13] The issue of wanting the language to become other than his own is at the heart of the two graphical poems that are surely Herbert's most famous. Here is "Easter Wings":

> Lord, who createdst man in wealth and store,
>   Though foolishly he lost the same,
>   Decaying more and more,
>   Till he became
>   Most poore:
>   With thee
>   Oh let me rise
>   As larks, harmoniously,
>   And sing this day thy victories:
> Then shall the fall further the flight in me.

> My tender age in sorrow did beginne:
>   And still with sicknesses and shame

Thou didst so punish sinne,
    That I became
        Most thinne.
        With thee
    Let me combine
And feel this day thy victorie:
For, if I imp my wing on thine
Affliction shall advance the flight in me.

                          ("Easter Wings")

Though it is tempting to say that the shape of the poem is aligned with and furthers the goal of communicating the meaning of the poem, in fact this poem is very much about Herbert identifying the poem as the fruit of an estranged language within himself, namely, the words that come to him when "I imp my wing on thine." The "thin" self that Herbert is on his own (shrinking down to two syllables at the midpoint of the second—more autobiographically personal—stanza) is expanded when he imagines himself merging with God's own wing back out to the full iambic pentameter line that is normative in the English poetic tradition. It is in this light, I think, that we should look at the stanzaic shape, for if the shape is in some very obvious way witty and pleasing, it is also an abuse of language, a strange use or even abuse of words as they normally function to communicate—as evidenced by generations of undergraduates who remember the shape but remember absolutely nothing of what the poem signifies.

The same point of view sheds light on Herbert's other famous shape poem, "The Altar":

A broken A L T A R, Lord, thy servant reares,
Made of a heart, and cemented with teares:
Whose parts are as thy hand did frame;
No workmans tool hath touch'd the same.
        A H E A R T alone
        Is such a stone,
        As nothing but
        Thy pow'r doth cut.
        Wherefore each part
        Of my hard heart
        Meets in this frame,
        To praise thy Name;
That, if I chance to hold my peace,
These stones to praise thee may not cease.

O let thy blessed S A C R I F I C E be mine,
And sanctifie this A L T A R to be thine.

("The Altar")

The dynamism of this poem comes from the paradox that even as it builds a graphical altar it also says that the only real altar is the heart. But if—in good iconoclastic fashion—the poem demonstrates how susceptible the reader is to getting caught by the alluring image rather than paying attention to the "heart," which is the only real altar, the poem nonetheless imagines that the graphical word-altar is supplemental to the personal heart that may fail: "if I chance to hold my peace, / These stones to praise thee may not cease." How can a poem that is composed and created by a man nevertheless imagine persisting when that voice ceases? It is when the speaking voice falls away and its products, graphical marks on the page, are left as dead monuments, emblems of human communication that have ceased to work as communication, that language has become truly eternal. And as with "Easter Wings," this poem is marked by an abuse of language as stones rather than words whose meaning the speaker can stand behind. For if the shape is what counts, then any other set of words would serve just as well, and Herbert the poet disappears into the manual labor of the stonemason.[14] Herbert here anticipates twentieth-century language poets who also treat language as building materials rather than as a means of communication. And once graphics come into play, they have their own rhetoric and their own effects and their own unpredictabilities, and they can never be reduced to a speaker speaking words that simply "communicate."[15]

In Herbert's hands, poetic discourse becomes a distinctive form of language that insistently draws attention to itself as language, as a material reality with the secondary property of carrying meaning, and moreover a material reality that has the potential to persist after all human language communities (and therefore the meanings that it can carry) have passed away (as with the graphical poems). In that sense, Herbert's implicit theory of poetic language anticipates Roman Jakobson's argument that what defines the "poetic function" is language that points back to the material stuff of language itself.[16] For Jakobson, poetry entails a relative deemphasis of the "communicative" function of language (in which language is designed to convey meaning unproblematically, so that the materiality of the language disappears in the process of transferring an idea from the mind of the sender to the mind of the receiver) and a relative reemphasis on the language itself, the sonic and graphical stuff that language is made of.[17]

I want to insist on the virtuous circle between Herbert's theological/theoretical program of searching the socialized body for the material substrate of a future resurrection and the work of poetry that, as a medium, searches meaningful words for the strange, sonic, and graphical core that is ultimately not completely contained by communicative uses of language.[18] It is a connection made by Herbert in "The Flower," in which he compares his own experience of depression followed by rejuvenation to a flower dying in the fall and resprouting in the spring:

> Who would have thought my shrivel'd heart
> Could have recover'd greennesse? It was gone
>   Quite under ground; as flowers depart
> To see their mother-root, when they have blown;
>   Where they together
>   All the hard weather,
>   Dead to the world, keep house unknown.
>
> . . . .
>
>   And now in age I bud again,
> After so many deaths I live and write;
>   I once more smell the dew and rain,
> And relish versing: O my onely light,
>   It cannot be
>   That I am he
>   On whom thy tempests fell all night.
>
> ("The Flower," 7–14, 36–42)

Here Herbert discovers a hidden, secret source of life, the "mother root" of his own life. Rediscovering himself as a living, material thing is central to his resurrection-driven poetics. And here he aligns it with a renewed attention to writing. It is in writing that he discovers himself as living body and vice versa. The life that Herbert embraces here is the life of poetry, the life of writing, and the self that Herbert finds being reborn in his writing is the self that is associated with a vigor that inheres in the body. Interestingly, his new vision of himself is also a new vision of the natural world, as having life in the midst of death. The coincidence of seeing the self in a new light and seeing the natural world in a new light is a logical consequence of the way, for Herbert, language is at one and the same time an act of a socially constructed speaker speaking about a socially constructed world and an act that discloses a presocial material reality both inside the language and in the world that the language carves up and describes, so that if poetry uses language to uncover a different self than the socially constructed speaker, then poetry must at the same time uncover a different conception of the natural world. As we shall see in the next chapter, the connection of reinvented, nonsocialized self and reinvented, nonsocialized natural world is at the heart of the poetry of Herbert's great disciple Henry Vaughan. But the connection certainly appears here in "The Flower."

In Herbert we see distinctively avant-gardist techniques in which the signifier draws attention to itself and is used to enact a displacement from social life (including the language community in which it operates). To the extent that poems thematize this process they also fail to enact it fully, but the point is that these two tendencies are dialectically held together. There is a tendency to *say* that the human person subject to resurrection is at an angle to the social world in his or her very flesh and to *enact* a displacement from the social world when language functioning to transmit meaning within a language community is decommissioned, thereby moving in the direction of sound and concrete poetry full of linguistic procedures that draw attention to themselves and by so doing move away from simple communicative functionality.

I have several times described the formal effects of Herbert's poetry as avant-garde, and I now want to explore this claim at greater length. There is a strong sense in which Herbert anticipates avant-garde aesthetics as theorized by Renato Poggioli and most especially by Peter Bürger in *The Theory of the Avant-Garde.*[19] For Bürger, twentieth-century avant-gardism is fundamentally an attack on any notion of art as separate, closed, and autonomous.[20] Avant-gardism punctures the sacred apartness of art, crashing art back into the world, creating immediate, visceral, often deranging experiences in readers and creating communities around an experience of art that is sometimes quite hostile to traditional canons of beauty and to the traditional artistic function of representation. Bürger therefore sees avant-gardism as the last chapter in a long history of the rise of the category of autonomous art. Though Bürger does not recount this history, it is well established. This narrative begins with the historical emergence of autonomous art from "auratic" art (to use Walter Benjamin's term) through the courtly art of the sixteenth and early seventeenth centuries, whose aim is to shore up the status and prestige of patrons.[21] A major leap forward comes with the emergence in the eighteenth century of a market for cultural goods, a market that rapidly splits between a market for popular or mass culture and a "restricted" or "inverted" market (to use Pierre Bourdieu's terms) where sales do not count and that caters to other artists and to highly sophisticated elites who exchange money for cultural capital.[22] The notion of an autonomous domain of culture that stands apart from the world is ultimately supported by this restricted market and its institutions (including journals, schools, and museums).

As Bürger sees it, twentieth-century avant-garde art fully recognizes the autonomous subsystem of art and turns against it, attacking it through techniques that deprive art of its ability to stand apart from society in institutionalized artistic purity. Thus, avant-gardism attacks the idea of a precious and closed work of art. In place of the closed work of art, avant-garde techniques offer montage, collage, systematic attacks on the canons of beauty, and efforts to deform the norms of sense-making and interpretation. In short, avant-gardism attacks art as an institution by denying the sacred separateness or apartness of art vis-à-vis the shabby ordinariness of everyday life governed by economic imperatives.

But Bürger's most central claim about avant-gardism is that its desire to break with the sacred apartness of art leads avant-garde artists to try to reconnect art to the everyday world by seeing art as a way of creating social communities or new forms of selfhood, new forms of interpersonal sociability—even in preference to creating a work that can persist in time, thus the penchant in avant-garde groups for "manifestoes" and fleeting "happenings" that annihilate the space between art as object and its social reception. For avant-gardists, art must create persons and communities rather than being a quasi-sacred object that represents the world or that is simply beautiful in its own right. Thus, for Bürger, avant-gardism is a movement that recognizes the full extent of autonomy or separateness that art has achieved and then reacts against it, attempting to use art as the basis for reconstructing experimental lifestyles and forms of social praxis—in essence, a form of politics (or maybe antipolitics).

One objection to my effort to use Bürger as a framework for understanding Herbert's project is that in the early modern period there is, as of yet, no fully autonomous art. In Bürger's account, avant-garde art only arises as a result of and reaction against a fully autonomous art that emerges over the course of the nineteenth century. For him, the avant-garde movements of the early twentieth century represent the moment when art and artists become self-consciously aware of the full extent and implications of an autonomous domain of art and begin to turn against it. He writes:

> It is my thesis that certain general categories of the work of art were first made recognizable in their generality by the avant-garde, that it is consequently from the standpoint of the avant-garde that the preceding phases in the development of art as a phenomenon in

bourgeois society can be understood. . . . My second thesis is this: with the historical avant-garde movements, the social subsystem that is art enters the stage of self-criticism. . . . The avant-garde turns against both—the distribution apparatus upon which the work of art depends, and the status of art within bourgeois society as defined by autonomy. Only after art, in nineteenth-century Aestheticism, has altogether detached itself from the praxis of life can the aesthetic develop "purely." But the other side of autonomy, art's lack of social impact, also becomes recognizable. The avant-gardiste protest, whose aim it is to reintegrate art into the praxis of life, reveals the nexus between autonomy and the absence of any consequences.

(19–22)

A fully autonomous domain for art does not exist in the early modern period. Yet there are strong tendencies pushing in that direction. The best New Historicism (from Montrose to Helgerson) was able to identify moments when a limited artistic autonomy appeared (often in complex struggles with extra-political agendas and concerns). Jonathan Goldberg posits an "Elizabethan high literariness" built, in part, on the sexual formations that he explores in *Sodometries*.[23] In Harry Berger Jr.'s account of the *Faerie Queene*, that epic is one of the main guideposts in the history of the emergence of literary autonomy. We might say the same of the Petrarchan and pastoral traditions more generally and their mutations, including within the *Faerie Queene* and within the history of the sonnet in England.[24] Both the Petrarchan and the pastoral traditions define a coherent set of conventions, images, and language uses that are self-consciously artful and therefore "apart" from conventional social life, conventions, and language uses. They also both have an imaginary locational quality, seemingly opening an imaginary space that seems to stand in for the world of art. The Elizabethan and Jacobean theater has even more institutionalized locational power, very literally defining a space apart in which imaginary worlds flower (not least imaginary worlds driven by the continuing power of the Petrarchan and pastoral traditions). The early modern theater draws on the autonomy achieved by theater in classical antiquity, the autochthonous theater traditions of the English Middle Ages, as well as the commercial basis of the theater (a commercialism that, only a few decades later, starts to represent a limit upon aesthetic autonomy). While neither Petrarchan/pastoral poetry nor early modern English drama achieves the full autonomy of what eventually constitutes the "social subsystem that is art," they nevertheless point to artistic practices that are set apart and whose apartness defines their freedom yet also sketches their potential powerlessness (as in the hint of impotence in Prospero's power on the theater-island or, closer to home for this book, the hints at effete silliness and empty prettiness that haunt the lyric expressions of the Petrarchan and pastoral traditions).

I have suggested that in Herbert's poetry it is the courtly Petrarchan tradition that comes closest to defining an autonomous domain, and he repeatedly writes poems in which the florid beauty of standard poems is contrasted to his own. In doing so, he suggests that he himself sees his poetry as a reaction against any such closed or separate art. I have suggested that if we look at the effects generated by his poetry on readers, we can see something very like Bürger's sense of "the avant-gardiste protest, whose aim it is to reintegrate art into the praxis of life." Thus, even if there is no fully autonomous "social sub-system of art" in Herbert's social universe, there is nevertheless a dialectical process that posits autonomy as well as the reaction to autonomy in which poetry explodes out into the world in the form of yearning to transcend the merely artistic. This anti-autonomy moment can be seen in Herbert's impulse to use his poetry to liberate a voice that is rooted in an alien materiality and that seeks to connect with the alien self of readers and the alienness of the world itself, that part of the world that cannot be represented in straightforward representational-referential language. Moreover, it should be obvious that there is at least a family resemblance between the techniques of montage, collage, systematic attacks on the canons of beauty, and efforts to deform the norms of sense-making and interpretation that characterize twentieth-century avant-garde artists and Herbert's poems as I have described them. But what is more strikingly avant-gardist about Herbert's poetry is its evident drive to create experiences, to rewire persons, to create communities, even to inspire new artistic production. Thus, I want to contemplate the notion of Herbert's poems—and especially the posthumous 1633 publication of *The Temple*—as a "happening" in seventeenth-century literary culture.

As I have already discussed, the most dominant "market" for poetry in Herbert's world is the genteel, essentially aristocratic exchanges in which courtiers show off their talents by circulating witty poems. Herbert conceptualizes these circuits of poetic exchange as the world of "Louely enchanting language, sugar-cane" ("The Forerunners," 19), and he always frames this world as the antithesis of what his own poems attempt to do. The notion of sugared sonnets invokes the witty, competitive circuits of coterie exchange, in which the goal is always to advance one's social status or visibility, often by wittily replying to other poets, typically using the erotic language of the Petrarchan tradition. Throughout his life, Herbert was surrounded by this kind of market, starting with the intellectual circle led by his own mother, Magdalene Herbert, a circle that included Donne. For Malcolmson, Herbert's poetry is always in dialogue with these coterie circuits, even or especially when it most disavows this interest. But I have suggested that we should take seriously Herbert's frequent assertions that he understands his project to be at odds with self-regarding displays of wittiness.

To some extent, Herbert sees his poetry as departing from the realm of "sugar-cane" sonnets because of their explicitly religious content (as opposed to erotic content, though in Herbert's poetry the distinction is not very stable). But at a deeper level, Herbert's poems depart from the realm of witty, competitive "coterie" poetry because of the deranging formal techniques that I have described and that aim to prevent the poems from becoming simply beautiful or "sweet." As I have suggested, these formal techniques are designed to make the voice of Herbert's poems feel alien or strange to the biographical person of Herbert, creating not a super-witty version of Herbert that the biographical Herbert might get credit for but a super-strange version of Herbert that the biographical Herbert might not fully recognize as himself. To a considerable extent, this dark "self-fashioning" project of Herbert's takes place in continuous conflict with the project of sugary sonnets as he understands it, so that, for Herbert, the domain of court poetry and the domain defined by his own poetry are dialectically tied together.

Moreover, in terms of Bürger's analysis of avant-garde aesthetics, Herbert's attack on the realm of sugared sonnets is also an attack on conventional ways in which readers receive or respond to a poem. That reader response was a vexed issue for Herbert is obvious in the history of the publication of his poems. Herbert did not publish or actively circulate his poems, at least in written form. According to Izaak Walton's early biography, on his deathbed Herbert sent the sole, handwritten copy of his poems to his friend Nicholas Ferrar, advising him to publish it only "if he can think it may turn to the advantage of any dejected poor Soul" and otherwise to burn it.[25] Herbert's own wish to evaluate his poems only in terms of whether readers connect to them in an intense, personal way does point to how these poems have in fact affected readers, often prompting them to treat Herbert (both as man and as poet) as a pattern that they then imitate in their lives or in their poetry. Barnabas Olney, in the preface to *Herbert's Remains*, his collection of Herbert's practical writing and aphorisms, writes that Herbert was "a Peer to the primitive Saints, and more than a pattern to his own age."[26] This notion that Herbert—man and

poet alike—is a "pattern" that propels itself into the minds, bodies, con-
duct, and even voices of those who come into contact with him has proven
to be true throughout the reception of Herbert's poetry. After Ferrar received the poems, they were copied by his nieces Anna and Mary Collett
(in a manuscript that survives; the original in Herbert's hand is lost), and
in that form they were conveyed to Thomas Buck, the Cambridge University printer, and published in 1633 (the same year that Donne's *Songs and
Sonnets* were published, also posthumously).

In that printed form Herbert's poetry proved almost irresistible as a
pattern for readers who often attested to their "conversion" both to the
religious life that Herbert lived and to the particular kind of poetry that
he wrote.[27] Thus, Christopher Harvey's imitative collection *The Synagogue*
was printed together with every edition of Herbert's poems printed after
1641, thereby indicating that the most appropriate response to Herbert's
verse is the imitation of his "pattern." It set the tone for other readers.
Ralph Knevet's "A Gallery to the Temple" circulated widely in manuscript,
but perhaps the most spectacular pattern imitator was Henry Vaughan,
whose 1655 second edition of his collection *Silex Scintillans* (which I discuss in the next chapter) contains a preface citing the influence of "the
blessed man, Mr. *George Herbert*, whose holy *life* and *verse* gained many
pious converts (of whom I am the least)."[28] The elision of the difference
between the life and the verse is characteristic of the way readers respond
to Herbert, whose poetry may convert to a renewed commitment to Christianity but whose verse converts to the impulse to write in a distinctly
Herbertian style. Another minor poet, Joshua Poole, a student of Barnabas Oley, went on to write *The English Parnassus, or, A helpe to English
poesie containing a collection of all rhyming monosyllables, the choicest epithets, and phrases: with some general forms upon all occasions, subjects,
and theams, alphabeticaly digested: together with a short institution to
English poesie, by way of a preface*, which begins with a long proem that
celebrates "Herbert's church":

> Many have been, which Pulpits did eschew,
> Converted from the Poets reading pew,
> And those that seldome do salute the porch
> Of Solomon, will come to Herbert's church.[29]

Here "Herbert's church" is simultaneously a religious and a poetic for-
mation, into which Poole's pedagogic text is supposed to induct readers.
Another, more scientifically minded poet, William Croune, adapted Herbert's poems in ways designed to make them more compatible with the

new affirmative spirit of scientific inquiry.[30] Even in North America a "church" of Herbert can be found in such writers as Edward Taylor and Philip Pain.[31] And no doubt seventeenth-century archives of personal and unpublished writing are also full of other, personal instances of readers being impelled to write in the voice of Herbert.

Thus, as much as Herbert's poetics is driven by the impulse to force words out of his mouth that do not seem like his "own," that effect is precisely what his seventeenth-century readers experienced as well, presenting themselves, often, as nearly powerless to resist generating the strange, poetic Herbert voice in their own mouths. And if these are only the best-known and most direct imitators of Herbert's voice, other seventeenth-century discourses also contain evidence of the powerful allure of the Herbert voice, as, for instance, in Walton's *The Compleat Angler* (1655), when Piscator assumes that a lover of Herbert's "Vertue" might also enjoy a poem by one who has imitated Herbert "most excellently" and then recites Harvey's poem "The Book of Common Prayer."[32]

Herbert's poetry is less a stable object waiting quietly between its printed covers to be read as it is a "happening" in the culture, one that creates "conversions" to new ways of being, both as an individual and in relation to others. If the "conversion" that Vaughan speaks of is a religious conversion (or, given the nonoptionality of Christianity in early modern England, a renewed recommitment to Christianity), then it is equally a conversion to the life of poetry, to the practices in language that Herbert pioneered and that give rise to the distinct effect of forcing a strange voice to come out of the reader's (now become writer's) own mouth.

These poetic "conversions" are driven by the sound and the distinctive formal effects that Herbert pioneered. It seems as if the sound, the attack, the rhythms of Herbert are what got under the skin of readers, who then felt moved to write poems of their own, repeating those distinctive sounds and rhythms. Indeed, it is through the sound and formal effects that most readers today continue to relate to Herbert, especially in view of the continuing history of secularization, which has put his religious "message" ever further beyond the pale. From this formalist perspective, Herbert's practice is reminiscent of Paul Valéry's interest in the moment when an artistic text

> is no longer one of those intended to teach us something and to vanish as soon as that something is understood; its effect is to make us live a different life, breathe according to this second life; and it implies a state or a world in which the objects and beings found there, or rather their images, have other freedoms and other ties

than those in the practical world . . . all this gives us the idea of an enchanted nature, subjected as by a spell to the whims, the magic and the power of language.[33]

No doubt for some readers today, reading their religion in poetic form is a kind of nostalgia; in other words, some of Herbert's continuing popularity is accounted for by the fact that his religious poetry allows self-avowed secular readers to consume religion, we might even say to "practice" religion, but in a secularized form. But I think an equally important explanation for his continuing popularity, especially among poetically inclined readers, is the formal games that his poetry invites, all of which move against any simple articulation of a Christian message. Instead, his poems "make us live a different life, breathe according to this second life" triggered by an encounter with a strange, language-saturated consciousness that, in turn, invites further poetic work in "answer," as it were, to Herbert's poems. Thus, in line with Bürger's definition of avant-gardism, Herbert's poems are marked by an effort to engage in social praxis, first and foremost by creating a new person in the poet himself, by allowing the poet to find a new, strange voice that is his yet not his, and second by creating new communities around the poetry, communities like that which (on his deathbed) Herbert hoped his poetry might call into being, communities that operate at a tangent to any church because they are defined only in an aleatory realm of art.

I have claimed that Herbert's poems should be seen not as closed and perfect works of art but as "cultural happenings" whose goal is to transfer a new pattern to readers and thereby to "convert" readers to a new lifestyle, one both Christian and at the same time poetic. In the final section of this chapter I want to argue that part and parcel of this Herbertian lifestyle is a distinctive relationship to the emotions, an "emotional style" that is associated with writing and reading poetry.

In the history of English Christianity, Herbert is often (though not always) seen as an early pietist who emphasizes the importance of emotions and emotional life in "genuine" religious experience. Richard Strier, for one, sees Herbert in this tradition and argues that Herbert values emotions because they testify to the sincerity of a person's religious convictions, as in "Sion," in which Herbert addresses God to say that "All Solomons sea of brasse and world of stone / Is not so deare to thee as one good grone" (17–18). Though pietism as a concept is associated especially with John Wesley (1703–1791) and thus the religious movements of the eighteenth century, this idea has important precursors in seventeenth-century

Calvinism, which combats the despair created by its radical predestinarianism by developing techniques of introspection and self-examination designed to uncover evidence that God is working in and through the believer. These techniques, including introspective prayer and diary keeping, are especially likely to fixate upon the emotions as the scene where God's interest in one appears.[34]

It is certainly true that part of the appeal of Herbert's poems is the intimate picture of his emotional life that they give, ranging from moments of despair and depression to moments of joy and elation. Indeed, Herbert emphasized the personal nature of the poems, describing them as "a picture of the many spiritual conflicts that have passed between God and my soul, before I could subject mine to the will of Jesus, my Master, in whose service I have now found perfect freedom."[35] This sense of emotional authenticity is also suggested by the title under which they were posthumously published, a title chosen not by Herbert but by Nicholas Ferrar, *The Temple: Sacred Poems and Private Ejaculations*, with their implied promise of giving access to the "private" life of Herbert the man. The assumption here is that the emotions testify to the distinctive personality of the person navigating the world; to really know Herbert is to know his emotional state, which is supposedly what the poems make available to readers.

But the question of "who" is the subject of the emotions Herbert describes in his poetry is a complex one. In other words, the question of whether emotions are sincere in the sense of testifying to the truth of the person is very much an open question. In the Renaissance, a humoral understanding of emotional life is still very available, in which emotions are understood to be caused by fluids in the body rather than by some psychologized personality. One example appears in the opening poem of the collection, "The Church-porche," in which the whole of England is personified and imagined to be "full of sloth":

> O England! full of sin, but most of sloth;
> Spit out thy phlegm, and fill thy breast with glory;
>
> ("The Church-porche," 91–92)

Here therapy for sloth requires spitting out the phlegm that threatens to clog the self. Michael Schoenfeldt has noted how often Herbert utilizes a humoral imaginary, including in the Eucharistic poems, where eating the Eucharist is imagined to create a physical change in the body.[36] But Schoenfeldt has also noted the interest in stoic self-discipline and self-management that pervades many of Herbert's poems. From a humoral standpoint, emotions do not testify to an authentic or sincere self so much as they point to the physical state of the body and its openness to being influenced by material forces in the world, but that perspective also opens the door to a new kind of "self-fashioning" through corporeal self-discipline.

Though Herbert is not ultimately a humoralist, humoralism is nonetheless an important starting point for understanding his emotional politics. For one of the chief goals and effects of Herbert's poetry is to effect a limited detachment or estrangement from his emotions, a shift to seeing emotions as having a nonsubjective quality, as they do in humoral theory. Thus, in "Affliction (III)" Herbert writes:

> MY heart did heave, and there came forth, *O God!*
> By that I knew that thou wast in the grief,
> To guide and govern it to my relief,
>   Making a scepter of the rod:
>   Hadst thou not had thy part,
> Sure the unruly sigh had broke my heart.
>
> ("Affliction [III]," 1–6)

Despair is a "rod" that corrects Herbert, and it is used by God to "guide and govern it [Herbert's heart] to my relief." As ever, Herbert is interested in speech that is not consciously intended—he is interested in the spontaneous "O God" that is not so much language as it is a nearly automatic groaning sound. But the main point here is that grief is reinterpreted as evidence of God's shaping power and interest in Herbert. God becomes an almost humoral force working within Herbert's heart, and this recognition is quite comforting to Herbert because it shows that God has a care for Herbert.

Herbert often imagines that God is responsible for his negative emotions; indeed, for Herbert, there is comfort in thinking that this is so because it is evidence of God's active involvement in his life. This point of view involves reconceptualizing negative emotions as a beneficent torture. This associates Herbert with a long Christian tradition that values asceticism and even pain as transformative. There is something masochistic in Herbert, but it does not seem like a simple preference for pain or a desire for an ecstasy born of pain. Margaret Miles argues that within the long history of Christian asceticism, bodily practices that inflict pain are not primarily valued as a way of creating pain or as a way of creating ecstasy but as a way of reorienting the self away from the world (inscribed silently upon the very body and its primary experience) and toward God.[37] Schoenfeldt notes "the chilling images, which recur with unsettling frequency throughout *The Temple*, of God as a torturer, imposing upon his creatures immense if ultimately salutary suffering. God's actions share a remarkable consonance with the cruelties practiced by the governments of Renaissance England."[38] But in light of Miles's model of asceticism we can say that for Herbert pain and negative emotions are valued as a way of decommissioning the body's unconscious, habituated imbrication in a social world. For Herbert, paying attention to the emotions becomes a way of catching sight of himself in a new light, recognizing how his self is captured by the social world, which makes him care about and thus emote in relation to worldly things, but also recognizing himself as something that is finally not fully one with the world, including in its basic emotional life.

Seeing the emotions as the terrain in which the self is alternately captured by the social world and then also able to set itself apart from the social world is the right perspective for understanding Herbert's emotional politics. And this perspective helps us see that negative emotions and positive emotions can and do appear on either side of the self-as-captured-by-the-world/self-as-able-to-transcend-the-world divide. In "Home," for example, the world creates a powerful joy that solders the self into its concerns, an experience Herbert describes by saying that the world "chains us by the teeth," until this joy is blasted by a God-given grief.

> With one small sigh thou gav'st me th' other day
>   I blasted all the joyes about me:
> And scouling on them as they pin'd away,
>   Now come again, said I, and flout me.
>
> ("Home," 43–46)

Here the joy of making it in the world is a killing joy, and the antidote is a sigh that displaces or separates the self from the world by which it is otherwise engulfed. In this context, joy is an emotion felt by the socialized historically situated person who does not see a horizon beyond this world. This joy solders the self to the world as though that world and the self and the connection between the two were forever. Grief is a beneficent crisis in the self and its conventional emotional relationship to the world.[39]

But if the appeal of emotional pain, including grief and despair, is that it separates the self from the world that captures it, then intense joy can function just as well to decommission the self from the social matrices it inhabits. Rather than any simple joy=bad (because worldly) and grief=good (because divine) equation, many of Herbert's poems set up a contrast between a bad form of joy (because it is worldly, and thus killing) and a good joy (because it testifies to the living, corporeal reality of the person in whom God takes an interest).[40] One example is "The Invitation," which is an invitation to take the Eucharist. In this poem one kind of joy, beneficent joy, literally drives out another, killing form of joy:

> Come ye hither all, whom joy
> > Doth destroy,
> While ye graze without your bounds:
> Here is joy that drowneth quite
> > Your delight,
> As a floud the lower grounds.
>
> ("The Invitation," 19–24)

The bad joy of the world is bad because it derives from an unconditional, unlimited, appetitive attachment to the world—it "Doth destroy" because it impels people to "graze without your bounds." The joy that the Eucharist elicits and that the poem celebrates is instead animated by a limited transcendence or detachment of self from world, and this other kind of joy drowns worldly joy. The poem goes on to make the parallel point about the subjective experience of love:

> Come ye hither all, whose love
> > Is your dove,
> And exalts you to the skie:
> Here is love, which having breath
> > Ev'n in death,
> After death can never die.
>
> ("The Invitation," 25–30)

When love is your dove (a bad rhyme that automatically evokes the entire Petrarchan tradition, treating it as a kind of joke), the effect is an explosion of self: Love "exalts you to the skie." It is a false transcendence of the world into heaven built on an egoistic negation of the reality of death, which will come as a shock to such dovey lovers. To this experience of love, the other love the poem describes is poison. And, connecting back to the onto-stories of resurrection that I examine throughout this book, this love points to a different transcendence of the world rooted in touching the body that is living, that will die, and that will live again.

In "The Banquet" Herbert starts with a humoral imaginary inflected into the Eucharist, where partaking of the communion wine brings "sweet and sacred cheer." Here drinking wine and eating bread create a sweetness in his soul. "O what sweetnesse from the bowl / Fills my soul," he exclaims. He goes on to ask, "Or hath sweetness in the bread / Made a head / To subdue the smell of sin" ("The Banquet," 7–8, 13–15), and connects the power of the communion wine and bread to create positive emotional states to the power of herbs and flowers and (in a Paracelsian imaginary) ethereal minerals (derived from "stars") to effect psychological change. But after posing the question of whether mere physical substances can create the positive emotional experience he feels, he decides that it is God alone who can infuse sweetness:

> Doubtlese, neither starre nor flower
> > Hath the power
> Such a sweetnesse to impart:
> Onely God, who gives perfumes,
> > Flesh assumes,
> And with it perfumes my heart.

> ("The Banquet," 19–24)

Similarly, in "Josephs Coat," God has the power both to "bring / My *joys* to *weep*, and now my *griefs* to sing" (13–14).

The fact that Herbert can see either joy or despair as evidence of worldliness or of divine intervention suggests a unique vision of emotional life in general. Herbert refuses to see his emotions as wholly humoral, that is, as needing mechanical management, nor does he see them as wholly cognitive, that is, as the expression of judgments by a sovereign self about the world. Rather, Herbert comes to understand the emotions as disclosing something very primal about the way he inhabits the world. Specifically, the emotions are signs of, on the one hand, the way the material body is itself conditioned by a social life that is historical and therefore destined to pass away (and that shows up in joy or grief) and, on the other hand, of the self as fundamentally other to the social life of persons, namely, as the scene of a strange and irreducibly fleshly life that is the precondition for yet also transcends any social conditioning (and that can itself show up as either joy or grief). In short, Herbert sees emotions as neither humoral nor cognitive but as a mode of disclosure—they disclose how the self inhabits a fleeting social and historical world that is destined to pass away.

Herbert's poetry creates a gap in his own emotional life: His emotional tone is no longer something he is completely absorbed by but instead becomes an object of reflection. Paying attention to the emotions creates a gap between Herbert the socialized person consumed by the world and Herbert as the substrate who is separable from that socialized person. Through Herbert's formally experimental poetry, emotions are not merely recollected in tranquility; they are reevaluated for the way they do and do not connect self and world via the body. And if Herbert's poems are a "happening" that invites readers into the lifestyle of poetry, the detached, informational, and transformational relationship to the emotions is part and parcel of that lifestyle.

Throughout this book I claim that there is a symbiotic relationship between the discourse of materialist and immanent resurrection and the poetry that picks it up, in which the poetry is fertilized by resurrection beliefs but at the same time transforms resurrection beliefs into a kind of critical theory that allows key assumptions of a rising secular modernity to be rethought. The critical-theoretical effect of Herbert's poetry is to raise doubts about the highly buffered, autonomous self that is associated with the body/soul dualism that powers the dominant path of secularization. Herbert's poems are finally a kind of therapy for making the self aware of the extent to which it has been captured and defined by the historical social world, and by doing so they also make the self aware of a vibrant, material life that is "other" to the conventional identities that the social world imposes. It is this project that also powers Herbert's distinctive thought about the emotions. The life of poetry to which Herbert's poems have converted so many readers is characterized by an alienated, distanced relationship to the self, including its emotional life.[41] The poems are a record of Herbert gaining an awareness—and at the same time they are an engine for making readers gain awareness—of the emotional life as what makes socialization possible and therefore also what makes it possible to see around the corner of socialization. It is a notion grasped in the history of phenomenology as the reality of "mood." As Jonathan Flatley remarks: "Mood arises out of and discloses to us this situatedness. And if we attend to it, mood can help us to see the 'thereness' of our 'there,' the particularity of our position in a given situation, the givenness of that situation and the necessity of always finding ourselves in some there."[42] In humans, mood is the emotional background that makes it possible to care about things in the world in many different ways. Herbert's poems are designed to make him and his readers aware of the background moods that glue us to the social world and by doing so to effect a limited detachment from the social world. Herbert's poems are a research program designed to bring to light the part of Herbert that is at the heart of all social conditioning yet always separate from social conditioning. And an essential part of this research program is to interrogate or listen to the emotions phenomenologically for what they reveal of the kind of thing Herbert is before (and as the precondition of) being captured by the social world that stamps him with personhood.

Herbert's poems are therefore a reminder of a life that is rooted in a body never fully co-opted by the identities and projects conferred by the social world upon a socialized self created by that conferral. If Herbert's poetry, under the strong influence of the most materialist theory of resurrection, is a cultural happening that defines a poetic pattern that jumps from Herbert's poetry into the minds and mouths of his readers, then not the least important effect of that is to create a new emotional style that is inseparable from the lifestyle of poetry. As we will see in the next chapter, one of Herbert's chief disciples, Henry Vaughan, adopts Herbert's emotional style and develops it into a systematic project of searching himself, as he puts it in "Vanity of Spirit," for the "Traces, and sounds of a strange kind" that already now point to the reality of the resurrection body within the self as well as in the material world of natural and man-made objects.[43]

3 / Luminous Stuff: The Resurrection of the Flesh in Vaughan's Religious Verse

Herbert's commitment to seeking the resurrection body within the conventionally social self and the way this search drives a distinctively avant-garde poetics had a significant influence on the poets of the seventeenth century that came after him. In this chapter and the next I want to examine one of Herbert's most important "disciples," Henry Vaughan. In this chapter I will focus on Vaughan's collection of formally experimental religious verse entitled *Silex Scintillans* ("the flashing flint" in Welsh), which he published in two volumes, the first in 1650 and the second in 1655. In the next chapter I will examine some of Vaughan's religious and medical writings. In both chapters I will track the impact of the "onto-story" (as Jane Bennett might term it) of fleshly resurrection upon the way Vaughan understands and represents his own bodily life and the bodily life of other persons and natural objects.[1] For Vaughan, the onto-story of an immanent material resurrection drives a distinctive vision of the self and its relationship to the natural world, and this vision is expressed through an avant-garde poetics that reprises and even intensifies the experimental work of Herbert. Vaughan values formally experimental poetry because it reveals within himself a strange bodily form of life that is at odds with any socially conditioned sense of self. And more than Herbert, Vaughan also extends this perspective to the material stuff in the world—to animals and natural objects—using his poetry to reveal a natural world full of a vibrant, numinous materiality that exceeds human meanings, a fact that accounts for the way his poetry has often been understood as anticipating Romanticism.

I argued in the Introduction that given the secularizing pressures in the seventeenth century, resurrection beliefs are gradually recast in a dualist form that endorses a disenchanted natural world subject to the laws of nature and a vision of the self as mentalistic and therefore highly autonomous and buffered from the social and natural worlds. Donne and Herbert return to the most material and immanent vision of resurrection in order to invest their poetry with an avant-garde power that generates and expresses a vision of the self as the scene of a strange, vibrant material life that it also shares with the natural world. Vaughan's thinking about resurrection is also based on a return to the increasingly outré or even decommissioned idea of corporeal resurrection. In the run-up to the English Civil War, a thoroughgoing body/soul dualism becomes the default view for the Puritans against whom Vaughan positioned himself both ecclesially and politically, and like other anti-Puritans, Vaughan defines himself in part through his rejection of all forms of body/soul dualism. Vaughan's bedrock principle is that the body is the person and the person is the body, so that for the person to have a postmortem life the body would have to be reassembled. This view leads Vaughan to embrace mortalism, the theory that the death of the body is the total death of the person, so that for a protracted period of time after death the person will not exist in any form. Only at the apocalyptic end time will God put bodies back together, and then deceased persons will live anew. This is a view that Vaughan holds in common with Milton, who articulates it in *De Doctrina Christiana* (i.13) and, implicitly, in *Paradise Lost* (as in Adam's "All of me then shall die" at 10.792).

But what invests the idea of corporeal resurrection with its critical power is that Vaughan bends it back in time from an apocalyptic future and into the here and now. For Vaughan, the resurrection of the body is not only something that will happen in the future but also something that begins to happen in the here and now, transforming the biological underpinning of human life so that even in the here and now it is possible to catch a glimpse of the future resurrection body. This perspective sees the resurrection of the body as *immanent* in the sense of *within the creation as it exists right now*, following the resurrection of Christ as the "first fruits" (1 Cor. 15:20) of a more general process.[2] For Vaughan, as for Paul, the agency of divine creation is breaking into history now and is, indeed, doing so in the self's own body. This thinking is apocalyptic, but in a very special sense. It does not imagine the apocalypse as utterly different but as importantly continuous with the now. Indeed, this perspective imagines the apocalypse as already here, though still veiled and still incomplete.[3]

From this materialist and immanent perspective, death is still total death, but corporeal life in the here and now is, if properly grasped, a partial preexperience of the kind of corporeal life that will be generalized at the resurrection. Vaughan's theory of immanent materialist resurrection therefore leads him, as he puts it in "Vanity of Spirit," to "search myself" in order to uncover "Traces, and sounds of a strange kind" that already now anticipate this resurrection life.[4] And as with Donne and Herbert, Vaughan's theologically informed approach remains of interest today for the critical effects it produces, which strongly anticipate Jane Bennett's notion that things are invested with a vibrant "thing-power."[5] Vaughan's poetry develops this basic theoretical stance in two distinctive directions, both of which I will summarize briefly before turning to the specifics of his poetry.

First, Vaughan's poems articulate a somewhat unhinged perspective on the historical and social indices of personal identity; they do so in order to gain sight of a mysterious materiality that Vaughan posits beneath the veneer of socialized selfhood. Vaughan's poems express an awareness of how he is claimed by the historical world, which is full of voices that demand to be answered in "Distraction." But drawing attention to the extent to which he is claimed by the social world is designed to bring to light the material substrate of his own body, a material substrate that remains outside social life because it is never fully absorbed in social roles and identities. And though we (in our modern biological frame of reference) think of the material substrate of the social and historical person as the thing that causes the death of the person by becoming diseased, Vaughan's perspective is the reverse: From his immanent apocalyptic stance, it is the socially and historically conditioned self that must necessarily die, just as (eventually) the entire historical and social world must pass away. For him, the only thing that could possibly survive such symbolic death is precisely the material thing, the "raw" body, the flesh left over after symbolic death and that he sees as the substrate of resurrection. It is true that the raw body and the socialized, historicized body are, for Vaughan, one and the same. But precisely because they are one and the same, it is possible to contemplate the socialized, historicized body in a poetic light that makes that same social substance appear as a "raw" body. Vaughan's poems strip the flesh bare of its symbolic and social attributes in order to reveal the flesh as other than a conventional identity in a social and historical world. For Vaughan, the flesh is what anticipates a resurrected life precisely because it is *other* to the historical person who will die. The goal of Vaughan's poems is to shift our perspective past the self that is historically situated and shaped by social life in order to see the self as endowed with a strangely material recalcitrance. This material thing is neither a social identity nor dead matter; rather, it is the living, pulsing substrate upon which his contingent, local identities are mounted and that will be left after they die away. Identifying with this underlying fleshly substrate (as Vaughan seeks to do in and through his poetry) is, paradoxically, a way of preexperiencing the future of corporeal resurrection.[6]

Second, and relatedly, Vaughan's poems articulate a somewhat unhinged perspective on the external natural world and the ways it exceeds the meanings that humans impose upon it. Because Vaughan's theory of immanent resurrection extends also to the entire creation (something that is strongly prefigured in Paul's letter to the Romans), he believes that he can see the seeds and signs of resurrection unfolding in the natural world; in his poems birds, bees, plants, sticks, feathers, rocks, magnets, and rainbows are all endowed with a strange, numinous power. In the light of an immanent process of resurrection, the material stuff of nature appears alien in its beauty, endowed with a strange pulsating life that points beyond the contingent, human, historical world where these things have names and human valuations. Vaughan contrasts the numinous "staidness" of natural things ("Man," 9) to the sociological absorption and "business" ("Man," 11) of human beings. Contemplating nature, therefore, again draws attention to the unnaturalness of human beings' socialized, historical life. Like the Romantics after him, Vaughan articulates an experience of nature as other or alien in order to use that experience of nature as a way of unhinging the human self from its conventional mooring in the social and cultural world.

In the run-up to the English Civil War Vaughan had been a witty, royalist cavalier writing classically balanced verses that celebrated the cavalier ideals of friendship and the good life, in the tradition of Jonson. Like much cavalier poetry, Vaughan's early poetry functioned as a weapon within the culture war that preceded the actual war. Prewar cavalier poetry was designed to allow like-minded poets and readers to differentiate themselves from the tastes and cultural ethos of the Puritan middle classes. But for Vaughan, his cavalier phase was followed by a dramatic turn to religious poetry (and a return to his native Wales). This turn to religious poetry remains somewhat mysterious. Vaughan claimed it had been triggered by reading the poetry of Herbert, though it seems also to have been aligned with a major health crisis and the disastrous fortunes of the king's party in the Civil War (in which Vaughan appears to have fought).[7]

Like many other religious poets, Vaughan is sometimes quite conventional. Given that religious poets work within a well-defined tradition, they end up reassembling the pieces of the tradition in predictable ways. Such poems are not only poetically conventional but also theologically

conventional, and since the theological default in Puritan England is body/
soul dualism, the most conventional poems in *Silex Scintillans* do sometimes articulate body/soul dualism and the concomitant view that the soul
is resurrected immediately after death even if the body must wait until
the general resurrection. One example is "The Burial of an Infant" (which
imitates Ben Jonson's "On My First Daughter"):

> Sweetly didst thou expire: thy soul
> Flew home unstained by his new kin,
> For ere thou knew'st how to be foul,
> Death *weaned* thee from the world, and sin.
> ("The Burial of an Infant," 5–8)

Here the death of the body is a liberation; the soul ascends immediately
to its "home," leaving the body in the ground, waiting to be reassembled at some future apocalyptic moment. When it appears in Vaughan's
poems, dualism is often associated with another person's death (rather
than his own imagined death); dualism offers the easiest form of consolation because it allows one to imagine that the death of the other is
not really death at all, since the essential part of him or her lives on
uninterrupted.

But in Vaughan's collection, the unambiguously dualist poems are a
minority, mostly clustered at the beginning of the sequence. Moreover,
even poems that begin with a dualist position often undercut this position by equating the living biological body with the person. One poem
that begins with dualism but then moves forcefully away from it is
"Burial." This poem begins with the notion of the body as a mere house
for a separable soul but ends with the speaker's inability to imagine himself apart from that body, whose material stuff will be scattered across the
world after his death. Addressing himself to Christ, Vaughan begins,

> O thou! The first fruits of the dead
>   And their dark bed,
> When I am cast into that deep
>   And senseless sleep
>   The wages of my sin,
>   O then,
> Thou great Preserver of all men!
>   Watch o'er that loose
>   And empty house,
>   Which I sometimes lived in.
> ("Burial," 1–10)

Already here there is a tension between the metaphor of a house that a detachable soul has left behind and the metaphor of death as sleep in which the self remains tied to the body.[8] In the third stanza the speaker gives up any notion of a self that is detachable from the body by describing his "I" being dissolved into little bits that are blown around the world, holding only to the hope that Christ will remain "faithful, and just" to these bits and reassemble them at the end times:

> And nothing can, I hourly see,
>   Drive thee from me,
> Thou art the same, faithful, and just
>   In life, or dust:
>   Though then (thus crumbled) I stray
>   In blasts,
> Or exhalations, and wastes
>   Beyond all eyes
>   Yet thy love spies
> That change, and knows thy clay.
>
> ("Burial," 21–30)

Here Vaughan abandons himself to total death (it is not only an incidental body but the essence of him, his very "I," that "stray[s] / In blasts"), trusting only that God will be able to spy out and reassemble the parts when the time comes: "yet thy love spies / that change, and knows thy clay." It is noteworthy that Vaughan imagines the reanimating love of God to be directed toward the "clay," a word usually devalued in the tradition as the inert carrier for personhood. Here the clay is tantamount to the person himself, and though the clay is utterly dispersed at death, Vaughan looks forward to an end time in which his body (and thus his person) will be reassembled.

The view Vaughan articulates here is mortalism; human death is total and complete until an apocalyptic end time in which the human person will live again by being corporeally reassembled. The poem ends by highlighting its orientation to the apocalyptic future when persons will live again by inviting the coming of the Lord: "Lord haste, Lord come, / O come Lord *Jesus* quickly!" (39–40).[9] The mortalism we see in this poem is shared by Milton; to some extent, it is the only logically plausible account of actual death that a nondualist theory of resurrection can generate.

But mortalism is defined by its focus on the future (the period between death and resurrection), whereas what is most distinctive and most interesting about Vaughan's poetry is that he bends an expected future resurrection of the flesh into the here and now. Vaughan's poems allow the future (in which clay will be reassembled) into the present (where the self feels the clay already animate with a strange, otherworldly life). This is a view that plays an important part in Paul's epistles, including the verses that Vaughan quotes as an epigraph to "Burial": "And not only they [plants and animals in the natural world], but our selves also, which have the first fruits of the spirit, even we ourselves groan within our selves waiting for the adoption, to wit, the redemption of our body" (Rom. 8:23). For Paul the human body—and, indeed, all of creation—is pregnant with the first fruits of the spirit that lead ultimately to corporeal resurrection. It is as if the resurrection body were already inside the body as it exists now. To use Bynam's resonant phrase, Paul's understanding of resurrection makes the matter of the body "pregnant with potential for otherness."[10] This same perspective leads Vaughan to investigate how the future of fleshly resurrection appears as a distinctive subjective experience in the here and now.

One vocabulary Vaughan often uses for the experience of catching sight of the resurrection body that is already a part of the conventional, socialized body is the notion of a seed that is secretly growing and budding. Vaughan is drawing on Paul's account of resurrection in 1 Corinthians 15, though he inflects the language in a distinctive way. The notion of resurrection as the sprouting of a seed that is already now inside the human body (or a seed that simply is the human body understood in a new way) appears in "The Seed Growing Secretly," a poem that explores the tension between the conventional life of the person, a life destined to come to an end at death, and a second, secret life that is already present and that points beyond death. The same idea appears in "Disorder and Frailty," in which Vaughan imagines that "That seed, which thou / In me didst sow," does "bud" and sprout only to be subsequently attacked by flies and poison and blasts in this worldly life so that:

> Not one poor shoot
> But the bare root
> Hid under ground survives the fall.
> *Alas, frail weed!*[11]

("Disorder and Frailty," 27–30)

The poem evokes the spectacle of a body internally riven into two separate forms of life: conventionally human life and a second, somewhat alien life that experiences the world as hostile. The same model appears in "The Sap," in which Vaughan imagines that ingesting the blood of Christ (he seems to be imagining communion) nourishes a "secret life" (31) that transcends decay: "who but truly tastes it, no decay / Can touch him any way" (29–30).

Yet it is obvious in both poems that these two forms of life—the worldly life on the one hand and the seed or bud or sap that anticipates resurrection on the other—are coincident in Vaughan's one body. Vaughan never imagines that there is a special organ inside his body that is already made of the stuff of resurrection and that will live while the rest of the body will die and be dispersed; rather, he imagines that the very body that will decay and die is at the same time, if properly understood, the seed of resurrection that has already sprouted.[12]

"Repentance" thematizes the interconnectedness of the animated flesh and the socialized person that will die. Vaughan describes a complex dynamic in which purely material life comes first but leads to another, secondary, historically and socially conditioned life that represents a distinctively human falling away from the first:

> Lord, since thou didst in this vile clay
>   That sacred Ray
> Thy spirit plant, quickning the whole
> With that one grain's infused wealth,
> My forward flesh creept on, and subtly stole
> Both growth, and power; checking the health
>   And heat of thine:
>
> ("Repentance," 1–7)

Here the divine life principle planted in "this vile clay" quickens the whole body, but once quickened the body is set in motion against the divine life principle with which it began. The natural organic growth of the body is an expression of the divine seed within it, but this organic growth gives rise to a second, socialized life that rebels against the underlying life of that divine seed. The same situation appears in "I walked the other day," in which Vaughan suggests that by looking carefully at the secondary cocoon of earthly life, one can still catch sight of the future life of resurrection (with which earthly life began).

> O thou! Whose spirit did at first inflame
>   And warm the dead,
> And by a sacred incubation fed
>   With life this frame
> Which once had neither being, form, nor name,
>   Grant I may so
>   Thy steps track here below,
> That in these masques and shadows I may see
>   Thy sacred way,
>
> ("I walked the other day," 43–51)

The masques and shadows of this life are the social and historical life that veils the life of the flesh, which was initially granted and "by a sacred incubation fed." But if the masques and shadows of historical life block access to the originary moment in which God's spirit "did at first in-flame / And warm the dead," they are also the very thing that allows the reader to regain this perspective, for it is in these masques and shadows that the speaker hopes to see "Thy sacred way."

Throughout his poems Vaughan's technique for separating out an experience of the resurrection body from experiences of the conventionally social body is to travel "backward" (one of Vaughan's favorite notions) through the socialized life of the socially recognized person to catch sight of an underlying natural life of the flesh that Vaughan understands as giving rise to but also transcending the social life of the person. As he puts it in his highly canonized "The Retreat":

> Some men a forward motion love,
> But I by backward steps would move;
> And when this dust falls to the urn,
> In that state I came, return.
>
> ("The Retreat," 29–32)

As I have already noted, our modern medical frame of reference assumes that it is the underlying material body of the person that causes death. For Vaughan, the opposite is true: The socialized life of the person will die, as the contingent social and historical world that the person inhabits comes to an end, and only the underlying raw animated body (which first comes to light through the process of being reduced to dust) survives this transition. Odd as it sounds, for Vaughan the material stuff left over after the death of the socially recognized person is the stuff of resurrection, and feeling the presence of an animated corpse within the still living social self is therefore a preexperience of resurrection.

Vaughan believes that animals and plants also contain the seed of resurrection. Indeed, in many poems Vaughan suggests that animals and plants are closer now to their resurrection state than he is because he is subject to the characteristically human falling away from his natural thingness that he describes having to undo in "The Retreat." In other words, he, like all humans, is thrown into a contingent but compelling social world that seizes the body and defines a socialized identity. It is precisely because he is subject to this falling away that he is ultimately able to become self-conscious about the numinous and transcendent thingness of his body. For Vaughan, losing touch with the natural body that subtends the human person is the precondition for ultimately recognizing and bringing to light this natural thingness.

The distinctively human falling away from a primary state of luminous life that appears in "The Retreat" is theorized by Vaughan as "busyness," a word that, together with its cognate "busy," plays an important role throughout the *Silex* sequence. For Vaughan, the word "business" (and the notion of being "busy") has three interconnected meanings:

1. Running to and fro or even being blown to and fro in the world (that is, it suggests a kind of passive busyness)
2. Making a living, doing what it takes to get and stay ahead in a slippery social world, being "in" business, so to speak
3. Building and maintaining a socialized personal identity, a self

For Vaughan, getting busy, giving oneself over to business, obscures the natural life of the flesh that is the substrate of resurrection. Paradoxically, however, human business is also the very thing that allows a distinctively human experience of uncovering the substrate of resurrection within the self. "Business" as sociological embeddedness is like a veil that blocks seeing natural life, but it is also the lens through which humans can encounter the core of natural life. Only by seeing business as business, by seeing the way the world catches the self, so to speak, can the self catch sight of the natural fleshly life that subtends the social persona without ever being fully exhausted by the social persona. The process Vaughan's poems seek to enact is precisely this self-conscious detachment of the self from business—in other words, from the self's social coordinates—in order to catch sight of the natural life that anticipates the life of the resurrected body.

Thus, in "Man" Vaughan contrasts the stillness and staidness of animals and plants to the roaming and ranging and "business" that characterizes human life. Vaughan marvels at the "steadfastness . . . / Of some mean things which here below reside" ("Man," 1–2)—he names birds, bees, and magnets, and in other poems he includes plants and even sticks, feathers, rainbows, stars, and rocks in this category—and wishes that humans could share this form of life:

> I would (said I) my God would give
> The staidness of these things to man! for these
> To his divine appointments ever cleave,
>   And no new business breaks their peace;
>
> ("Man," 8–11)

Birds and bees have no "business" to break their peace. By contrast to these staid things, "Man hath still either toys, or care, / He hath no root, nor to one place is tied, / But ever restless and irregular / About this earth doth run and ride" ("Man," 15–18). It goes without saying that Vaughan's claim about humans being "restless and irregular" is echoed in his metrical and stanzaic pattern, 8A 10B 10A 8B 10C 6A 10C, which, like so many of his patterns, holds out the hope of resolving into a pleasing rhyme or metrical pattern only to disappoint that hope.

Yet if nonhuman life is superior to human life because it never loses itself in business, it is also inferior because insofar as it never loses itself it can never come to awareness of itself as enlivened materiality. The point of the poem is that while there is a peaceful, staid life that nonhuman animals and plants (and magnets and rocks) have and that humans lack, the business (and sociological busyness) of humans is in some dark way essential to the distinctive part humans play in the divine order:

> Man is the shuttle, to whose winding quest
>   And passage through these looms
> God ordered motion, but ordained no rest.
>
> ("Man," 26–28)

Though there may be some slight glance here at the fall and punishment of Adam's seed (for which God might be imagined to have "ordered motion, but ordained no rest"), the punishment of earthly life is not a frequent concern of Vaughan's. Rather, it seems that the God-ordered motion he describes here is part and parcel of the distinctive, divinely ordained human quest to catch glimpses of resurrection unfolding within human and natural bodies in the here and now. Vaughan makes the point explicit in "The Pursuit":

> Lord! What a busy, restless thing
>   Hast thou made man!
> Each day, and hour he is on wing,
>   Rests not a span;
>
> .   .   .   .
>
> Hadst thou given to this active dust
>   A state untired,
> The lost son had not left the husk
>   Nor home desired;
> That was thy secret, and it is
>   thy mercy too,
> For when all fails to bring to bliss
>   then this must do.
>
> ("The Pursuit," 1–4, 9–16)

Vaughan points to the paradox that if God had created humans to be less restless, the prodigal would never have left home (he "had not left the husk"), but, at the same time, he would never have known home, in the sense of yearning to return to it and then, in fact, returning to it ("Nor home desired"). In the final line, the "this" that succeeds when all else fails is the very business that also causes the alienation of man from God.

In "Distraction," which immediately precedes "The Pursuit" in the sequence, Vaughan expresses the same insight not as a general proposition about "Man" but as a specific proposition about himself, and he makes it clear that business is the condition of his own social identity, of the kind of "I" he is in the world. This busy "I" is the block to seeing the natural resurrection body within, but it is also the precondition of seeing and acknowledging the natural life of the flesh that is also the self and that points forward to resurrection.

> O knit me that am crumbled dust!
> Is all dispersed, and cheap?
> Give for a handful, but a thought
> And it is bought;
> Hadst thou
> Made me a star, a pearl, or a rain-bow
> The beams I then had shot
> My light had lessened not,
> But now
> I find my self the less, the more I grow;
> The world
> Is full of voices; Man is called, and hurled
> By each, he answers all,
> Knows every note, and call,
> Hence, still
> Fresh dotage tempts, or old usurps his will.
> Yet, hadst thou clipped my wings, when coffined in
> This quickened mass of sin,
> And saved that light, which freely thou
> Didst then bestow,
> I fear
> I should have spurned, and said thou didst forbear;
> Or that thy store was less,
> But now since thou didst bless
> So much,
> I grieve, my God! that thou hast made me such.
> I grieve?
> O, yes! thou know'st I do; come, and relieve

And tame, and keep down with thy light
Dust that would rise, and dim my sight,
    Lest left alone too long
    Amidst the noise, and throng,
        Oppressed I
Striving to save the whole, by parcels die.

                           ("Distraction")

The word "I" appears nine times in this poem, and its identity is inseparable from the experience of being lost in a world that is "full of voices" that demand to be answered. This is a disadvantage as compared to stars, pearls, and rainbows, for these things do not lose their luster as they live, whereas the "I" of this poem feels itself to be growing less as it lives. Yet this process of self-expenditure is the essential precondition for a human understanding of being, and the speaker knows that if God had made him "staid" he should have been lessened. Coming to see the "crumbled dust" that is "dispersed, and cheap" as the result of human life having spent itself into a social world of voices is the precondition for recognizing the body that is natural but not social, a knowing that is not available to stars, pearls, and rainbows. In the concluding lines Vaughan asks for help in settling the dust that aspires to get busy and warns himself and God that Vaughan's efforts to shore up the whole amid the "noise, and throng" (that is, his efforts to save the self with a unified identity that is always challenged by the world) are precisely what lead to death in "parcels" rather than the revivifying encounter with the natural resurrection body within.

It is true that there are poems in which Vaughan simply wishes to escape the human predicament and become part of the nonhuman creation, as in "And do they so?" in which he writes, "I would I were a stone, or tree, / Or flower by pedigree" (11–12), and in "Thou that know'st for whom I mourn" Vaughan writes that "I have known thy slightest things / A feather, or a shell, / A stick, or rod which some chance brings / The best of us excell" (21–24).[13] But the basic vision of these poems is that it is only a distinctively human life, afflicted with socialization, that makes possible a conscious recognition of the luminousness of the natural body that is intertwined with the socialized body. For Vaughan, it is in waking up from the necessary slumber of the socialized self that the self comes to recognize within itself the natural stuff that is the precondition for all socialized identity but that is at the same time different from all socialized identity. And if the socialized identity is destined to pass away (through one's actual death or through the little deaths, so to speak, of failures and disappointments in the world), then that will only leave behind the natural stuff ("dust," as "Distraction" conceives it) that is not part of history and that is therefore not subject to death and decay in the same way the social person is. For Vaughan, human being achieves a self-conscious embrace of its natural thingness only through a detour of necessarily losing itself in a social world that people are socialized into and that is the precondition of being human.

It will be no surprise that for Vaughan the most fundamental sign of the human being's socialization is the acquisition of language. Vaughan represents language as a fall into the social world and, at the same time, as the very tool that enables a distinctively human grasp of the natural substrate of resurrection. In "The Retreat" he aligns the fall from mere being with the acquisition of language when he bemoans the moment that "I taught my tongue to wound / My conscience with a sinful sound" (15–16). But this is, of course, also the precondition for his poetry. Vaughan understands the purpose of poetic language, as opposed to everyday language, to be transforming language from a tool of imbrication into the social world into a tool of uncovering the material stuff that is the seed of a hypothetical future resurrection.

Vaughan frequently thematizes or addresses his own verse, and, like Herbert's poems, sometimes Vaughan's comments seem to operate within Stanley Fish's paradigm of the "self-consuming artifact," in which the poet aims to erase his own work so as to point directly to God's ineffable glory. In "Joy" Vaughan commands his verse to "Be dumb, coarse measures, jar no more; to me / There is no discord, but your harmony" (1–2). God takes no account of Vaughan's poetry ("He weighs not your forced accents") because he "can have / A lesson played him by a wind or wave" (7–8). Significantly, the main problem Vaughan can imagine with his own verse is that from God's eternal perspective his "numbers tell their days" (9), meaning that his (human) poetry will eventually seem dated.[14] Since his poetry depends upon the existence of a historically contingent community of human readers who share Vaughan's language, Vaughan's "numbers" will eventually become defunct, a problem that natural sounds like wind and wave do not have. The fact that Vaughan probably learned Welsh before he learned English and remained proudly aware of the marginal status of this linguistic community throughout his life helps explain his interest in the historical contingency of functioning language communities. But if Vaughan's numbers tell their days, then in doing so they also highlight what they have in common with natural sounds like the wind or the wave. After all, as much as language functions within a historically contingent language community it is also composed of material bits, sounds and graphical marks that have a material persistence beyond their usefulness in communication and that are highlighted by Vaughan's formal experiments.

Throughout *Silex* Vaughan's formal experiments aim to arrest the silent, automatic functioning of a language community that attaches a meaning to a sound or a mark. This poetic denaturalization of membership in a language community also makes readers aware of the contingency of the whole conceptual universe defined by the language community they inhabit. By highlighting the power of language to organize and shape a world of meanings, Vaughan's poems invite readers to imagine what the things of the world—including the self—might look like outside the particular conceptual fabric delivered by membership in a particular language community that is destined to pass away.

Vaughan's experimental, avant-garde poetics is driven by the goal of creating a pause between sound or graphical mark and meaning and thus creating an awareness of "things" (including the "thing" that every human person is) beyond the envelope of meaning projected by a human language. Though Vaughan's formal experiments are so exuberant as to defy cataloging, it is possible to identify at least four recurring patterns, each of which is designed to push against the grain of communication in order to reveal the material stuff that lies beneath (and outside the naming power) of communicative language:[15]

1. The most prominent formal technique Vaughan uses to draw attention to the graphical and sonic stuff of language before it acquires sense is his use of metrical patterns that are so complex as to require an almost geometrical attention to the shaped lines on the page and a musical attention to the number of syllables and patterns of stresses and rhymes in the words, a process that is quite different from understanding what the poem's words say or represent. Moreover, once the reader has identified the metrical pattern it often seems to impose itself so forcefully on the reading experience as to bracket the meaning of the words and therefore the meaning of the poem as a whole. There are many examples of this approach to form in the *Silex* sequence.

2. Relatedly, Vaughan writes poems that have a repeating unit within a larger cloud of language that is otherwise disorganized. One example is "Distraction." On the face of it, this poem appears to be a mash of lines with different lengths that have no discernible metrical pattern to them at all. But closer inspection reveals that there are two metrical units that are repeated: a unit of 10, 6, 6, 2 syllables and a unit of 10, 6, 8, 2 syllables, each of which is repeated twice.

Moreover, the complexity of the interplay between metrical anarchy and the two repeating metrical clusters is itself at odds with the completely regular rhyming couplets that run throughout the poem but are hard to hear in light of the variance of line lengths. Here again the formal properties can be appreciated only at the cost of bracketing the actual meaning that these English words convey to a speaker of the English language.

3. A related technique (borrowed from Herbert) that Vaughan uses to draw attention to the material stuff of language is to repeat words or phrases either within lines or from (near) the end of one line to (near) the beginning of the next line. One example is "Love Sick," in which he wishes that God would make "man" into a star:

> A star that would ne'er set, but ever rise,
> So rise and run, as to out-run these skies,
> These narrow skies (narrow to me) that bar,
> So bar me in[.]
>
> ("Love Sick," 5–8)

These repeated sounds do not emphasize the meaning of the words so much as denature them by drawing so much attention to themselves that they threaten to overshadow the reading mind's engagement with the meaning of the words. In conjunction with the end rhymes, the density of repeating sounds in the poem creates a sonic tapestry that drives the reader forward in an almost trance-like way.

4. Finally, like many other Protestant poets, including Herbert, but with a distinctive effect, Vaughan composes poems out of fragments cobbled together from other texts, especially the Bible. By shredding the Bible and recombining its fragments, Vaughan transforms bits of language that communicate in their original, sacred context into a poetic structure that reveals the material substance of language, which can be broken up and rearranged. One example is "Son-days," which is composed of short fragments divided by semicolons rather than being woven into actual sentences, a technique that highlights the fragments of ready-made language in the poem. Though written at a time when Anglican Communion service was outlawed, Vaughan imagines Sunday worship as:

> The pulleys unto headlong man; time's bower;
>   The narrow way;
> Transplanted Paradise; God's walking hour;
>   The cool o'the day;

The creatures' Jubilee; God's parle with dust;
Heaven here[.]

("Son-days," 9–14)

This fractured poem is constructed of snippets of well-known and well-worn biblical language (such as "The cool o'the day," a phrase Vaughan has liberated from Genesis 3:8). Language that is used up in its original context in the Bible (as well as in worshipful uses of the Bible and every day, semiconscious quotations from the Bible) is here made to reveal a material weight that persists, like the persistence of sound after a bell has been struck.

These techniques of formal estranging remind readers that the communicative and representational language that, *in itself,* disappears as soon as it has functioned to transfer a message is, at the same time, suffused with a material presence that lasts past its functioning to communicate meaning. Language contains something within it, the material stuff upon which the will to communicate is mounted, and that material stuff invites us to imagine what will survive even when the particular messages that have been mounted on it have all disappeared and therefore to consider what the world will look like outside that particular functioning language. If language use is the thing that defines socialized human life as opposed to the life of things and animals, then because language is itself structured by the conflict between the merely historical and the transhistorically material, contemplating language (as Vaughan's poetry does) opens the door to a distinctively human consciousness of stuff below or beyond the conceptualizations that language delivers, the immanent material stuff that is the seed of resurrection. As such, Vaughan's formal experimentation turns his poetry into a tool for bringing to light a deranging materiality at the heart of the world and the human person.

The way Vaughan turns language against itself in his poetry may point to a distinctive theory of language in general, one marked by a certain kind of humility. On the one hand, it is obvious that language is an instrumental tool that humans wield to impose meaning on the world. Within a given language community, language situates objects and persons. But on the other hand, language also always marks its own limitations, in the fact that the question of the meaningfulness of things in the world is never definitely established. One of the goals of deconstruction was to reveal the way language creates meaning and also undermines meaning at the same time. Indeed, Jane Bennett cites Derrida precisely to make the point that as much as language is the essential precondition for bringing things into the human world, it also points to the fact that there is something irreducibly strange and even resistant to human meaningfulness in all named or spoken-of things and that the underlying awareness of this fact is precisely what makes language possible in the first place. Thus, dismissing naming theories of language in *Vibrant Matter*, Bennett writes that "Jacques Derrida offers an alternative to this consciousness-centered thinking by figuring trajectory as 'messianicity.' Messianicity is the open-ended *promissory* quality of a claim, image, or entity. This unspecified promise is for Derrida the very condition of possibility of phenomenality: things in the world appear to us at all only because they tantalize and hold us in suspense, alluding to a fullness that is elsewhere, to a future that, apparently, is on the way" (32). For Bennett the Enlightenment (the dream of universal human reason) is characterized by progressively marginalizing or distancing this fact. She writes that with what she terms "a burst of willfulness" Hegel moves "toward the view that 'things' are constituted by the categories of reason" so that "every determinateness, i.e. all content and filling . . . [becomes] a human entity and (mere) idea." As such, "the status of 'things' shifts from that of 'objects' to 'notions' or mental representations of objects. Objects-turned-notions are second-order being, the products of the categories that organized an identity for an originally chaotic cluster of elements" (37). It is precisely this movement that Vaughan's poems, through their experimental poetics, subvert or at least problematize and slow down. To put it in Derridean terms, by relentlessly foregrounding the signifier, Vaughan's poems make the reader aware of the limits of signification.

This is precisely the effect of Vaughan's poetry, and it is undertaken in the grip of his commitment to the resurrection of the flesh. As we have seen, Vaughan theorizes the body as the scene of deep, social habituation and conditioning but also, in its material vibrancy, as exceeding or escaping this social habituation and conditioning. His formally experimental poetry is a tool for bringing this vibrant materiality to light and thus effecting at least a limited transcendence of the social and historical world. As such, Vaughan's poems contain a distinctive theory of the nature, function, and purpose of poetic language. To see the force of Vaughan's implicit theory of poetic language, it is useful to begin with a modern counterpoint, namely, Susan Stewart's theory of poetry in her *Poetry and the Fate of the Senses*.[16] Stewart frames poetry as a process of taking preverbal, visceral, and essentially subjective experiences and putting them into language, which therefore renders them intersubjective. For Stewart, poetry takes the isolated, dark self and projects it into a shared world where experience is at least potentially intersubjective and, moreover, where the possibility of having the self's own experiences recognized by another makes the speaker into a socially validated self—a person. For Stewart, poems make persons eternal by eternizing a particular, intersubjective world within which the person's subjective experience is recognized and affirmed as having meaning. Stewart argues that all formal elements of poetry (meter, rhythm, rhyme, and so forth) are designed to convey private, inner experience (including experience of the body) into a shared world and in doing so to affirm a shared, intersubjective world in which the speaking "I" has a place. Though Stewart does admit that formal patterns sometimes disrupt or undermine a poem's ability to communicate, she nevertheless sees formal elements in poetry as fundamentally geared toward conveying meaning to others. And though Stewart would not put it this way, when a poem is looked at from a position *within* the horizon of a functioning language community, all the elements of the poem (including the formal elements) are presumed to convey meaning. This is a feature of the mindset of being *inside* a language community and looking at a textual artifact from within that horizon. A competent reader imputes meaning to anything he or she recognizes as his or her language.[17] Imputing meaning to (any and all) bits of language (including formally patterned language) is what it means to be a member of a language community.

As against Stewart, I suggest that the formal experiments in *Silex* are designed to liberate readers from an automatic, unconscious membership within a language community that extends the presumption of meaningfulness to textual artifacts (and, not incidentally, also projects a linguistic conceptual matrix onto the social world). Vaughan essentially understands language as double: on the one hand, historically situated, functioning to communicate meaning within a contingent language community that is destined to pass away; on the other hand, endowed with a materiality that cannot be completely mastered for communication and that has the potential to persist after all human language communities have passed away. It is this material dimension of all language that poetic language is designed to highlight. As Roman Jakobson argues, the formal elements of poetry have the effect of pointing back to the material stuff of language. For Jakobson, poetry entails a relative de-emphasis of the "communicative" function of language (in which language is designed to convey meaning) and a relative re-emphasis on the language itself, the sonic and graphical stuff that language is made of. Poetic language is crafted in such a way as to draw attention to the language itself, and this self-reflective structure is what Jakobson famously calls the "poetic function."

Jakobson argues that poetic language has the effect of highlighting or emphasizing whatever meanings the language conveys or making those meanings more memorable, as when the poetic function is deployed in advertising jingles. But if we reflect on the purpose or function of poetic language in the context of Vaughan's understanding of immanent, material resurrection, then we can say that poetic language foregrounds the material, graphical, and sonic stuff that language is made out of and that has a material reality separate from the meaning it conveys within a particular language community and thus suspends the everyday meaningfulness of the world. As Paul Valéry puts it in a famous sentence that Jakobson quotes: "Poetry is a prolonged hesitation between sound and sense."[18] To read a Vaughan poem, as opposed to a bit of everyday communicative language, is to see the sonic stuff in the hesitation before sounds acquire sense. When readers pay attention to the formal patterns of Vaughan's verse, they do not encounter *mere* rhythm and sound and graphical shapes, as though the poems were music or graphical art. Rather, they encounter rhythms and sounds and graphical shapes that are on the cusp of being invested with meaning within a particular language community, the one that they in fact inhabit. And when readers recognize that they inhabit a particular language community that is about to invest this sonic stuff with meaning, they also see that it could be different, that they could inhabit some other language community that would make these poems meaningless, but also, and more radically, that their language community could pass out of existence altogether, since, after all, everything passes out of existence. By introducing a hesitation between sound and sense, poetry makes readers see the material stuff that is not *yet* language, and that is analogous to (and also makes you aware of or brings into focus) the material stuff that subtends persons and recognizable, namable things in the world, all of which material stuff will persist even after this contingent historical world has died away.

This perspective puts us in a position to read one of Vaughan's most wonderful poems, "The Book," in which he contemplates the physical thing that the linguistic artifact of his Bible is.[19] Here Vaughan focuses on the material stuff that makes up his Bible rather than the words in the book and what those words mean:

Eternal God! Maker of all
That have lived here, since the man's fall;
The Rock of ages! In whose shade
They live unseen, when here they fade.

Thou knew'st this *paper*, when it was
Mere *seed*, and after that but *grass*;
Before 'twas *dressed* or *spun*, and when
Made *linen*, who did *wear* it then:
What were their lives, their thoughts & deeds
Whether good *corn*, or fruitless *weeds*.

Thou knew'st this *tree*, when a green *shade*
Covered it, since a *cover* made,
And where it flourished, grew and spread,
As if it never should be dead.

Thou knew'st this harmless *beast*, when he
Did live and feed by thy decree
On each green thing; then slept (well fed)
Clothed with this *skin*, which now lies spread
A *covering* o'er this aged book,
Which makes me wisely weep and look
On my own dust; mere dust it is,
But not so dry and clean as this.
Thou knew'st and saw'st them all and though
Now scattered thus, dost know them so.

   O knowing, glorious spirit! when
Thou shalt restore trees, beasts and men,
When thou shalt make all new again,
Destroying only death and pain,
Give him among thy works a place,
Who in them loved and sought thy face.

("The Book")

Though in other poems Vaughan is perfectly willing to treat the Bible as
"life's guide," as he puts it in "To the Holy Bible," in "The Book" Vaughan
does not treat it as functioning language that transmits messages. Rather,
Vaughan responds to the stuff that the book is made out of, the once living and now dead (and eventually to be reanimated) stuff that he highlights in italics and in which he can see a model of resurrection—the paper
in which he still sees the seed that sprouted only to be harvested and spun
into clothing before being made into paper; the wooden cover in which
he can still see the quiet shade of the forest; the leather binding in which
he can still see the "harmless *beast*, when he / Did live and feed by thy decree." Vaughan treats the Bible as a decommissioned linguistic artifact

that brings to light the materials out of which it is made (wood, fiber, skin). And as Vaughan passes backward from the tool fashioned out of language for human communicative purposes to an encounter with the raw stuff that composes the Bible, this raw stuff acquires the luminous sheen of all natural stuff in Vaughan's poetics, pointing to the past but also forward to a future when "Thou shalt restore trees, beasts and men, / When thou shalt make all new again."[20]

This poem conjures up a resurrection future in which this Bible—indeed all artifactual, printed texts, including this very poem—will cease to exist insofar as their constituent parts will be redistributed to the bodies of their original owners. If the forest is to rise again, the paper must cease to be. But though Vaughan's poem here brushes up against the metaphysical thickets of how raw material that was shared by different bodies over time will be allocated at the resurrection, this poem, like so many of Vaughan's poems, derives its power from the way it bends its apocalyptic orientation into the now, into a deranging and transforming experience of his physical Bible as it lies before him. In the here and now, Vaughan suggests, the most proper use of the privileged linguistic artifact that is the Bible is not to decode it for messages but rather to use it to touch the underlying stuff of which it is composed, the material stuff of the physical book and its printed words, and by doing so to touch the material stuff of the self, too. Vaughan writes that this book "makes me wisely weep and look / On my own dust; mere dust it is, / But not so dry and clean as this." It is a use of the Bible that is essentially mediated by encountering the Bible through the medium of Vaughan's poetry.

In earlier chapters I have argued that under the pressure of the onto-story of immanent and materialist resurrection, Donne and Herbert anticipate early twentieth-century avant-garde poetry as theorized by Peter Bürger. For Bürger, avant-garde poetry is characterized by a turn against the classically closed work of art that represents the world and instead sees poetry as a cultural "happening" that creates new communities and social experiences around itself. Vaughan's own poetry was triggered as an intense response to reading Herbert's poetry (a "conversion," as Vaughan put it himself), and Vaughan's own poetry is also designed to seize readers and to change how they perceive themselves, others, and the natural world. For Vaughan the most fundamental sign of the human being's socialization is the acquisition of language. By naming things and persons, language brings things and persons into the world of human meanings, but by doing so language also occludes the thingly otherness of both things and persons. Thus, Vaughan represents the acquisition of language as a fall away from a mystical oneness with the numinous thingness of the natural world and into the social and historical world. At the same time, however, language is, for Vaughan, the very tool that enables a distinctively human grasp of the natural substrate of resurrection. Through language it becomes possible to name things yet also to become aware of the part of things that remains other or alien to the human conceptual frameworks that they are inducted into by language. And it is in this context that Vaughan is especially interested in language's doubleness: On the one hand, it is historically situated, functioning to communicate meaning within a contingent language community destined to pass away; on the other hand, however, it is composed of matter (sounds, graphical marks) that are never completely subordinated to human communicative purposes. As Vaughan puts it in "Vanity of Spirit," the material traces of language are destined to live on as "hieroglyphics quite dismembered,/And broken letters, scarce remembered" (23–24). By inviting readers to look upon his poems as though they were themselves already half-denatured, halfway to being hieroglyphs, Vaughan detaches readers from the particular language community in which words have the power to classify and catalog and carve the world (including human beings) into a particular historical shape.[21] By doing so, the poems force readers to contemplate the material stuff of the world and of persons in a manner that transcends any particular historical and linguistic world. By liberating readers from automatic, unconscious membership in a historical language community, Vaughan's poems trigger an intense consciousness of the material stuff below or beyond the conceptualizations that language delivers, the immanent material stuff that is the seed of resurrection. In the next chapter I examine more explicitly what the consequences of Vaughan's take on resurrection are for how he understands and theorizes human subjectivity, including emotional experience.

4 / The Feeling of Being a Body: Resurrection and Habitus in Vaughan's Medical Writings

More explicitly than in the previous chapter, I will here examine the way Vaughan's vision of material and immanent resurrection could open the door to a distinctive kind of "critical theory" about selfhood, identity, and the social world. To do so I look at some of Vaughan's devotional and religious "self-help" writings, and I especially focus on Vaughan's translation of a hermetic medical treatise into English, a project that Vaughan undertook out of professional interest, since he worked for most of his life as a physician. In examining this treatise and Vaughan's own additions to it, we can see how Vaughan's immanent corporeal resurrectionist commitment to finding the "seeds" of resurrection in the socialized body is transposed in his devotional and medical writings into a theory that posits an essential core of bodily life—what the hermetic tradition terms the "radical balsam"—that is sickened when it is penetrated and rewired by the social and historical world. The goal of Vaughan's devotional writings and medicine alike is to rewire the self so that it reduces its investment in the historical and social world by having its life directed by the hypothetical essential core, a move that I see as analogous to his poetic search for the seeds and signs of a "resurrection body" within himself that I examined in the previous chapter. I will suggest that when resurrection thought is translated into medical and therapeutic terms, it becomes the site for a kind of organic theory work that produces powerful insights into the self's habituated relationship to the social world and that this work strongly anticipates Bourdieu's theory of habitus and a Heideggerian phenomenology of the body. The conclusion of the chapter is that Vaughan's theoretical work transforms materialist resurrection into a distinctive way of understanding, relating to, and managing individual identity, emotional life, and sexual desire.

Part of the reason Vaughan's materialist resurrection ideas function to produce such anticipatory insights is that they emerge as a response to the complex secularization process that pushes in the direction of assuming a thoroughgoing mind/body dualism. The dualist separation of mind and body that emerged as the cutting edge of seventeenth-century secularism has been repeated, as it were, in the history of scholarship on early modern culture, a scholarship that has oscillated between wholly mentalistic and wholly materialistic approaches to understanding early modern representations of the person. Thus, in the past twenty years or so many influential scholars have attempted to reconstruct how early modern subjects understood their own bodily and emotional life through the early modern discourse of Galenic humoralism, itself inherited from classical antiquity.[1] The central conviction of Galenic/humoral discourse is that the body is a porous container for fluids that mechanically determine the health and emotional state of the person. Pioneering scholars like Paster, Schoenfeldt, Floyd-Wilson, and Smith touched off a tidal wave of subsequent studies that impute to early modern culture a basically mechanistic picture of the human person.[2] This approach has produced what I see as an equal but opposite reaction, in the form of cognitivist accounts of emotional experience as resulting from judgments by a highly autonomous and "buffered" self about its situation in the world. This approach has been especially evident as a strand in Shakespeare studies, associated, for example, with the work of Mary Thomas Crane and Arthur F. Kinney, among others.[3] I see humoral and cognitivist approaches as mirror images of each other, in that each assumes a fundamental distinction between mind and body, with the humoralists focused on the side of the body and the cognitivists on the side of the mind.

I argue that in Vaughan's therapeutic writing he arrives at a different perspective from either humoralism or cognitivism by grounding his thinking on the materialist and immanent version of resurrection.[4] Insofar as Vaughan interprets himself and others in light of an immanent, materialist theory of resurrection, he declines to see emotional and somatic life as the result of fluid hydraulics, but neither does he imagine a sovereign mind making judgments about what matters to the self in the world. Instead, he develops an understanding of emotional and somatic experience as the fruit of deep, unconscious habituation into a historical world, as signs of how the embodied self is captured by a contingent social and historical world. Moreover, within Vaughan's resurrectionist theory, this way of treating somatic and emotional life is inseparable from the project of gaining awareness of another dimension of bodily life, a pulsating vital core that is (1) the very thing that is socialized but also at the same time (2) deeply resistant to socialization and understandable as the seed or sign of a future resurrection.

Thus, as against both humoralist approaches and cognitivist approaches, Vaughan's resurrectionist theory bypasses any mind/body dualism and posits, instead, a distinction between two forms of embodied experience, on the one hand, a historically conditioned and deeply habituated dimension of bodily life and, on the other hand, an experience of the body as the very thing that transcends a particular historical moment. As Vaughan's form of resurrectionist thought makes him aware of how much of bodily life (even at its seemingly most spontaneous and "natural") is the fruit of deep, unaware habituation into a contingent social world, it delivers what we, in retrospect, can understand as a sociological framework on the self and the world, one that strongly anticipates both Pierre Bourdieu's cultural sociology and his important notion of "habitus" and at the same time phenomenological accounts of emotions.

But what does it mean to take the resurrection of the flesh "seriously" as a theoretical starting point within Vaughan's therapeutic writings? As I have suggested, one way of understanding this vision of the body as infused with a strange, nonmasterable life is as an early modern anticipation of Jane Bennett's notion of "vibrant materialism," in which things—natural and manufactured alike—are imagined to have a kind of agency and in which this fact leads to a reconceptualization (and indeed a humiliation) of any fantasy of the self as a sovereign agent. This perspective is most fully and influentially developed in her 2010 book *Vibrant Matter*, but that work is grounded on her earlier work, including her book on Henry David Thoreau. Bennett's earlier book on Thoreau clarifies the ontological status of her claims to the real existence of "vibrant matter" and in doing so helps clarify my understanding of how the idea of the resurrection of the body and its flesh functions as "critical theory" in Vaughan's therapeutic writings.

In *Thoreau's Nature: Ethics, Politics, and the Wild* Bennett argues that Thoreau sees nature as a deranging wildness that opens the door to a form of subjectivity at odds with the "they-world" (the world defined by alienating social pressures) and which she terms "sojourning."[5] But in the central chapter of the book, "Writing a Heteroverse," she takes on the vexed question of the status of the wild that Thoreau posits and decides that it is best to think of it as a fable or even a mythology, and she comes to see Thoreau as "an idealizer who pronounces the world as Wild" (59). She reports that whereas at first she took Thoreau to be a naïve romantic, as she read further she was not so sure: "More sustained engagement with his writing, however, made the question of the status he assigns to Nature more difficult to answer. While he sometimes seems to posit Nature, universe, character, and the Wild as pre-discursive 'facts,' he also uses these terms in ways that mark them as figures in a fable" (59) but not "simply a fiction" (60) either. Thus, Bennett emphasizes the tactical or strategic quality of Thoreau's writing, the way it is oriented toward producing certain effects (rather than making positivistic truth claims). She writes:

> [My goal is to] examine Thoreau's project of self-fashioning, a project designed to weaken the voice of the They within him. As a substitute for the dulling comfort provided by a conventional identity, Thoreau seeks the sublime experience of a "universe," of a self capable of fleeting moments of unity with Nature. . . . I describe Thoreau's quest as a series of eight techniques: moving inward, idealizing a friend, keeping quiet, going outside, microvisioning, living doubly, hoeing beans, and eating with care. These exercises are to be practiced daily until they become second nature. Taken as a group they display how Thoreau's art of the self combines bodily discipline with relaxation of intellect, and how it mixes intellectual rigor with flight of fancy.
>
> (16–17)

Here Bennett emphasizes that Thoreau's nature is not so much a scientific fact as it is a useful fiction, one valuable for the subjective effects it produces. He writes in order "to cultivate an *as if* stance" (58); he writes so that he and we can feel the self "as if" his vision of nature as "wild" were true. And above all, this "art of the self" is expressed in his writing because "his faith in the transformative power of imagination leads him to choose writing as his primary means of transcendence" (67).

To some extent, over her career, Bennett moves in the direction of treating the agency of the natural world as real, so that by the time she writes *Vibrant Matter* she has mostly jettisoned the attention to the hypothetical or "as if" quality of positing that the natural world is resistant to the projects of the self that she still emphasizes in the book on Thoreau. That said, this perspective certainly still appears in those moments in which she frames vibrant materialism as "a speculative onto-story" or a "tale [that] hazards an account of materiality" (4). And I want to suggest that this is precisely the status of resurrection in Vaughan's religious and medical writing. Vaughan uses the idea of the resurrection of the body and its flesh as an onto-story or a fable that hazards an account of materiality. I argue that Vaughan uses the notion of the resurrection of the body and its flesh as a way of injecting the kind of vibrant materiality that Bennett traces in the natural world into the heart of the self, which thereby becomes strange and even alien to itself. Bennett anticipates such an "injection" of a "vibrant materiality" perspective into the heart of the self when in *Vibrant Matter* she writes that "it is easy to acknowledge that humans are composed of various material parts (the minerality of our bones, or the metal of our blood, or the electricity of our neurons). But it is more challenging to conceive of these materials as lively and self-organizing, rather than as passive or mechanical means under the direction of something nonmaterial, that is an active soul or mind" (10). She reminds readers of the "the 'it' inside the 'I,'" (60) or, as she puts it in *Unthinking Faith and Enlightenment: Nature and the State in a Post-Hegelian Era*, her earlier book about religious faith and the Enlightenment, "within the intention-bearing subject, the author of actions, is there not an 'internal' exteriority that can take the form of inexplicable impulses, fury, depression, disease?"[6] In *Vibrant Matter*, Bennett argues that "vital materiality . . . captures an 'alien' quality of our own flesh, and in so doing reminds humans of the very *radical* character of the (fractious) kinship between the human and the nonhuman" (112), mentioning, as an example, the millions of bacteria that live in the crook of her elbow and that lead her to wonder whether "if we were more attentive to the indispensable foreigners that we are, would we continue to produce and consume in the same violently reckless ways?" (113).

In view of her ecological politics, Bennett says that this perspective of seeing an alien self inside the self is valuable for the way it humbles a self that threatens to run roughshod across the natural world; as she puts it, "the task is to engage effectively and sustainably this enchanting and dangerous matter-energy [i.e., the self as agent]" (xix), and she asks, "what are some tactics for cultivating the experience of our *selves* as vibrant matter?" (xix). I will suggest that for Vaughan, the idea of the resurrection of the body and its flesh is valuable precisely for the new vision of the self it makes possible, a vision attentive both to the dimension of the self captured by the social world and saturated by socialized meaning and the dimension of the self that is deeply alien and resistant in its recalcitrant materiality. The "as if" quality of the starting point of taking seriously a future in which the body and its flesh will be resurrected notwithstanding, I argue that the theory that ensues is in important ways "more true" than either the humoralist or cognitivist accounts of self and emotional life. What Vaughan adds, and what we can add by listening to his ideas, is a sociological account of how the self is wired and defined by the historical and social world together with a phenomenological account of how to attain awareness of what underlies bodily life.

My argument in this chapter moves in two waves. First, I will critique humoral and cognitive scholarly approaches to emotional life, and I will sketch out a theoretical alternative that draws heavily on Bourdieuvian cultural sociology and (sometimes implicitly) Heideggerian phenomenology. Second, I will argue that the place where Vaughan does this kind of protosociological "theorizing" of embodiment and emotional life is in the discourse of resurrection that I have been examining in this book. To illustrate this intellectual history argument, in the second half of this chapter I will analyze Henry Vaughan's translation of a German medical treatise by the alchemical thinker Heinrich Nolle. Since we know something of Vaughan's background beliefs about resurrection from his poetry and religious writings, we will be in a position to see how those background beliefs condition the explicitly nondualist and implicitly sociological account of the body and emotional life that emerges in the additions he made to his translation of the Nolle text. Looking at this Vaughan/Nolle text will also allow us to address an important convergence between resurrectionist thinking and the protoscientific discourse of hermetic thought and thus to situate the role of resurrection beliefs within the rising edifice of early modern protoscience.

Before turning to the kind of alternative thinking about the embodied (and emotion-experiencing) self that I see in Vaughan's resurrection discourse, I want to examine the current scholarship on humoralism and cognitivism in some detail. At the heart of much of the scholarship on humoralism lie two questions that are logically separate but that are, in practice, often conflated:

1. How did early modern theorists of the emotions conceptualize and describe the emotions?
2. How did early modern people engaged in the practice of everyday life actually experience and interpret their emotional life?

Many early modern writers did in fact turn to the classical discourse of the humors to conceptualize somatic and emotional life and to propose therapies for sickness or emotional dysfunction. The modern scholarly program devoted to answering the first question is ironic in that it does not ask if the humoral theories espoused by early modern writers actually corresponded to the real experiences of real people in early modern England. Rather, the scholarly program organized around the first question simply describes how early modern writers working in the humoral tradition imagined emotional life.

The second question is quite different from the first: It does not seek to describe how early modern theorists theorized the emotions; rather, it inquires what the actual emotional experience of early modern subjects was like. Why did early modern people experience the emotions they did? How did those emotions feel? How did early modern subjects interpret or understand their emotional life? To address this second set of concerns we need more than an ironic theory of the emotions. Rather, we need a theory of early modern emotional life that is true as an account of actual emotional experience. Such a theory may well require us to set aside some or even much of early modern humoral discourse as a red herring.

In the practice of scholarship, answers to the first question (how did early modern theorists theorize the emotions?) are often made to seem like answers to the second question (what did early modern emotions feel like?). It is, of course, true that early modern humoral discourse must have captured some of the ways people experienced their own emotions in early modern England; to be persuasive as a theory, early modern Galenic humoralism would have to match everyday experience, at least for the elite readers of treatises on the passions. But at the same time, treating answers to the first question as answers to the second question often ends up creating a picture of early modern emotional life that is almost unimaginably strange to us. This strangeness is typically explained by the hypothesis that people's experience of themselves as embodied and as emotion producing has changed dramatically from the early modern period to today and that work that recovers the strangeness of the early modern experience is worthwhile precisely because it expands our imaginative understanding of human life and human experience. While this is doubtless at least partly true, it also covers up the methodological conflation of the two very different questions I articulated above.

To evaluate whether (or to what extent) early modern humoral discourse in fact gives us an account of how early modern people experienced their somatic and emotional lives, we have to assess whether humoral theory is a logically or empirically plausible account of anybody's somatic and emotional life. The cognitivist approach that has been dominant in psychology and that has started to play an increasingly important role in scholarship on early modern emotions sees the humoral model as radically underplaying the role of subjective judgment in producing emotion. From the cognitive standpoint, the self cares about many things in many different ways, and it is judgments by the self about what matters to it that account for emotions, both positive, when the self's concerns are advanced, and negative, when the self's concerns are blocked. By contrast, the humoral approach is radically anticognitivist insofar as it sees felt emotions as the mechanical result of the fluid makeup of the body, and it sees changes to the makeup of the body as the path to changing emotional life. From the cognitivist standpoint, what is wrong with the humoral model is that it is too mechanistic or hydraulic, blunting the role that subjective judgments about the world play in producing an emotional life that is (and, therefore, *feels*) saturated with subjective thought.

Of course, a major reason that many scholars have been so drawn to the humoral model is precisely because it challenges the Cartesian vision of the autonomous, thinking self posited by cognitivist accounts of emotional life. For these scholars, the cognitivist model is wrong precisely because it overvalues the conscious, judging mind, when at least some of emotional life seems very bodily and to have a certain autopilot quality to it. But endorsing the humoral vision of an essentially mechanical emotional life is not a critique of the Cartesian account but an equal and opposite reaction to it. Indeed, Descartes himself endorses a completely mechanical account of emotional experience as the necessary counterpart to his purely cognitivist account of mental life; it is part of what places him at the cutting edge of early modern secularization. Whereas the humors provide a purely mechanistic, almost robotic account of the emotional life (making no appeal to mind at all), the cognitive approach posits a disembodied mind as the ultimate explanation for emotional life. What both approaches share is a commitment to the fundamental separateness of mind and body. Pure humoralism and pure cognitivism are mirror images of each other, both fundamentally committed to mind/body dualism.

One theoretical model that allows us to move beyond the sterile debate between the mirror images of humoralism versus cognitivism is Pierre Bourdieu's cultural sociology.[7] On the face of it, Bourdieuvian sociology does not project a theory of emotions at all. In fact, however, a theory of emotions is implicit in Bourdieu's account.[8] Bourdieu's sociology provides a powerful perspective on emotions by evading any differentiation of the mind and the body, pointing instead to a primordial state in which people are socially imbricated and habituated within a particular social world. For Bourdieu, most of life is unconscious and habitual, the product of unaware socialization. From this perspective, it is wrong to imagine that human beings fundamentally operate by making conscious judgments about what matters to them in the world and what they wish for (as the cognitivists assume). When this kind of abstract, reflective consciousness appears at all, it appears in a secondary way, upon the foundation of the vast, silent sea of an unconscious, habituated form of life. For Bourdieu, people are born into a particular quadrant of the social world and are socialized into skillfully dealing with it. It is only when things go awry or when people move from one area of the social world to another—only, in other words, when people find themselves not at home anymore—that people bring their practice to reflective consciousness and try to articulate explicit rules and criteria for defining their own goals and possibilities. As Bourdieu sees people, they are habit machines who are born into particular social worlds; their habits reflect their social world and glue them into it.

On Bourdieu's account, people habitually (and therefore unconsciously) care about many things, wishing for or holding onto some things and disavowing or spurning others. These attitudes do not require conscious judgments. They are implicit judgments; they are inscribed in the body in an almost automated way, and one of the main ways one's habituated situatedness appears in the world is through emotional responses. Bourdieu uses the term "habitus" for this constitutive habituated way of caring about the world that manifests itself as a textured emotional life. From this standpoint, emotional responses are not "triggered" by conscious or even unconscious judgments about the world (as the cognitivist theory would have it), nor are they the product of purely physical forces in the body (as the humoralists would have it); rather, these emotional responses simply are the ways that the subject is habituated into a social world. From a Bourdieuvian perspective, emotional experiences do not require a mentalistic judgment about a world that is separate from the self; rather, emotional responses follow from the unconscious, skillful ways of dealing with a social world that one has in virtue of being social. People are born and socialized into a particular corner of a particular social world, and because of the situation they are in, things matter to them implicitly or habitually, and these implicit or habitual connections between selves and other people and things in their world define emotional states that "work," as if on autopilot. This autopilot quality is what the scholarship on humoralism imagines that it captures when it buys into an early modern discourse that describes merely physical substances as generating emotional experience. But to describe the emotions as the result of ("dumb," as it were) humoral imbalances is to deprive them of the weighty (if implicit) meaningfulness that they always have for people whose lives are habitual patterns within particular social worlds, a meaningfulness, in other words, that comes from the fact that people always are in a situation in which things matter and in which emotional life is one measure of who and what matters and how.

The scholarship on humoralism blunts this implicit, habituated meaningfulness of emotional experience, and this blunting falsifies the phenomenology of emotional experience, the way it must have been felt and experienced in early modern England just as it is experienced now, because of the basic ontological reality of humans as socially embedded and socially habituated. My complaint about the scholarship on humoralism is that it is too ironic, refusing to take a philosophical stand on the ontological question of emotional life (where it comes from, how it relates body and mind, how it relates the individual and his or her social horizon). Absent a nonironic theory of emotional life, current scholarship often adopts a bad-faith, ironic sensibility, describing early modern culture as though it were free to define the experience of emotions on the basis of a false belief, namely, that the humors mechanically determine emotional experience. While such scholarship is often right in its reconstruction of early modern humoral discourse, it is surely wrong in its (explicit or implicit) claim that this discourse provides a window into how emotions were experienced and understood in day-to-day life. What humoral scholarship lacks is attention to the fact that people's real emotional experience always takes place within a horizon of intelligibility provided by a social world defined by concrete, practical, habituated life. That is as true today as it would have been in the early modern period, so that understanding the spectrum of emotional experiences and how people related to them in early modern England would require more than raiding literary texts for snippets of humoral (or, for that matter, cognitivist) metaphorical thinking. Rather, it would require reconstructing (or "objectifying," as Bourdieu would put it) the entire (conflicted) social universe that early modern people were habituated into and that provided the horizon of intelligibility for their emotional experience just as much as the social world we are habituated into provides the horizon of intelligibility for our emotional experience.

As an explicit theoretical discourse, Bourdieuvian cultural sociology is obviously not present in early modern England, but early modern culture does nonetheless contain some discursive antecedents to the kind of Bourdieuvian theoretical approach I have just sketched. Quite surprisingly, the early modern discourse that comes closest to theorizing emotions in the way Bourdieu would is the onto-story of the resurrection of the flesh. I see early modern resurrection beliefs as the site of a primary, spontaneous theory-work that parallels the theorizing I have attributed to Bourdieu. This is because belief in the resurrection of the body forces people to theorize how (and to what extent) the embodied self is embedded in a contingent social world that affects and conditions all corporeal experiences, including emotional responses, and how (and to what extent) the embodied self can be imagined as separable from the contingent social world it inhabits. If we examine early modern resurrection discourse we can therefore recover precisely what is left out by scholarly programs focused on the discourse of the humors as well as by scholarly programs that adopt a cognitivist stance, namely, the sociological sensibility that is essential if we are to understand what it felt like to be embodied and to experience emotions in early modern England.

Some of these claims may seem to fly in the face of the seemingly commonsense assumption that resurrection is primarily a liberation of a transhistorically pure soul from the body. But as I have tried to show in the Introduction, in the early modern period ideas about resurrection are quite conflicted. As should be evident by now, the body/soul dualism that emerged in the scholastic Middle Ages and that plays an important part in Calvinist and Puritan writings is nevertheless always in tension with resurrection theories that are monist in insisting that the person is the body and the body is the person so that if the person is to live again, the body must live again. From this point of view, death cannot be the liberation of the separable soul; it is the true and total death of the person (a position sometimes called mortalism) until the apocalyptic future in which the body is reconstructed and the person lives again. Moreover, while much resurrection thought is apocalyptic, there is a powerful countercurrent—which we have seen in Donne, Herbert, and Vaughan and which is strengthened by secularizing pressures that focus on immanent time—that insists that resurrection is somehow immanent in the creation we have now, in the sense of already unfolding in the here and now so that it is possible to catch sight of the "seed" of a future resurrection. As such, the resurrection of the flesh is what Jane Bennett might term a fable, but one that is valued for the productive theoretical insights and the new perspectives on the self and the world that it makes possible. Looking at the self in the light of the fable of the resurrection of the flesh has the effect of forcing attention quite insistently to the body, yet seeing the body as split between a sociologically conditioned set of experiences that must, per force, be left behind at resurrection and a fleshly life that is other than the life of the socialized person yet nevertheless his or her very essence insofar as it is precisely what shall be (hypothetically) resurrected. We have already seen this point of view in Vaughan's poetry. I now want to argue that by looking at some of his medical writings we can see an explicit theoretical articulation of this principle.

As I noted in the previous chapter, Vaughan holds an explicitly monist and immanent understanding of resurrection. He denies that the soul can live on separately from its body, so that, for him, any postdeath life is utterly dependent on the apocalyptic reconstruction of the body. Vaughan therefore rejects any comforting fantasies of souls continuing to live after the death of the body, as it were, by ascending directly to heaven. For him, death is total and complete until the end of time, when bodies will be re-made. But at the same time, implicit in his poetry is the belief that it is possible, based on careful reflection on the experience of the body as it exists here and now, to catch sight of what a resurrected body will be like.[9] Much of his verse is, in fact, devoted to searching himself in order to dis-cover the material reality of a resurrection body that is already within himself and that displaces him from his conventional sociological coor-dinates. Vaughan's goal in his poetry, in other words, is to uncover "Traces, and sounds of a strange kind," as he puts it in "Vanity of Spirit."[10] Bypass-ing any soul/body distinction, Vaughan's searching analysis of himself splits his bodily life into two: on the one hand, a socialized and histori-cized life and, on the other hand, a life that, in its material strangeness, is alien to his time and place and therefore the substrate of resurrection.

In his poetry and also in the medical and devotional writing that I fo-cus on in this chapter, Vaughan's search for the physical signs of a future resurrected life is heavily indebted to the important language of "seeds" that derives from Paul's great statement on resurrection in 1 Corinthians 15 (which I give here in the King James Authorized translation that Vaughan used):

> But someone will ask, "How are the dead raised? With what kind of body do they come?" Fool! What you sow does not come to life unless it dies. And as for what you sow, you do not sow the body that is to be, but a bare seed, perhaps of wheat or of some other grain. But God gives it a body as he has chosen, and to each kind of seed its own body.
>
> (1 Cor. 15:36–39)

The seed metaphor Vaughan derives from Paul leads Vaughan to see res-urrection as beginning in the here and now, with a part of the physical body already now containing the potential for resurrection. This perspec-tive can be termed an "immanent eschatology of the body" because it sees the resurrection of the body as immanent in the sense of *within the creation as it exists now*, following the resurrection of Christ as the "first fruits" (as Paul puts it in 1 Corinthians 15) of a more general process.[11] As Vaughan argues in his 1652 collection of prayers and meditations entitled *The Mount of Olives*, death is total death, yet it is possible even now to see the corporeal trace of a future resurrection: "Grant I beseech thee that this Celestial seed may take root in me, and be effectual to my salvation;

Watch over my heart, O Lord, and hedge it in with thy grace, that the fowles which descend in the shadows of the Evening may not pick it out" (21). For Vaughan, therefore, there is a natural body that will die, but within that body there is already now a seed that can "take root" within the self and thereby anticipate (now, in this life) what the resurrection of the whole body will be like in the future.

The notion of a seed or essential core that is present within the body—that is, indeed, the animating principle of all bodily life—and that anticipates a postresurrection body is a recurring principle in Vaughan's writing. The transformative potential inherent in the language of seeds is one that we are only beginning to be aware of. In addition to its prominence in Christian discourse, the language of seeds also appears in classical discourses of generation and change and in protobiological discourses of reproduction. Indeed, the language of seeds is a powerful entry point into early modern culture precisely because it fuses these different discourses into a sometimes unstable whole. Jonathan Goldberg's magisterial *The Seeds of Things: Theorizing Sexuality and Materiality in Renaissance Representations* traces some of these discursive connections and uses them to generate a brilliantly unsettling entry point into early modern culture.

My concern here is to describe how the "seed" language functions within a Pauline frame of reference to bring to consciousness a sociological sensibility about the embodied self and its experience of bodily life, including the emotions. In Vaughan's poetry as well as in his religious and medical writing, the assumption that the seed of the resurrection body is already now within the socialized self affects how emotions are understood and experienced. Since one of the privileged ways people gain awareness of their bodies is through emotional experience, from the perspective of seeking the "celestial seed" within the self, emotions are interpreted as signs of the degree and quality of attachment to the social and historical world. From the perspective of the immanent eschatology of the body, when the self undergoes emotional experience, that experience must be queried as to the information it gives about, first, the part of the embodied self that is a habitually and conventionally social self and, second, about the part of the embodied self that is not a conventionally, habitually social self but is instead pointing forward through time to an apocalyptic future. From this perspective, somatic and emotional experience is not understood mechanically but informationally; it gives information about two separate things.

First, somatic and emotional experience gives information about the part of the embodied self that is socially habituated. Rather than seeing the body as mechanical, the immanent corporeal resurrection perspective understands emotional experiences to testify to the degree and quality of situatedness in the world. From this perspective, the person is born and socialized into a corner of a social world and, because of the situation he or she is in, things matter to him or her implicitly or habitually. These implicit or habituated responses define connections between the person and the people and things in his or her world. In contrast to the humoral view, the resurrection perspective does not imagine everyday emotions to be mechanical or automated (nor, in contrast to a cognitivist account, are they understood to be voluntaristic, the result of "mere" judgments); rather, they are understood as encoding information about the way the self is caught by the social world. As Vaughan puts it in the dedication to Sir Charles Egerton in one of his religious self-help books, *Flores Solitudines* (1654), emotions testify to the implicatedness of the self in the world, for "Man himselfe in his outward part, which was taken out of the world, feeles the like passions with the world."[12]

This perspective on the embodied self strongly anticipates the Bourdieuvian notion of habitus. But from the standpoint of corporeal, immanent resurrection theory, seeing the body as socially habituated is only the necessary condition for touching the vital principle or resurrection seed within that is never fully subordinated to a historically and socially conditioned form of life.

Therefore, second, somatic and emotional experience gives information about the part of the embodied self that is not socially habituated, the part of the self that remains *other* to a socially defined identity, the part of the self that is the "celestial seed" of a future resurrection of the flesh. From the standpoint of immanent resurrection, persons become aware of the socialized, habituated world in them, and in becoming aware of it they are detached from it. But this newly conscious perspective on the self and its emotional life is experienced as a new set of emotional possibilities that point to the positive presence of something within the self that is moving away from being socially conditioned by the world. The quasi-sociological detachment from the social world produced by the search for a resurrection body within produces its own distinctive emotional life.[13] For instance, Vaughan ends *The Mount of Olives* with a partial translation of St. Jerome's "Life of Paulus," in which he emphasizes that the desert fathers had

> here upon earth already begun the heavenly life; and regenerate Prophets who were indued not onely with holy habits, but had received therewith the Spirit of promise: for I have known many of

them that were so free from malice, perverse thoughtfulnesse and suspition, as if they had never known that there were such evill wayes to be followed in the world. Such a great tranquillity of mind, and such a powerful love or longing after goodnesse had wholly possessed them.

(108)

The possibility of becoming "regenerate" amounts to cultivating the "celestial seed," which Vaughan here terms the "Spirit of promise," so that the body is infused with the spirit in a way that anticipates resurrection. Cultivating the resurrection body in the here and now aims for a transformation in which the self is detached from the conventional world, and this detachment is experienced as a radical transformation of emotional life in which some new emotional experiences become dominant and other emotional experiences wither away.

It should be obvious how far we are from the mechanistic humoral account of emotional life, in which emotions represent physical substances sloshing around in the body and in which a cure to somatic or emotional discomfort is to change the makeup of these fluids. It should be equally clear how far we are from any cognitivist account, in which emotions represent judgments by an autonomous self about what is conducive or antithetical to its wishes. If we approach early modern emotional life through the framework of resurrection, we begin to see a theoretical account in which the emotions are not mechanical fluids but instead are understood and *felt* to testify to the degree and quality of embeddedness in the historical social world and the degree and quality of displacement from the historical social world and in which changing the emotions means effecting a change in the basic way a person is habituated into the world as reflected in the emotions—that is, change in what Vaughan calls the "habits" and what Bourdieu calls "habitus."

Whereas in much of the book I have focused on how poetry, especially the most avant-garde poetry, is a privileged carrier of the immanent corporeal resurrectionist perspective, here I want to investigate how this perspective appears in some protoscientific discourses. The Christian idea of resurrection represents a challenge to an increasingly mechanical understanding of the natural world as being governed by laws of physics. Various important early modern natural philosophers try to face this concern by trying to find a mechanism of resurrection within the physical world itself, leading (for example in Leibniz) to theories of stamens or embryos as the smallest physical unit of a person capable of regenerating that person (an approach open to the attack that it results in an under-standing of resurrection as replication rather than identical re-creation).[14] Gradually this project of finding a physical basis for resurrection is dis-carded in favor of a thoroughgoing dualism where resurrection is a matter of the soul living again, and the question of how the body will be recon-structed is gradually banished to the margins of scientific inquiry.

Nevertheless, it is worth noting that within emerging seventeenth-century science there is an oppositional countertradition, namely, vital-ism, especially when vitalism is coassembled with Paracelsian science. In fact, a vitalist tradition in which matter is infused with life persists in the face of the increasingly thoroughgoing dualism of early modern empiri-cism, which posits a material world devoid of supernatural or psychic forces and that can be measured and analyzed according to the new em-pirical methods. This vitalist tradition is often coassembled with a theo-retically distinct body of scientific views, namely, the early modern hermetic thought associated with Paracelsus.[15] One feature of Paracelsian thought is the interest in what it terms the "astral body," which is the es-sence or core of material things yet different in kind from conventional matter. This early modern rival science can, in fact, be coassembled with immanent corporeal resurrectionism, whereby the astral body is trans-formed into the resurrection body that is imagined to be already inside the conventionally socialized body that will necessarily die.

So far in this chapter I have outlined a somewhat speculative account of how immanent corporeal resurrectionism could lead people to under-stand and value their own somatic and emotional life in ways that antici-pate the sociological concept of habitus. Now I want to argue that this speculative account is explicitly articulated in the hermetic science that Vaughan was very influenced by. Vaughan functioned as a community physician for much of his life, and he published several therapeutic texts. One of them is a translation and extension of a medical treatise by the German hermetic writer Heinrich Nolle entitled *Hermetical physick: or, The right way to preserve, and to restore health.* This text is interesting because it shows how immanent, materialist resurrectionism conditions an understanding of the life of the body and its emotional experience even in a relatively secular register, namely, a medical therapeutic discourse.

Hermetical physick is animated by an explicit (and amusing) hostility to the "Dogmatical" (49) or "vulgar Philosophy" of Galenic humoralism.[16] But rather than dismissing humoralism outright, the text recontextual-izes humoral discourse as one pole of a two-pole theory of life that is heavily indebted to the notion of corporeal resurrection and the vision of a seed of resurrection that lies within the historical and socialized body.

The effect of this recontextualization is precisely to endow humoralism with a sociological horizon. What appears in explicitly religious discourse as a conflict between the body caught by a historically contingent social world and the seed that is already pointing forward to resurrection appears in Vaughan's medical writing as a conflict between an essential core that seeks eternal life and an envelope of humoral life that is understood as the product of unaware socialization.

The Nolle/Vaughan text is striking for its explicit attack on humoralism on the grounds that it is a "bare received Theorie" disconnected from empirical observation. In contrast to this theory, the Nolle/Vaughan text advocates careful empirical observation that

> layes open the most private and abstruse closets of nature, it doth
> most exquisitely search and find out the natures of health and
> sickness, it provides most elaborate and effectuall Medicines,
> teacheth the just Dose of them, and surpasseth by many degrees the
> vulgar Philosophy, and that faculty which is grounded upon the
> principles of the common, supposititious knowledge, that is to say, it
> doth much exceed and out do the Galenical Physick. . . . Now all the
> knowledge of the Hermetists, proceeds from a laborious manual
> disquisition and search into nature, but the Galenists insist wholly
> upon a bare received Theorie and prescribed Receits, giving all at
> adventure and will not be perswaded to inquire further then the
> mouth of their leader.
>
> (3–4)

Vaughan criticizes the Galenists for believing in their dogma as against what can be learned from careful empirical observation of the body that "layes open the most private and abstruse closets of nature." And what looking into the most private and abstruse closets of nature reveals is not the fluid dynamics of four humors entering in varying states of equilibrium or disequilibrium but a single, homogeneous principle of life that he calls the "radical seed," the "radical balsam," or, sometimes, the "radical humor." "The Radical seed, is the innate balsame of the body, which if it be advantaged with perfect digestion, will yeeld effusion, and a balsame of the same nature as it selfe. In this balsame the body lives as in his proper seed" (28). This is the central conviction of Vaughan's medicine: that all human bodies have within themselves an identical core, a substance that is the essence of life and that attempts to maintain itself through time. It is a perspective that maps readily (and at times, as I will show, explicitly) onto the Pauline vocabulary of the seed of resurrection. From this perspective, sickness always has the same structure: It is always a weakening of the one underlying substance of life, the radical seed. Vaughan does not understand the body as a mechanism that can get out of whack in many different ways (as the Galenists do), nor does he imagine that there are many varieties of bodies, each requiring its own kind of medicine (its own "prescribed Receits"). In place of the Galenic/humoral approach of applying many different medicines to adjust many different kinds of bodies back into a static balance, for Vaughan the goal of medicine is to strengthen the dynamic, inner principle of the "radical seed" or the "radical balsam."

According to Vaughan, when it is strong, this radical seed has the quasi-alchemical ability to digest the stuff a person eats and the stuff a person's body produces into more of itself. Vaughan understands sickness not as bodily humors getting out of balance but as this inner principle losing its vigor and its ability to digest what is alien into more of itself. He writes, "Therefore, because health depends upon the strength and vigour of the radical balsame, sicknesse must needs proceed from the weaknesse and indisposition of it" (32). And because of his singular conception of human life, Vaughan believes that there is a universal medicine that would cure any disease by strengthening this one principle:

> This universall Cure is performed by a naturall medicinall Balsame, consentaneous to the nature of man, which resolves, discusseth and consumes the Seminary tinctures of all impurities and diseases: but corroborates, confirms, and conserves the innate humane Balsame; for (as Paracelsus teacheth) so long as the radicall humour keepes in its due quantity and proportion, no Disease or indisposition can be perceived. And in this way of Cure, the pluralities, particularities, and orderly Rules of Symptoms and Prognosticks, have no place for all Diseases (what ever they be) are universally & perfectly cured by this one universall medicine.
>
> (85–87)

This rather strange idea of a universal medicine is logically necessary given Vaughan's picture of human life as basically always the same: an inner principle—the balsam or radical seed or, in this passage, "radical humor"—attempting to maintain its vigor. The universal medicine is understood as being of the same substance as the radical seed (it is "consentaneous to the nature of man") so that giving it to a patient would amount to feeding the radical seed with more of itself.

But after noting the theoretical possibility of a universal medicine that would strengthen the radical seed directly, Vaughan turns his attention to treating the symptoms that occur when the radical core weakens. "Next to the universall, is the particular cure, by which the roots of diseases, and the Seminal tinctures themselves, are not always taken away; but the bitter fruits of them, the Symptoms." For Vaughan, symptoms are caused when the core is no longer strong enough to transform a hostile environment into more of itself, "when," as Vaughan puts it, "our internal natural Alchymist is insufficient of himselfe to separate the pure from the impure" (99). For Vaughan, as for early modern Galenists, impurities in the environment enter into the body through food but also through more occult mechanisms. When the radical seed is not strong enough to digest them into more of itself, these impurities accumulate on the periphery of the radical seed and produce essentially humoral symptoms, which Vaughan thinks are indeed correctly theorized by Galenic thought. Vaughan/Nolle write that their goal is to merge the best of Galenic medicine with their own theory of the radical seed. Having shown the errors of Galenism ("their Errours being first laid aside"), they will now salvage those Galenic ideas they find useful: "I unite it with the Physick of the more sober Galenists, that theirs by consoclation with ours, may become perfect and irreprehensible." But more than a merger of equals, what the treatise accomplishes is a massive recontextualization of Galenic symptomology as one pole of a two-pole theory in which the essentially non-humoral core of life gives rise to an envelope of humoral life that can then sicken the whole organism. After all, for Vaughan/Nolle, it is not the balance of humors but the strength of the radical seed that defines the essential health of the person: "the radical Balsame [is] the vital seed, and the very root or fundamentall of humane nature." But this radical seed is, at the same time, surrounded by a second life that functions humorally.

Thus, the picture that Vaughan offers is one in which a radical core of life energizes a secondary form of life, a humoral envelope that can turn back on the core and suffocate it when the core becomes weakened. In place of the Galenic/humoral vision of the human being as *essentially* a container of humors that need to be mechanically balanced against one another to arrive at a more or less neutral state (mere dogmatism or even a scholarly "hallucination" [49], as Vaughan would have it), Vaughan sees the human body as internally divided between (1) the *essential* core of the radical seed that aims for perpetuation and that transforms what the body ingests and the fluids the body produces into more of itself and (2) a veneer of humoral life that creates symptoms only when the inner core weakens. The job of the physician is to assist the in-dwelling process of perfection by applying the one universal drug that will strengthen the radical seed by feeding it more of itself. And when the universal cure is not available, the physician can treat the symptoms of humoral imbalance that arise on the periphery, as it were, of the self's essential core.

It should be obvious how readily the Vaughan/Nolle physiological model maps onto Vaughan's understanding of resurrection, in which there is a bifurcation between the embodied person as he or she exists now and the "seed" of a future resurrection that is already present inside the body as its animating principle. In place of the resurrection body we have in *Hermetical physick* the radical seed or radical balsam, and around that we have the humoral veneer that envelops and sickens the radical balsam. Indeed, in *Hermetical physick* Vaughan notes that when a physician strengthens the radical balsam, he is doing the work of resurrection before the actual day of resurrection, when the "Almighty Physician himselfe will be pleased to heal us" (89). In fact, Vaughan's model of strengthening the radical balsam by applying the universal medicine (if only a physician could find the universal medicine!) blurs the line between medicine and resurrection so much so that he worries that a physician equipped with the universal drug might accidentally produce eternal life before death, so that he is forced to affirm that in such a case God would intervene arbitrarily to ensure that medical interventions do not "carry us alive beyond those bounds, which the very Father of life will not have us to transpasse" (106).

But none of this would seem to point to a sociological sensibility on the self and its corporeal life that I have claimed resides within resurrection discourse. In fact, however, Vaughan connects the humoral body that grows out of the radical seed to a historically contingent social life. For Vaughan, the humoral envelope that surrounds and sickens the radical seed is, in fact, the place where the social world digs into the self and re-wires it, where the social world becomes flesh. Thus, instead of a simple model of a radical seed enveloped by hostile humoral life Vaughan actually gives us a model of a transhistorical radical seed that aims for eternal self-perpetuation enveloped by a socialized and historicized fleshly life that derives from a particular social and historical world. In essence, weakness in the radical seed makes the person vulnerable to being penetrated and rewired by the social world. This social perspective is suggested by the fact that Vaughan begins his discussion with a whole series of what I would term "lifestyle cures." Some of these cures are very much in line with standard Galenic practice, which is concerned with managing what is brought into the body through eating and drinking and with managing the effects of exercise and sleep habits. Thus Vaughan offers such narrow lifestyle cures as "Eat not greedily, and drink not immoderately" (20). But Vaughan goes on to offer lifestyle cures that indict a whole

European way of life and its supposed superiority over the "Salvages, Barbarians, and Canibals" (17). In fact, the treatise suggests that curing the diseases of the humoral envelope requires a cultural reform program and a vast change in lifestyle that is designed to effect at least a limited detachment of the self from the historical and social world it inhabits.

Vaughan's focus on a broad reorientation of self and world is suggested by the fact that his discussion of therapies begins with the admonition to "Lead a pious and an holy life" (11), "For Piety (as the Apostle teacheth) is profitable for all things, having the promise of this present life, and of that which is to come" (12). But for Vaughan/Nolle, piety is not a narrowly religious matter, for it amounts to a wholesale rewiring of the self and its relation to a historical world. "Wonder not therefore, that so many in this age perish so suddainly and so soon. Impiety now bears the sway: true and unfeigned charity hath no place to abide in; Perjury, Treachery, Tyranny, Usury and Avarice, or (where these are not,) a vicious, lascivious, and loose life, are every where in request" (12). What Vaughan accomplishes through his attacks on the European form of life is to socialize the humoral envelope that grows when the radical seed weakens and loses its quasi-alchemical capacity to digest everything alien it encounters into more of itself. Lifestyle causes trouble by ensconcing itself in the humoral part of the body that is at odds with the radical seed, the part of the body that is aiming for perfect and everlasting bodily life. The life of the humors is a life embedded in a social universe, and the goal of the physician is to effect a limited detachment of the body from its habitual, mindless imbrication in social life, which strengthens the flesh at the expense of that within the body that aims for transcendence of time.

Thus, from Vaughan's perspective, therapeutic interventions are not designed to restore mechanical balance (the goal of Galenic medicine) but to effect a wholesale rewiring of the self so that the life of the body will not be directed by the socialized flesh but by the radical seed or radical balsam, the principle within that seeks eternal life. And from this perspective, somatic experience (including emotion) is informational. It gives information about the relationship of the self to a contingent historical world. This information is important for Vaughan's medicine because he understands health to be a medically assisted displacement from this contingent historical world.

I want to end my discussion by looking more specifically at the implications of this model for reconstructing early modern emotional life as a felt reality. It is striking that one of the only extensive additions Vaughan makes to his translation of the Nolle treatise is a "note" that highlights the importance of the felt emotion of joy in the context of sexual experi-ence.[17] Vaughan adds his marginal note to a section entitled "Use not too frequently, the permissions of Marriage." In the original Latin treatise written by Nolle, the thinking about the health effects of sex (for men) is quite mechanical; the expenditure of procreative "seed" is understood as an expenditure of essential life force, and, if done immoderately, it can cause death. It might be tempting to see this seed as precisely the radical seed that Vaughan's resurrection somatics posit as the core of life, but this is where Vaughan adds a corrective supplement to the original text. Vaughan's supplemental comment tells the story of a man who, after a long courtship, gains the love of an especially "handsome" woman and is then found dead the morning after his wedding. The mechanical ac-count that the original Nolle text proposes would cast this as an instance in which too much emission of semen has led to death. But Vaughan steps back from that account and in its place posits the crucial mediating role of emotions, especially what he terms "excessive joy":

> It was not long before the publishing of this peece, that I was told by a very noble Gentleman, that in his late travailes in France, he was acquainted with a young French Physician, who for a long time had beene suiter to a very handsome Lady, and having at length gained her consent, was married to her, but his Nuptial bed proved his Grave, for on the next morning he was found dead. It was the Gentlemans opinion, that this sad accident might be caused by an excessive joy, and for my part I subscribe to it; for a violent joy hath oftentimes done the worke of death: this comes to passe by an extreame attenuation, and diffusion of the animal spirits, which passing all into the exterior parts, leave the heart destitute, whence followes suffocation and death. Scaliger Exercit. 310. gives the reason of this violent effusion and dissipation of the Spirits: Quia similia maxime cuprint inter se uniri, ideo spiritus, veluti exire conantur ad objectum illud externum . . . atum ac jucundum, ut videlicet cum eo vniantur, Illud{que} sibi maxime simile reddant. If any will suspect, that together with this excessive joy, there was a concurrency of the other excess mentioned by my Author, I permit him his liberty, but certainly I thinke he will be deceived.
>
> (29)

The "other excess mentioned by my Author" is the purely mechanical ex-penditure of semen. But bypassing any simple expenditure-of-semen-equals-death theory as too mechanistic, Vaughan adds another, to us strange cause of death: "excessive joy . . . for a violent joy hath oftentimes done the worke of death."[18] Vaughan cites Scaliger for an explanation of the killing power of joy; the Scaliger citation reads (in my translation): "Because similar things principally desire to be united among themselves, on that account spirits, for example, try to go out to that external object which is agreeable and pleasing, so that, of course, they may be united with it, and may give back that thing that is especially similar to them."[19] The quotation suggests that Vaughan (following Scaliger) understands joy to be a movement of a part of the self out into the world with an enervating immediacy. For Vaughan, joy is the *feeling* of the self investing itself into a world that is essentially alien and contingent, and no matter how pleasurable the feeling, joy also contains a pain that is built upon the recognition that it ties you to a contingent world. Indeed, too much joy has the power to kill (separate from the mechanical emission of seed as a cause of death) because of the excessive growth into the world, the overattachment to the world that it betokens.

From this perspective, excessive joy does not admit of a simple humoral-hydraulic response. The solution to the Frenchman's problem is not to refrain from emitting more fluid semen. That is too simple, for the underlying problem is that his body is fundamentally *caught* by a social world that implants itself into the self and that thereby causes the self to implant itself into the world. The solution is to effect a slow and gradual retraining of the basic habits by which the self is in the world. Indeed, the treatise as a whole never suggests that it is possible *simply* to free one's self from the world that is bored into it at the level of quasi-humoral emotions. Rather, the only way out is a gradual retraining program, and the treatise's lifestyle precepts, including the sexual ones, must be seen as part of a program of transformation (rather than a simple process of purging the self of emotions or the fluid imbalances that cause emotions).

One way of understanding Vaughan's marginal comment about "killing joy" is that it opens up a field a sexuality not governed by Nolle's mechanical imagery of sex as physical emission of the radical seed.[20] Leo Bersani has taught us to see sexuality as a beneficent crisis of selfhood, and killing joy would seem to qualify as such a crisis.[21] But Vaughan's vision also seems to depart from Bersani's account insofar as Vaughan sees killing joy not as a beneficent death of the person but as a kind of explosive screwing of the self into the world. The joy of having a handsome woman, that vision of the self in the world, is itself deadly from the standpoint of the radical seed that is the body's only real health. Indeed, the kind of transcendence of self that Vaughan aims for (his account of "health") is a transcendence in the other direction, as it were, not out into the social world but back into the body, into the core of the body in all its pulsating, living strangeness, something that excess joy takes you away from by admitting the siren call of the world. The field of sexuality that Vaughan opens up here is marked by the notion of the body as socialized yet as potentially unhinged from that social connectedness, a vision that ultimately derives from his belief in a corporeal resurrection. This resurrection-inflected perspective sees somatic experience, including the emotions, as the terrain on which persons become aware of and therefore become capable of transforming, the nexus between self and world.

I have argued that the resurrection beliefs that animate Vaughan's poetry provide him with a distinctive framework for understanding somatic and emotional life as socially habituated. I have also argued that this discourse is one that we should take seriously because it makes it possible to reconstruct the felt reality of at least some emotional life in the early modern world. Indeed, I have argued that the "official" discourse of humoralism is, to some extent, a red herring, at least if our scholarly interest is in recovering the phenomenological experience of early modern emotional life. Implicitly, I have suggested that to the extent that contemporary scholars are interested in recovering the felt reality of early modern bodily and emotional life, they should bypass humoral discourse in favor of reconstructing a Bourdieuvian vision of the social world: that people are unconsciously habituated into in ways that "show up" as quasi-automatic emotional responses. I have argued that though Bourdieuvian sociology is not present as a discourse in early modern England, an analogous kind of theory-work is done, somewhat surprisingly, by the discourse of the resurrection of the flesh, especially when that discourse is informed by the most immanent and materialist commitments. I have argued that Vaughan's translation of the Nolle treatise is a site where the protosociological vision granted by a corporeal, immanent resurrectionism is "secularized," so to speak, into an alternative kind of "scientific" theory that might be deserving of scholarly attention as a sociologically savvy rival to humoralist theory. In that sense, this chapter makes explicit the theoretical stakes of the discourse of resurrection as it appears in the avant-garde poetry that I have examined in the rest of this book and to whose eclipse in *Volpone*, Ben Jonson's great play about early capitalism, I turn now.

5 / Resurrection, Dualism, and Legal Personhood: Bodily Presence in Ben Jonson

With the advent of secular modernity, the ancient hope for a resurrection of the flesh undergoes a massive reorientation toward body/soul dualism, in which the soul is equated with the essence of the person and is understood to be capable of survival in a purely disembodied form, where it awaits its eventual reunion with the body. The residual idea of the body as essential to the self and the self as essentially bodily, together with a residual interest in the body as the scene in which an experience of transcendence breaks into the here and now, is preserved in various dissenting discourses, first and foremost among which is avant-garde poetry, although I have also identified some sermons, treatises on the humors, and one strand of hermetic medical theory as harboring this immanent corporeal resurrectionist thinking as well.

In English avant-garde poetry of the seventeenth century this materialist resurrectionism is repurposed as the source of potent aesthetic power and as a kind of "critical theory" that allows for poets and readers to fashion a perspective on selfhood and agency that dissents quite strikingly from the "buffered" self associated with the mainstream of the secularization process. Donne, Herbert, and Vaughan value the most materialist view on resurrection for its ability to act as leverage for poetic explorations of forms of subjectivity and agency that are fully conditioned by the experience of being a body and therefore being vulnerable and continuous with other bodies and even the natural world. Anticipating the "new materialism" associated with Jane Bennett and others, this materialist and immanent resurrectionism acts to foreground the material vibrancy and "thing-power" at the heart of persons. A virtuous circle exists between this theoretical project of reconceptualizing personhood in relation to the body and the poetic project of fashioning a discourse capable of gesturing toward the human person beyond any of the contingent historical identities and meanings inscribed on the body. I have thus suggested a connection between the "materialism" of the decommissioned idea of fleshly resurrection and the insistent formalism of seventeenth-century poetry.

This chapter represents a turn in a new direction associated with the distinctive ways in which resurrection and secularization function in the work of Ben Jonson. Because Jonson holds an avowedly dualist and apocalyptic understanding of resurrection (in contrast to Donne, at least in part, and certainly in contrast to Herbert and Vaughan), he is much more in alignment with the mainstream of the secularizing process as it transforms Christian ideas. Jonson very much endorses the idea of a separable, noncorporeal soul that is the essence of the person and that is capable of a postmortem life immediately upon death.[1] In other words, whereas Donne, Herbert, and Vaughan examine the critical effects of a materialist and immanent understanding of resurrection, Jonson works within the mainstream of Christian discourse as it responds to secularizing pressures by moving in the direction of a thoroughgoing soul/body dualism. This dualism plays an important role in Jonson's poetry of praise, especially when that poetry is directed to the dead, insofar as it animates a project of "reducing" the person to disembodied information, as though providing a list of a person's symbolic attributes (his or her worldly achievements, qualities, and social connections) might itself constitute a kind of immortality (or at least persistence) in the world even in the face of death. In a sense, Jonson's dualism is aligned with his classicism insofar as his poetry of praise returns to the ancient idea of immortality through reputation and the important role the poet plays in maintaining that reputation. In shifting from bodily presence to symbolic reputation, Jonson is following his own commitment to the idea that the disembodied soul is the essence of the person. Just as the soul lives on (in a purely disembodied form) in a putative heaven, so too the reputation of the person lives on (in a purely disembodied form) in an earthly life in which the body has died.

However, in Jonson's poetry of praise this serene double dualism (soul safely in heaven, reputation safely made on earth) is nevertheless troubled by his inability to turn completely away from the body. In fact, if the body and its thingly vibrant power is not built into Jonson's "official" theory of the person then it nevertheless reappears in his poetry of praise in the form of a persistent fear that even if he memorializes the memory of a person after his or her death he is nevertheless missing something. In a sense, Jonson honors both sides of dualism and comes to believe that, even if the soul is in heaven and the reputation maintained on earth, the missing body creates a gap in the world that will only be healed at the final apocalyptic resurrection, when the (still) living soul will be reattached to "its" (reanimated) body. And in the gap between the now of death and the future of reunion between immortal soul and body, Jonson proposes that his own poetry—in its formal weightiness and intertextual, cross-temporal density—can step in to act as a kind of ersatz body for the remembered person until he or she regains his or her actual body. In that sense, though Jonson begins with a sunny dualism, he ends up opening his poems, at least in part, to the kinds of attention to the reality of the body that characterize the work of the avowed materialists I have examined previously. Moreover, this opening to the body (in Jonson's case, via the backdoor, as it were) animates a spirit of formal poetic experimentation also reminiscent of the experimental energies that Donne, Herbert, and Vaughan expend in the service of using their poetry to seek out the fleshly life that transcends the conventionally socialized life of legible persons.

But in the second half of the chapter I "must change / Those Notes to Tragic" (as Milton puts it in *Paradise Lost*), for I follow a very different future in Jonson's play *Volpone*, his satire on some of the forces animating early capitalism in England in the seventeenth century. While the rest of this book is undertaken in the spirit of utopian recovery of a materialist counterdiscourse of the self-as-body that is still valuable as a tool for thinking today, the center of gravity in my discussion of *Volpone* shifts to a future in which the dominant secularizing trend toward thoroughgoing dualism wins and displaces the countervailing materialist energies I have been exploring. In particular, I will argue that *Volpone* charts the massive cultural shift in which a fully dualist understanding of resurrection eventually becomes hegemonic and is institutionalized in secular form as a model of legal personhood where the essence of the person is not his or her bodily life but his will as enshrined in legal documents, legal frameworks, and legal institutions that allow the individual's disembodied will to survive past the limit of death. In *Volpone* Jonson charts his culture's increasing fascination with the idea that the essence of the person or selfhood exists in a disembodied form, including in a network of legal institutions and especially legally entitled wealth (or "substance") that enables the person-as-agent to survive the death of the person-as-body.

But even here, just as is the case in Jonson's poetry of praise, where the body haunts a basically disembodied conception of human presence, so, too, in *Volpone* the character of Volpone is there precisely to satirize the willingness of the other characters to reduce their bodily substance to the merely symbolic substance of legally entitled wealth. As the other characters in the play invest more and more fully in a disembodied understanding of substance as wealth, Volpone becomes an ever more intensely bodily force, eventually stalking the play as an undead body (literally), as though to remind the characters in the play and the audience watching it of a very different way of understanding personhood and agency. Nevertheless, I conclude by arguing that the final scene of the play, in which the Venetian magistrate court separates Volpone's wealth and status from his body and casts his body into jail to await death, signals the end of the historical period in which the dominant, essentially dualist path of secularization is haunted by a counterdiscourse that insists on the sometimes deranging force of the body in all its strange, animated liveliness and announces the thoroughgoing, legally mediated dualism of the future we have come to inhabit.

As I have already suggested, one of the major differences between Jonson and the other poets I have examined is that Jonson is an avowed dualist, consistently representing resurrection as a two-stage process in which the soul ascends to heaven first, followed only later by the reconstruction of the body. That religious position is, in turn, associated with a certain vision of the person as disembodied in its essence, with the body only acting as a vehicle or home for the person. When it comes to the poetry of praise and especially the poetry of praise after death that aims to immortalize the person, this view of the person leads to an emphasis on the symbolic achievements or résumé of the person, which persists in the world even after the body has died. For Jonson, the confidence that the soul is in heaven is seconded, as it were, by the confidence that his poetry can immortalize the deceased person by acting as a record, a CV, a résumé of his or her achievements.

Nevertheless, I want to suggest that in Jonson's poetry this dualist perspective on personhood is shadowed by a powerful residual interest in the body as vital to the actual "presence" of the person. In other words, Jonson's disembodied understanding of the person and his ensuing confidence that language can represent (make present again) the essential qualities of the person are shadowed by the view that the symbolic representation of a person is incomplete, that it fails to recreate the real presence that the person had, and that that real presence was in some irreducible way bound up with the bodily life of the person. Thus, to the extent that in his poetry of praise, especially postmortem praise, Jonson's goal is to make the person present, the symbolic evocation of the person that his poetry can offer points to the missing body as the supplement that would be required to re-present the person. As a matter both of theology and aesthetics, Jonson's confident and sunny dualism is haunted by the dark fear that the separation of body and soul creates a gap in the ontological fabric of the world and that if his poetry is to re-present a person, then it must find a way to fill this gap.

This haunting wish for the body explains how often Jonson imagines his poetry of praise and memory as a funeral monument. This is a way of understanding his poetry that puts it into direct and unmediated contact with the body, or at least what remains of the body underneath the grave. But ultimately Jonson goes further, positing his poetry, in its material density and formal "thingness," as a stand-in for the missing or buried body. In essence, Jonson frames his poems as ersatz bodies that stand in for the missing body of the dead person. For Jonson, celebrating the memory of the person as a disembodied set of achievements (as his poetry of praise does do) leads him to put forward the hypothesis that, in their textual density and formal perfection, the poems themselves supplement those symbolic achievements, thus recreating the presence, the vibrant force, that the person had and that has now dissolved in the face of death.

For Jonson, memorial poems "do the work of resurrection" in the gap between death and the final resurrection, or, to put it another way, they supplement resurrection by creating a material presence that exists not fully on the timescale of eternity (Jonson still looks forward to eventual resurrection) but at least on a much longer timescale than the fleeting lives of human persons.[2] By continuing to think about agency, personhood, and identity in relation to a body, whether biological or textual, Jonson's poetry thus reveals a countersecularization impulse that is analogous to the discourse of materialist immanent resurrection I have been following in this book, but here that impulse appears in the midst of a consistently dualist (and thus mainstream) understanding of resurrection.

Unlike the other poets I have examined, who tend to devalue any notion of a fully disembodied soul-life separate from the life of the body, Jonson is fairly consistent in his belief in the possibility of an immediate continuing life for the soul of a person, and this dualist conception is valued, in part, because of the immediate consolation it provides for the death of loved ones, including his own children. As he puts it in the epigrammatic couplet "Of Death," "He that fears death, or mourns it, in the just, / Shows of the resurrection little trust."[3] This couplet does not specify a dualist understanding of the actual process of resurrection, but other poems leave little doubt that Jonson was able and willing to imagine that the soul lives on, as it were, in heaven immediately after the death of the body. One example is "On My First Daughter," in which Jonson posits the immediate continuing life of his daughter's soul even after her body's death:

Here lies to each her parents' ruth,
Mary, the daughter of their youth;
Yet, all heaven's gifts, being heaven's due,
It makes the father, less, to rue.
At six months' end, she parted hence
With safety of her innocence;
Whose soul heaven's queen (whose name she bears),
In comfort of her mother's tears,
Hath placed amongst her virgin train;
Where, while that severed doth remain,
This grave partakes the fleshly birth;
Which cover lightly, gentle earth.

("On My First Daughter")

Here the "soul" is imagined to be safely in heaven, in the "virgin train" of "heaven's queen." This is said to be a comfort to her mother, while the thought that she was a gift of heaven so that it is only just that heaven has demanded her back is said to be a comfort to her father.[4] In either case, the body is an afterthought; the poem begins by pointing to the grave that holds the body ("Here lies . . ."), but having found comfort in contemplating heaven, the speaker ends by thinking that the body is secondary, asking the earth to "cover lightly" the "fleshly birth" in the interim between death and the Resurrection.

A similarly dualist framework appears in "On My First Son":

Farewell, thou child of my right hand, and joy;
    My sin was too much hope of thee, loved boy.
Seven years thou wert lent to me, and I thee pay,
    Exacted by thy fate, on the just day.
Oh, could I lose all father now! For why
    Will man lament the state he should envy?
To have so soon 'scaped world's and flesh's rage,
    And if no other misery, yet age?

> Rest in soft peace, and, asked, say, here doth lie
>> Ben Jonson his best piece of poetry;
> For whose sake, henceforth, all his vows be such,
>> As what he loves may never like too much.

("On My First Son")

Though less pronounced than in the poem on his daughter, here the notion of a soul that lives on after the death of the boy appears with the idea that the boy was merely "lent" and that he is now in a state to be "envied," having "'scaped world's and flesh's rage, / And if no other misery, yet age." At the same time, this poem is less assertive in forcing attention to the happy soul, more caught, as it were, by the reality of physical death, whose evidence is the moldering body pointed at by the poem's most spectacular event, the moment when Jonson imagines the dead body speaking: "Rest in soft peace, and, asked, say, Here doth lie / Ben Jonson his best piece of poetry." On the one hand, in terms of tone, this claim suggests a sense that the real poetry to which Jonson has committed so much time and energy does not count for much when weighed against the fact of his boy's death. But on the other hand, it also points to some special role for poetry in memorializing the dead body in the here and now, on earth as it were, separate from his supposed continuing life in heaven. Through the poem the boy is imagined to speak again to the living. But if the poem preserves the boy's presence on earth, then the poem does so by foregrounding the dead body, the sign of death. It is a dead body that speaks, and the poem asserts that the dead body should be understood as a kind of poetry.

This equation of poetry and dead body makes sense in the context of the many poems in which Jonson imagines his poem as an epitaph literally covering the dead body, as in the poem called simply "An Epitaph," which also addresses the death of a child, this time unnamed:

> What beauty would have lovely styled,
> What manners pretty, nature mild,
> What wonder perfect, all were filed,
> Upon record, in this blessed child.
>> And till the coming of the soul
>> To fetch the flesh, we keep the roll.

("An Epitaph")

In a surprisingly bureaucratic turn on the Platonic notion that earthly phenomena are pale echoes of heavenly Platonic forms, Jonson imagines that beauties and manners instantiated in this child were "filed/Upon record," and Jonson then imagines that now that the child has died and, with it, the record of the Platonic ideals that it represented, "we" (readers of the poem, or the general public of people left behind at the death of the child) must take on the responsibility of keeping track of the qualities that the child had in life: "And, till the coming of the soul / To fetch the flesh, we keep the roll." The purpose of the poem is to keep this "roll," but as it does so it also (like all the epitaph poems) hovers around the now dead body rather than fleeing into some disembodied, purely informational or ideal space. Somehow, it is not enough to say that the soul is in heaven. The persistence of the fled soul is not the same as the persistence of the person as he or she lived, so that the soul's continuing life in heaven—posited here as much as in the poem on Jonson's daughter and to a lesser extent on his son—is less obviously comforting. The poem wants to preserve the living, present reality of the person as he or she lived, and this means keeping the "role" of what that person was in the world—but it also means keeping at least one eye on the body that is now in its grave. Here death has effected a real loss, a depersonalization, and even if some separable soul lives on, it now does not quite preserve the person without a body, or at least not quite in the way that would provide comfort from a human perspective. And it is somehow the poem that steps into this gap.

In the "Epitaph on Katherine, Lady Ogle" Jonson starts by saying that the "record" of her achievements are in heaven ("'Tis a record in heaven," [1]) but that Jonson's own poem has the function of making this heavenly record accessible; addressing her descendants, he says "read it [i.e., the heavenly record] here! [i.e., in this poem]" (2). In the poem about another death in the same aristocratic family, "To the Memory of the Most Honored Lady Jane, Eldest Daughter to Cuthbert, Lord Ogle: And Countess of Shrewsbury," Jonson starts by listing all the things about her that a funeral stone could do as well as this poem: she was "a noble countess, great / In blood, in birth, by match, and by her seat; / Religious, wise, chaste, loving, gracious, good" (3–5). But these sorts of indices of worldly identity *by themselves* are not satisfying, and Jonson will not make them the subject of his verse, for "every table in this church can say / A list of epithets: and praise this way" (7–8). Instead, his poem focuses on the fact that she had only one husband and did not remarry after his death.

This is a misogynistic point, in the sense that marital fidelity even after the death of the spouse seems the only quality for which Jonson thinks this woman should rightly be celebrated (just as the title of the poem emphasizes her father more than her). But I think the shift to fidelity is also valued because it shifts attention to the body that has now been

interred in the grave over which he is writing and where her husband
has been buried before her. This sets up a very Donnean picture of a
postresurrection reunion of these two lovers—in their shared tomb, in
"spite of death, next life, for her love's sake, / This second marriage, will
eternal make" (25–26). The two bodies await resurrection to enter into
an eternal second marriage. By generating this vision as the culmination
of his memorial poem, Jonson seems to prioritize keeping the body in
the foreground alongside (and inseparable from) the worldly qualities of
the person that the poem also rehearses. As I will suggest, this amounts to
a general model for Jonson's poetic project: He forces social identities
into proximity to the body that has now died, suggesting that without a
continuing connection to this body, a disembodied, purely informational account of someone's achievements is somehow inadequate to the
immortalization toward which his poetry of praise aims.

Jonson's wish to combine reciting a CV with continuing proximity to
the body explains his fondness for presenting his poetry as a funeral
plaque for a body that lies (in his imagination, at least) immediately beneath the words, as in "An Epitaph on Master Philip Gray," which begins
with "Reader, stay, / And if I had no more to say / But here doth lie, till the
last day, / All that is left of Philip Gray" (1–4). The "here" points ambigu-
ously to the grave on whose stone these words are inscribed but also to
the poem itself. In "An Epitaph on Henry L[ord] La Warr. To the Passer-
By" Jonson again imagines that his poem is the physical gravestone that
marks the grave that a person might pass by ("If, passenger, thou canst
but read, / Stay, drop a tear for him that's dead:" [1–2]). Moreover, not only
does the poem point down (as it were) to the now dead body, but it also
devotes much of its energy to a detailed and highly corporeal evocation
of "a disease, that loved no light / . . . / but crept like darkness through
his blood" (6–8). A detailed and sometimes gruesome medical report on
the progress of a fatal illness may seem like a strange way of memorializing someone, but it does what many of Jonson's poems do, which is to
force the reputation (in La Warr's case, his "love of action, and high arts"
[12]) back into the orbit of a body that was the condition of that reputation but also, in its sickness, became the enemy of that reputation. The
poem and the body imagined moldering in the grave enter into a logical
circle, each intensifying the experience of, and attention paid to, the other.

In "An Elegy on the Lady Jane Paulet, Marchion[ess] of Winton" Jonson again conjoins the memory of a deceased person's qualities with attention to the dead body, but here he explicitly adds his own physical
presence doing the work of poetry to the dynamic. On the one hand, this
poem is explicitly dualist, celebrating death as (immediate) entry to heaven

and imagining that Lady Jane Paulet even "now, through circumfused light, she looks / On nature's secrets, there, as her own books: / Speaks heaven's language, and discourseth free / To every order, every hierarchy; / Beholds her Maker, and in him doth see / What the beginnings of all beauties be" (69–74). Jonson invites the angels to sing for her: "Let angels sing her glories, who did call / Her spirit home, to her original;" (63–64). But there is a sense of something inadequate about merely asserting the happiness of this separated soul. For one thing, there is a hint of ineffability, as in Jonson's claim that the soul is beyond words: "Had I a thousand mouths, as many tongues / And voice to raise them from my brazen lungs, / I durst not aim at that [i.e., her soul]" (23–25). And if the soul in heaven is imagined as a good (if inexpressible) thing, then there is nevertheless a sense that something is missing that Jonson as poet *does* have enough tongue and voice to address. If the angels will sing her heavenly glory, then that seems to pose the question of what more Jonson's own singing can accomplish. I think that what Jonson's poem can add to the angel's song is to memorialize the real earthly presence of the person in a way that simple assertion of a soul's ascension to the "future life" of the "Christian" does not.

The poem famously (and quite unusually, for Jonson) begins with an almost gothic scene in which Jonson describes himself seeing the ghost of Lady Jane, a sight that freezes him in horror: "Stay, stay, I feel / A horror in me, all my blood is steel! / Stiff, stark, my joints 'gainst one another knock!" (7–9). A few lines later this frozen state is then reimagined as turning Jonson's whole body into a block of marble, like the marble of Lady Jane's funeral monument, upon which Jonson imagines Lady Jane's worldly achievements will be written. Addressing "Fame," Jonson asks:

> Alas, I am all marble! Write the rest
> Thou wouldst have written, fame, upon my breast:
> It is a large fair table, and a true,
> And the disposure will be something new,
> When I, who would the poet have become,
> At least may bear the inscription to her tomb.
> ("An Elegy on Lady Jane Paulet," 13–18)

This presentation of Jonson's own body as a writing surface, and his emphasis on his own corporeal largeness, represents a return of the repressed body.[5] To function as the poet, Jonson will literally become a funeral monument with Lady Jane's worldly achievements inscribed upon him. He imagines the source of the inscription to be not himself but a personified "fame": "Write the rest / Thou wouldst have written, fame, upon my breast:" (13–14). The poem itself as it exists in its published form is the record of this fantasmatical inscription, for Jonson (via fame) does in fact recite Lady Jane's CV, as it were, starting with her title ("marchioness / of Winchester") and her aristocratic pedigree.

Thus the poem imagines that the soul has entered heaven but then insistently asks what else is to be done in the world. Indeed, the poem's primal scene, in which a hungry ghost wanders, seemingly demanding something of the poet, also suggests a sense of dissatisfaction with the notion that the soul has left the world. It is as if the departure of the soul for heaven leaves a horrifying gap or void in this world, a gap or void that once was filled by the living, embodied person but that now, in death, the poem is intended to fill. And moreover, to perform this function Jonson himself, as poet, has to suffer a certain depersonalization in his own voice as he becomes marble and suffers himself to be written on. This points to a strange experience of creative work, perhaps somewhat at odds with the way Jonson is sometimes understood as a self-assertive author. But at the same time, there is something recognizably Jonsonian in his vision of himself as flesh become marble, the marble that is made into a (funeral) monument that then becomes a poem.

Many readers have felt that there is something strangely dispassionate or depersonalized or stony or marble-like in many of Jonson's poems of praise, whether memorials of dead people or celebrations of living people. While many of these poems do indeed contain specific claims about the worldly achievements and qualities of the people who are being celebrated, it is nonetheless noteworthy that Jonson is often reticent or perhaps haunted by a sense of the inadequacy of providing a purely informational list. There is a parallel with the implied inadequacy of simply imagining the soul in heaven; a similar inadequacy haunts any simple list of the worldly qualities of a person, and in both cases what is missing is the body and the real, bodily presence that comes with the person. As we have seen, in "To the Memory of the Most Honored Lady Jane, Eldest Daughter to Cuthbert, Lord Ogle: And Countess of Shrewsbury," even as Jonson does in fact deliver the lady's pedigree and achievements, he also hints at dissatisfaction with merely this, for, he says, actual gravestones can do just as well. It is as if he wants to be clear that poetry performs a different kind of memorialization than memorial plaques, and the odd formal depersonalization of many of his poems of praise is associated with that.

In a classic discussion, Stanley Fish has noted that many of Jonson's poems of praise do not say very much about the objects of praise.[6] Fish argues that this is a response to the problem of how a poet should relate to a patron, a problem Jonson faced much more explicitly in the case of his work writing masques. For Fish, Jonson ultimately affirms only that the object of praise is worthy of being praised alongside the many other objects of Jonson's praise, thus creating a kind of fraternity of worthies, each of whose honor redounds to the glory of the others in a "community of the same." I think there is something exaggerated about Fish's starting premise that Jonson does not say much that is concrete about the objects of his praise; Jonson does usually provide at least the outlines of a CV or résumé. But there is certainly something right about Fish's sense that there is something oddly formal and colorless about Jonson's mode of praise. It is certainly true that Jonson frequently points to some reticence about merely providing (disembodied) information, and it is also true that—as Fish notes—Jonson often gives special emphasis on the name of the person being praised as though just reciting the name might evoke the reality of the person in the world, rather than using words in the conventional way words operate to represent the person.

The praise poems to Robert Cecil, the first Earl of Salisbury, are characteristic in this regard. "To Robert, Earl of Salisbury" is a poem almost completely given over to the rhetorical question of "who could remain silent in view of your qualities and accomplishments?" but nevertheless remarkably light on spelling out what those qualities and accomplishments are. The answer the poem presents to its rhetorical question is that no one can remain silent, including Jonson, and the proof is the fact that this poem itself exists, concluding with "Cursed be his muse that could lie dumb or hid / To so true worth, though thou thyself forbid" (11–12). The companion poem to "To Robert" does not even evoke his name, being titled merely "To the same," though that empty title is followed by a subtitle that identifies the occasion of the poem as "Upon the accession of the Treasurership to him." But the poem's content is as self-referential as the previous one: It attempts to differentiate Jonson's motivation in writing the poem from the imputed motivations of other poets, namely, flattery and a desire for personal advancement.

By contrast, Jonson notes that the advancement of a man like Robert Cecil is a sign of the virtue of King James, and thus the poem becomes a tribute to King James more than to Cecil. The poem climaxes with a dramatic invocation of Cecil's name, which Jonson cites for its power to inspire a poem of praise directed past Cecil himself: "These, noblest Cecil, labored in my thought, / Wherein what wonder, see, thy name hath wrought: / That whilst I meant but thine to gratulate / I've sung the greater fortunes of our state" ("To the same," 15–18). It is unknown whether Cecil took a poem that ultimately does not say anything about him and his qualities as praise. But the wariness of reducing a person to a CV, the shift from praising the person to adopting a larger, more monumental perspective, is quite characteristic. The name of Cecil ("Where what wonder see thy name hath wrought!") is invoked as a means of ratcheting the poem up to a level of ambition that leaves the particular qualities of Cecil himself to fall away. A similar movement occurs at the intertextual level: In his edition of the poems, George Parfitt cites extensive embedded quotations within both poems, from Valerius Maximus and Pliny in the first poem and Pliny in the second. Thus, two poems that promise to be personal celebrations of a single human being instead become monumental in the sense that they memorialize an age and at the same time collapse the distinction between the ages by silently incorporating classical culture into its textual weave. From the standpoint of the individual praisee, Cecil, the only thing the poem really accomplishes is to enter his name into the monumentalizing and age-transcending tradition of self-consciously literary poetry. The same is true in the stately regularity of Jonson's iambs and his rhyming couplets.

The poems of praise are everywhere designed to transform or translate the fleeting life of a human person and his or her achievements into the abiding, textually mediated life of monumental poetry, a claim that is made explicitly in "To William, Lord Mounteagle," who prevented the Gunpowder Plot's success when he received an anonymous note warning him away from the House of Lords, though one would not know this from reading the poem. Without specifying any of Mounteagle's achievements or indeed any of his qualities, Jonson writes that England should "have raised / An obelisk or a column to thy name, / Or, if she would but modestly have praised / Thy fact, in brass or marble writ the same" (1–4). But because England did not raise a monument to Mounteagle, instead now Jonson's own poem will perform this monumentalizing function: "Lo, what my country should have done . . . / I, that am glad of thy great chance, here do! / And, proud my work shall outlast common deeds" (1, 5–6).

What is striking in Jonson's poetics of praise is the reticence to reduce a person to a list of accomplishments or qualities that the poem can list. Actually providing an account of someone's worldly qualities or achievements is often identified by Jonson as "flattery" (one of Jonson's most hated failings), but what flattery really means for Jonson is remaining tied to a particular time rather than aiming to "outlast common deeds" and achieving monumentality. To flatter someone is not to praise them in a way that transcends the here and now but rather to use a person's achievements to advance personal ambitions in the here and now. Flattery takes the achievements of another and bends them insistently back into time. By contrast, what Jonson understands the function of poetry to be is to memorialize the person in a way that transcends this moment, but, somewhat paradoxically, this requires a sacrifice of some of what made that person unique and particular—and sometimes it requires the sacrifice of everything but the name of the person.

Names have an especial interest for Jonson, and he uses them almost as talismans. Ian Donaldson asks, "What power does Jonson find in names, and why does he invoke them so insistently throughout the *Epigrams*?" Donaldson's answer is that Jonson creates a "pantheon of national worthies, men and women whose virtues are deserving commemoration."[7] But Jonson is haunted by the fear that in his poems of praise, the "real thing" will be left out, and I see this as a sign of his commitment to the resurrection of the flesh in all its strangeness in addition to his dualist sense that the dead person's soul is already now in heaven. And in that sense, the material, linguistic substance of the name comes to stand for the person. Jonson is operating with some kind of a fantasy that by allowing the name to ring out, by drawing attention to its material/metrical properties as sound waves in the air or letters on the page, it is somehow possible to touch the real presence of the person, as in one of his poems about Celia Boulstrode, in which he lists some of the distinctive qualities of the deceased but then asks his reader "Wouldst thou all?"—that is, do you want to touch the very essence of her person? And the answer to this implied request is simply to give her name for the first time in the poem (since it is not given in the title):

> Wouldst thou all?
> She was 'Sell Boulstred. In which name, I call
> Up so much truth, as could I it pursue
> Might make the *Fable of Good Women* true.
> ("Stay, view this stone," 11–14)

Here the name is the truth, and a name that by taking up three syllables and by drawing attention to the longer name that has been shortened to fit the meter becomes materially real and present.[8]

One poem that notably emphasizes the way the material name can stand in for the bodily presence of the deceased person is the elegy "On Margaret Ratcliffe," in which her name is spelled out acrostically along the left margin of the poem:

> Marble, weep, for thou dost cover
> A dead beauty underneath thee,

Rich as nature could bequeath thee:
Grant then, no rude hand remove her.
All the gazers on the skies
Read not in fair heaven's story,
Expresser truth, or truer glory,
Than they might in her bright eyes.

Rare as wonder was her wit;
And, like nectar, ever flowing:
Till time, strong by her bestowing,
Conquer'd hath both life and it;
Life, whose grief was out of fashion
In these times. Few so have rued
Fate in a brother. To conclude,
For wit, feature, and true passion,
Earth, thou hast not such another.

("On Margaret Ratcliffe")

The poem begins by evoking, even identifying with, the marble headstone that must "weep" because it covers "a dead beauty underneath thee." And this impulse toward physical weightiness as a way of marking the actual life of the person extends to the poem itself as a material production that spells out the name of the person as an acrostic (and, indeed, in the Folio version of the poem, the name only appears in the title and in the acrostic). As such, the poem marks the association of the body in the grave and the poem in its capacity to evoke the "wit, feature, and true passion," but it is also a poem in which the name of the deceased evokes her bodily presence through the real, material force the name acquires within the formal structure of the poem. The name-as-material especially appears in this poem insofar as the poem takes apart the name to reveal its innards, as it were, the alphabetical and phonemic elements that constitute it and that function as raw material out of which new language can be shaped, all without losing sight of the material reality of the building blocks themselves. The raw materials of language can be reassembled into new shapes and patterns just as the atoms or dust of the body can be used to make new bodies and things before the final resurrection, when God will magically sort all the matter back out into persons, including the person named in this poem.

When Jonson enters the part of a person that is already text into the textual weave of one of his poems of praise, the name attains a physical or corporeal density or reality that releases it from the fleeting world of talk to the poetic timeframe that passes the ages, even if it does not reach all the way to eternity (which is still understood to be the province of God, who will judge at the end of time, as Jonson says many times, for instance in "To Heaven"). For Jonson, the name that comes to be a material object (physical marks on the page, sound waves in the air) points toward the body not through representation (A stands for B) but through the fantasy of equation (A=B).

What these features suggest is that the real goal of Jonson's poetry is to become monumental and precisely by becoming monumental also to preserve the felt material reality of the person being described in addition to listing the dematerialized achievements of the person. In other words, the scene of Jonson becoming marble and feeling words inscribed upon his breast that then constitute the poem itself is quite indicative of his poetics, in which he has an urge to write poetry that ceases to be personal (merely his own poetry, in which *his* voice would appear) and instead enters into a depersonalized, formal realm that the memories of his dedicatees also enter. This same drive is very much in evidence in the 1616 Folio of his *Works*, which is frequently seen as an expression of unprecedented authorial self-assertion but that also contains a barely suppressed impulse to convert himself into a monument, into marble, and to do so even in the midst of his own life, for Jonson was only forty-four years old when he published this automonument. This impulse to create something that is physically, corporeally weighty is seen both in the sheer volume of the book but also at the level of the text in the frequent and sometimes frankly bizarre variations in typography, as if the text is drawing attention to its material-graphical reality.[9] For Jonson, this impulse certainly seems to contain at least some element of self-directed aggression, even an impulse to kill the (still quite young) living person.

But the payoff of converting himself (including his seemingly ephemeral plays) into the monument of the 1616 Folio is easy to name: immortality. And the payoff for those whom he writes about—whether the living or the dead—is similarly immortality. Somewhat paradoxically, Jonson sees the formal and depersonalized mode of language he developed for his poetry as having the power to evoke presence across time in a way that a mere informational list of achievements and qualities might not. After all, tombstones with their inscriptions fade and die, for they are as much subject to the passing of time as the human body is. Any actual representation of a person is subject to time insofar as representations only work as long as they are legible, and inscriptions may fade, and, moreover, the language community in which words have meaning may pass out of existence. It is, indeed, only in the realm of formally stylized poetry far removed from everyday speech that Jonson can imagine something close to (if not yet strictly identical to) eternity, the same quasi-eternity that he feels he sees in the Latin and Greek classics he still reads and often translates in ways that are acknowledged and unacknowledged and that account for much of the impersonal, stately power of his poetry.[10]

One well-known example is "To the Immortal Memory and Friendship of that Noble Pair, Sir Lucius Cary and Sir H. Morison." This poem is explicitly structured on the model of a Pindaric ode, and its text is composed of a dense weave of classical texts by Pliny, Seneca (heavily present in this poem), and Persius. Similarly, in "To Sir Horace Vere" Jonson structures the poem around the fact that both parts of Vere's name activate fragments of classical culture—the name Horace obviously evokes Jonson's favorite Roman poet, while the name "Vere" means "true" or "authentic" in Latin. Jonson writes:

> Which of thy names I take, not only bears
> > A Roman sound, but Roman virtue wears:
> Illustrous Vere, or Horace; fit to be
> > Sung by a Horace, or a muse as free;
> > > ("To Sir Horace Vere," 1–4)

And since Horace himself is notably absent, Jonson steps in to ensure that the "relish" of Vere's deeds "to eternity shall last."

Jonson frames his poetry (in its verbal density, formality, and nonrepresentationality) as a corporeal presence capable of carrying the memory of a worthy across time. In his poems, Jonson always imagines a point of actual physical resurrection in the future, but it is the potentially very long gap in time before that happens that he, through his poetry, aims to fill. By taking a record of worldly achievements and converting it into the timelessness of classically inspired (and often intertextually driven, even prewritten) poetry, Jonson uses his poetry to fill that gap before soul and body are reunited, and he imagines that in his textually dense poems the person actually exists again in an embodied form, even if embodied in a textual rather than biological body. In his poetry to the living, also, Jonson tries (preemptively, as it were) to convert the living person into a corporeal reality that might persist beyond whenever the living person addressed in the poem has died.

Jonson's double game of memorializing the person as information and using the material-linguistic body of the poem as a supplementary ersatz body endows his poetry with an avant-garde quality. In describing seventeenth-century poetry as avant-garde I have been drawing on Peter Bürger's understanding of the avant-garde as a turn against the notion of art as classically beautiful objects that stand apart from everyday life. Bürger argues that avant-garde artists aim to return art to the praxis of everyday life by making it part of communities or experiences in the world. Applying this definition of avant-garde to Jonson may seem wrong, since his commitment to something like the autonomy or the apartness of art is obvious, emblematized by his decision to publish a standard copy of many of his works in his *Works*. It is also obvious that Jonson does very definitely value the idea of art as a classical object, and his craftsmanship is obvious in the sculpted, closed quality of many of his poems. But at the same time, Jonson's insistence on drawing attention to the material presence of his poetry as an essential part of the experience of memorialization suggests an understanding of poetry as a force in the world that creates new experiences and communities in the world. Obviously, Jonson thinks that the material density of his poetry creates new experiences of community across the membrane, as it were, of death. But it is also equally obvious that Jonson's poetry created new communities in the world, in the form of intimate communities of readers who felt moved and even defined by their experience of Jonson (official and unofficial "Sons of Ben"). As Jonson conceptualizes them, his poems are material things that enact realities in the world, drawing readers into physically mediated relationships with one another and with the dead. So conceived, Jonson's poems are not merely beautiful objects or simple representations but things that work in the world, that create effects in readers.

But if Jonson's fantasy about text's ability to create presence in the world seems strange, then it is well to consider as an analogue our modern fantasies about the special incantatory power of "code," whether genetic code or computer-based code, as a kind of language that does not represent but that enacts presence in the world by creating tangible realities. This notion of "code" is a modern subset of the more general notion of performative language, which creates effects in the world. One obvious place where language as code appears is in the theater, which, as an institution, is committed to the portability and regenerability of persons based on nothing more material than the script. As we will see, this notion of script-as-code will reappear in *Volpone*. But *Volpone* also foregrounds what is surely the most important kind of performative, self-executing "code" in the modern, capitalist world, namely, legal instruments such as wills.

In the balance of this chapter I want to examine the way Jonson treats legal language in *Volpone*. I argue that Jonson picks up the same impulse that we see in his poetry, namely, to identify a special class of language that has the ability to do the work of resurrection in the interim before a soul and a body are reunited (as his specific beliefs would lead him to imagine). But whereas poetry is still quite concerned with the material reality of the body that lies under the grave and that is reflected in the material density of the text (with all the weight and even monumentality that text achieves as it appears in Jonson's formally wrought poetry), in *Volpone* legal discourse is imagined as capable of converting embodied personhood into the completely disembodied agency of the legal person, literally through a will. And if this fantasy is ridiculed in the play, its power is nonetheless revealed. *Volpone* shows the conversion of the complex, contested notion of resurrection into the completely disembodied fantasy of the legal person who exists as a nexus of legal documents and legal institutional frameworks and that comes, in secular modernity, to displace the old body-based antidualist discourses I have been studying. *Volpone* charts a culture-wide loss of the richness of the ideal of memorialization that Jonson posits in his poetry. In *Volpone* the only kind of immortality that counts is not monumental (that is, weighty, substantial, material, bodily) immortality but the immortality of substance as money entailed by legally binding documents such as wills, entails, and endowments. And though *Volpone* rails against this brave new world, it nevertheless has the force of prophecy, sketching the world that, to a considerable extent, we now inhabit.

The rise of capitalism in early modern Europe has been studied in terms of changes in monetary policy and in the use of credit, the emergence of trade networks on a global scale, the beginnings of colonial domination of the new world, and the rise of finance capital capable of disrupting traditional, local markets. Moreover, from Max Weber on, historians and sociologists of capitalism have also sought to portray the rise of capitalism as coincident with (and requiring) a new form of subjectivity that is inward, calculating, and ascetic. The rise of this new form of subjectivity has often been connected to Protestantism's emphasis on faith, the personal nature of the spiritual journey documented in spiritual diaries or account books, and, finally and perhaps most importantly, the valuation of individual reading and interpretation of scripture. The role of an acquisitive and highly buffered form of selfhood has obviously been an important starting point for criticism of early modern culture for a long time. All of these ways of understanding capitalism have been applied to *Volpone*.[11]

But I want to examine how Ben Jonson's play reveals the religious roots of another important component of early capitalism, what I term "legal personhood." Jonson guides his audience to the understanding that with the rise of capitalist forms of economy comes a new form of selfhood, one in which the self understands its life to exist in intersecting legal and institutional frameworks that, among other things, guarantee its claim on various abstract forms of wealth. Anchors of legal personhood include deeds to property, citizenship, and the legal entitlements that come with it, including the right to bring disagreements before a court, wealth transfers tied to marriage, and, most centrally in the play, the right to transfer wealth through a legal testament or will. Such legal instruments define a personhood that consists of legally entitled property that exists separately from the life of the embodied person and that, moreover, can persist after the death of the embodied person. Jonson's play reveals the roots of this legal personhood in the ancient Christian hope for a resurrection of the flesh. But the notion of "legal personhood" radically reduces the body's role in defining the self in the world. This new experience of self-as-legally-entitled-property reduces the constraints upon the self that the body brings with it, but it also reduces the possibilities for transcendence and transformation that come with a recognition of the body as an irreducible source of selfhood.

In one sense, such legal personhood has a history that stretches back very far, at least to the Justinian code.[12] But in another sense, the nature and importance of legal personhood change dramatically in the early modern period coincident with the rise of capitalism. I see two significant changes in the realm of legal personhood in the early modern period: first, a steady expansion of its claims from a very small number of people who had wealth sufficient to be inscribed in and regulated through the application of legal instruments to an increasingly large percentage of the population who vector at least some of their personal dealings through legal apparatuses and legal documents, and second, an increasing psychic investment in this legal personhood as truly and fully the scene of personhood *tout court* as people increasingly see their existence as legally codified persons as a primary source of selfhood. Evidence for these claims is first and foremost an increase in the legal infrastructure of everyday lives in legal archives, but this development also leaves a trace in the literary archives, for instance in the surprising quantity of early modern plays that involve plots centering on legal questions, especially inheritance.[13]

Such literary treatments are especially revealing in pointing to the emerging phenomenon of *identification* of the self with the legal person, the subjective experience of feeling the self's identity within legal personhood, and most specifically the idea of the self *as* its legally entitled wealth. And it is here that *Volpone* takes its place in literary history. In *Volpone*, first performed in 1606, a Venetian aristocrat named Volpone and his servant Mosca scam various personages in Venice out of their money and valuables by pretending that Volpone is about to die and willing to name anyone who pleases him as his sole heir. This leads various suitors to lavish Volpone with gifts and money in the hopes of being named his heir. In their pursuit of Volpone's wealth, the suitors even turn against their most fundamental family relationships, one suitor disinheriting his only son and another offering his own wife to Volpone for extramarital sex. This play is often seen as a satire on early capitalism that focuses on the deleterious effects of greed. I want to say instead (or also) that it is a satire on the willingness of people to see themselves and others as nothing but disembodied legal persons. By taking advantage of the willingness of the suitors to see themselves as disembodied legal persons, Mosca and Volpone diagnose an epochal shift in English and indeed European culture.

By conflating the hope for a life beyond death with the rise of legal personhood, the play reveals not only the increasing willingness of people to see themselves as legal persons but also the ways this model represents a transformative secularization of the ancient Christian hope for resurrection.[14] My key claim is that the rise of legal personhood is not a rejection of Christian religious thought about resurrection but a transformation of such religious thought. In fact, all the building blocks (or the shattered fragments?) of resurrection discourse are in place in the play—including the idea of immanent death, the question of what will happen to the body after death, the legal will, and the community of onlookers, as Maggie Vinter notes in her study of the play as an examination of the "good death."[15] But if resurrection is in the air, so to speak, it is in the air in a way that foregrounds the soul very much at the expense of the body. In the first half of this chapter I have suggested that Jonson's poetry preserves an essential relationship to the body; by contrast, the kind of afterlife that legal personhood provides in *Volpone* is essentially and fundamentally disembodied.

Initiating the play, Volpone announces his project, and he does so by invoking what will turn out to be a key term in the play's diagnosis of the new notion of legal personhood, namely, "substance."

> What should I do,
> But cocker up my genius, and live free
> To all delights my fortune calls me to?
> I have no wife, no parent, child, ally,
> To give my *substance* [my italics] to; but whom I make,
> Must be my heir:
>
> (1.1.70–75)[16]

The condition of possibility for Volpone's con-artistry is not simply that he has no heirs but that in the legal-institutional framework of Venice, the essence of a person's life, his or her "substance," is increasingly defined as wealth that can be the object of legal documents, notably the testament that transfers that substance to another person.

The notion of "substance" and the question of what it is appear many times in the play. Indeed, the play might almost be said to be haunted by the word "substance," a word that contains within itself the transfer from understanding the essence of the person as somehow bound up with the matter out of which he or she is made to understanding the essence of the person as his or her wealth. The word "substance" is a fundamental concept in Thomist theory in general and Thomist thinking on resurrection in particular. In Thomism "substance" is a technical term that refers to the material stuff that must be given shape and thus function, what Thomism calls a "soul." Here the soul is simply matter insofar as it is shaped and capable of performing functions, and the ancient Christian emphasis on resurrection of the flesh means that the soul has a complex dependency on the body for its reality. Much of the energy of Thomist thought about resurrection lies in puzzling out what is possible for a soul separate from the particular substance in which it is substantiated, especially in the interim between death and a hypothetical future resurrection. But that the substance of the person is essential to a future resurrection and that souls (as shapes) cannot live in a complete state separate from the material stuff in which they are instantiated is simply taken for granted in Thomist thought.[17]

In the aftermath of Thomism, in debates about resurrection, the word "substance" comes to refer to the thing that is most essential to the identity of the person, and slowly the word comes to mean "wealth," especially insofar as that wealth is legally entitled and can be transferred to the next generation at death. In *Volpone* we can see the meaning of the term drift toward legally entitled wealth as the essence of identity. Wealth is the substance that in a very real sense lives on after biological death has destroyed the physical substance of the person. This seems to be a secularized and also a disembodied understanding of substance very much at odds with the meaning of the technical term in Thomist theory.[18] The way the word haunts the play suggests the profound shift in which the essence of the person and how it is imagined changes from the (shaped) matter of the person to the wealth that is managed and controlled in legal documents such as legal wills.

In the context of the migration of the notion of substance from matter to money, the play *Volpone* attacks the suitors not on the grounds that they are greedy but on the grounds that they embrace a notion of "substance" as legally entitled wealth and therefore a notion of human personhood utterly divorced from the body. The suitors see their own identities as well as Volpone's identity as utterly divorced from the body; for them, the essence of substance is not the material stuff that constitutes the bodily life of the person but the person's legally structured wealth. That new conception of identity is the condition of possibility of and also the object of the attack launched by Volpone and Mosca's elaborate con game.

The suitors relate to Volpone only through the fantasy of the legal will he will write, and they relate to themselves only through the fantasy of being the potential beneficiary of this legal will. For them, a signature, a name inserted in one of the blank legal transfer documents Volpone keeps in his chest, has the power to change everything about who Volpone is, and, in the relation such a will sets up between a legally codified "Volpone" and his named heirs, it has the power to change everything about who or what they themselves are in the social world insofar as their own sense of self is invested fantasmatically in their real or imagined wealth. The idea of being written into a new identity (both for testator and beneficiary) is precisely what the shift to legal personhood makes possible. If you are made by written legal documents, then you can be remade by written legal documents. Voltore, for example, is a very old man who concedes nothing to his own impending death, focusing all his energy on being named in Volpone's will. He asks, "Am I inscribed his heir for certain?" What follows is an exchange with Mosca that emphasizes the power of a document to define a new sense of self.

> Voltore: But am I sole heir?
> Mosca: Without a partner, sir, confirmed this morning;
>   The wax is warm yet, and the ink scarce dry
>   Upon the parchment.
> Voltore: Happy, happy, me!
>
> (1.3.44)

Mosca assures Voltore that he is sole heir and—just to confirm the presence of resurrection theory in the background of the whole issue—compares him to the "rising sun" (1.3.37). Similarly, when Mosca promises to take Bonario to where his father is writing a will that will disown Bonario, Mosca says he will "Hear yourself written bastard; and professed / The common issue of the earth" (3.2.64–5). The ability of written legal instruments to make and remake persons, utterly separate from their embodied lives or any sense of family connections between embodied persons, is the condition of possibility for the whole play and its satirical energies.

That the suitors are driven by a self-conception as legal persons capable of being named in a will seems obvious enough, but this desire is quite different from the much more corporeal and pleasure-oriented greed that drives Volpone. Volpone and Mosca do not "buy into" the reduction of the person to disembodied legal personhood, for both of them in their interactions with each other and with other characters emphasize the role and importance of the body, especially in relation to pleasure.[19] It is in the face of the disembodied, legally vectored form of identity of the suitors that Volpone asserts the intensely *physical* desires that drive him. Volpone reaffirms his goal to "live free / to all delights that my fortune calls me to." For Volpone, delight is always delight of the body, in contrast to the obsessive, self-denying asceticism of the suitors, who invest everything they have in the hopes of a tenfold return to their legal person (even at considerable cost to the biological person). What is fundamentally driving Volpone and Mosca is a pursuit of pleasure, and pleasure is always pleasure of the body. This pleasure is a pleasure of physically touching and using things, beginning with the actual gold and silver and precious gems that Volpone fingers in the opening scene and extending to the bodies of the suitors and the persons the suitors proffer to Volpone and Mosca.

While the suitors are willing to trade everything for the promise of a return on their investments, Volpone and Mosca have something that is more important to them than any money, and that is corporeal life and its pleasures. Throughout the play, Volpone proudly affirms his sensuality and pursuit of pleasure:

> I will be troubled with no more. Prepare
> Me music, dances, banquets, all delights;
> The Turk is not more sensual in his pleasures,
> Than will Volpone.
>
> (1.5.86–89)

This interest in the body as the scene of pleasure accounts for the specific kind of eroticism that Volpone engages in. For Volpone, eroticism amounts to a practice of making the person (back) into a body when his or her identity threatens to become purely symbolic.[20] Indeed, for Volpone even the gulling that he and Mosca engage in is valuable because it makes them into bodies, as when they are overcome with fits of laughter. At one point Volpone asks Mosca, "Why dost thou laugh so, man?" to which Mosca replies, "I cannot choose, sir" (1.2.97–8). And Volpone says "Oh, I shall burst; / Let out my sides, let out my sides—" to which Mosca replies,

"Contain / your flux of laughter, sir;" (1.4.133–34). The gulling game they play is preeminently a game of and through the body. After one especially memorable and successful instance of Mosca gulling another character for Volpone's benefit, Volpone wishes that he could turn Mosca into Venus so that he could use him sexually: "Let me kiss thee" (1.4.137), Volpone says and, at the climax of their plotting, "Let me embrace thee. O that I could now / Transform thee to a Venus—" (5.3.103–4). Wishing to transform Mosca into Venus is not about enforcing a heteronormativity that does not exist in early modern England; after all, Volpone is anything but sexually heteronormative. Rather, the primary force of Volpone's wish to make Mosca into Venus is to give voice to the desire for some form of sexual pleasure rooted in an insistent foregrounding of the body and its vibrant life, that same life they touch when they are overwhelmed by fits of laughter.

Volpone's erotic drive is obviously most on display in his obsessive desire to physically touch and use Celia, a drive that ultimately leads to Volpone's downfall. After seeing Celia while dressed up as a mountebank, Volpone says that he has been wounded by laying eyes on her:

> Volpone: Oh, I am wounded!
> Mosca: Where, sir?
> Volpone: Not without;
> Those blows were nothing, I could bear them ever.
> But angry Cupid, bolting from her eyes,
> Hath shot himself into me like a flame,
> Where now he flings about his burning heat,
> As in a furnace an ambitious fire,
> Whose vent is stopped. The fight is all within me.
> I cannot live, except thou help me, Mosca;
> My liver melts, and I, without the hope
> Of some soft air from her refreshing breath,
> Am but a heap of cinders.
>
> (2.4.1–11)

When Celia's husband, Corvino, delivers Celia to Volpone, Volpone woos her with the promise of endless pleasures based on role play.[21] Here erotic role playing is a way of playing with symbolic identity and a way of delivering heightened pleasures of the body:

> Whilst, we, in changed shapes, act Ovid's tales,
> Thou, like Europa now, and I like Jove,
> Then I like Mars, and thou like Erycine,

So of the rest, till we have quite run through,
And wearied all the fables of the gods.
Then will I have thee in more modern forms,
Attired like some sprightly dame of France,
Brave Tuscan lady, or proud Spanish beauty;
Sometimes, unto the Persian Sophy's wife;
Or the Grand Signior's mistress; and, for change,
To one of our most artful courtesans,
Or some quick Negro, or cold Russian;
And I will meet thee in as many shapes;
Where we may, so, transfuse our wandering souls
Out at our lips, and score up sums of pleasures,

(3.7.221–35)

When Celia expresses surprise that a seemingly decrepit old man suddenly has such vigor, Volpone, invoking the language of resurrection, says that she has "raised him":

Why art thou 'mazed to see me thus revived?
Rather applaud thy beauty's miracle;
'Tis thy great work: that hath, not now alone,
But sundry times raised me, in several shapes
And, but this morning, like a mountebank;
To see thee at thy window: ay, before
I would have left my practice, for thy love,
In varying figures, I would have contended
With the blue Proteus, or the horned flood.
Now art thou welcome.

(3.7.145–55)

Celia's beauty has the power to "raise" Volpone, and this raising is associated with the theatrical guises he has adopted to see her and other women, as he recounts having dressed as a mountebank earlier to see her and on a previous occasion having acted the part of Antony in a play: "I am, now, as fresh, / As hot, as high, and in as jovial plight, / As when, in that so celebrated scene, / At recitation of our comedy, / For entertainment of the great Valois, / I acted young Antinous; and attracted / The eyes and ears of all the ladies present, / To admire each graceful gesture, note, and footing" (3.7.157–64). As this memory suggests, for Volpone eroticism and theatricality are in close proximity.

One important point is that acting, as Jonson represents it in his play, is centrally about the body, foregrounding the body and the self's relationship with the body. The bodies of Volpone and Mosca are the scene of pleasure, but they are also tools for acting. The body has to be contorted in order for Volpone to play his part, so much so that he needs Mosca's help to physically push his body into place: "Help, with your forced functions, this my posture" (1.2.126). Being an actor is an experience of how symbolic identity cannot exist except as a bodily state; as illustrated by Volpone and Mosca, the work of acting is preeminently a work on, through, and in the body. In *Volpone* acting is first and foremost a way of being embodied so that acting is a way of becoming more and not less aware of the body's role in securing any identity, just as the erotic playacting he proposes to Celia is.

Volpone suggests that Jonson sees acting as fundamentally an experience of the body (in its separateness from the roles that the actor plays). In acting the actor becomes aware of his or her body as the thing that enables social roles (or, in a theater context, characters) but also the thing that limits or undermines or escapes from these roles in some ultimate sense, a remainder before, during, and after the character's life on the stage. On the one hand many early modern critics of the theater saw the essence of the theater as its unreality, the fact that it is built on "shadows," as Prospero famously refers to his actors in *The Tempest*. But at its deepest level, acting and theater are about reaffirming the body. As Michael O'Connell notes, in the eyes of the antitheatrical Puritans, the problem is precisely that the theater provided vivid images for the eyes, especially the bodies of the actors, as "the illusion of presence is created by actual human bodies standing for other bodies."[22] For Volpone and Mosca, acting—whether when they gull their marks or when Volpone proposes erotic play with Celia—is a way of affirming that they *are* the body, by seeing it as the precondition for any of the specific sociosymbolic identities they inhabit. Acting is essentially a matter of taking a body and creating a character out of or on top of that body, and this experience creates an awareness in the other direction, as it were, that any sociosymbolic identity, no matter how seemingly essential, is contingently but inescapably inscribed in the body if it is to have any reality. And this is precisely where Jonson finds a persistent utopian force in Volpone and Mosca's acting, because it makes them and the audience aware of a disconnect between the "role" or "character"—the very thing that can be captured in legal personhood—and the body in which that role or character is instantiated.

That the issue of resurrection is what is at stake in acting is suggested by an epigram on the death of the great actor Richard Burbage (this epigram is not always attributed to Jonson, though Brandon S. Centerwall makes a persuasive case that it should be):

Tell me who can when a player dies
In which of his shapes againe hee shall rise?
What need hee stand att the judgement throne
Who hath a heaven and a hell of his own?
> Then feare not Burbage heavens angry rodd,
> When thy fellows are angels and old Hemmings is God.[23]

The point of this epigram is that Burbage has rehearsed for the final judgment in the plays he and his fellows have put on and in which Hemmings has played God. But the opening couplet raises the question of what the actual person of the actor is that will be raised, given that he has played so many different characters. From a resurrection standpoint, the actor touches the body as the thing that will be resurrected once all social roles and identities have been abolished at the apocalyptic end of history. Thus, there is a sense that in playing actors are rehearsing for the resurrection, and not only by engaging in mock judgments and pre-experiencing both heaven and hell. *Volpone* suggests that one reason that acting is a pre-experience of resurrection is precisely that by using the body to impersonate many different "shapes" the actor ends up with a hyperawareness of the body and its capacities for impersonation. From an eschatological standpoint, all conventional social identities are impersonations, beneath which lies the timeless reality of the body.

Part of the reason Volpone loves acting is because, contra the dualistically minded suitors who see Volpone as a legal person who can bequeath his substance to them and who see themselves as legal persons who can inherit, acting creates a heightened awareness of the body as that body subtends social and symbolic identities. Indeed, Volpone finally gets into trouble only when he divorces the role he plays from the body he uses to play that role, that is, when he stages his own death as a legal person only to then haunt the play as a (decommissioned) person, in order to see the effects of his supposed death on the suitors. On the one hand, Volpone's persistence as a body is a forceful counter to the dawning legalized dualism of Venice, but, on the other hand, by legally transferring his "substance" to Mosca, Volpone initiates a process of self-decorporealization and virtualization that he cannot ultimately contain:

Volpone: I will ha' thee put on a gown,
And take upon thee as thou wert mine heir;
Shew 'em a will: open that chest, and reach
Forth one of those that has the blanks. I'll straight
Put in thy name.

. . . .
Mosca: But, what, sir, if they ask
After the body?
Volpone: Say, it was corrupted.
Mosca: I'll say it stunk, sir; and was fain to have it
Coffined up instantly, and sent away.
Volpone: Anything, what thou wilt. Hold, here's my will.
Get thee a cap, a count-book, pen and ink,
Papers afore thee; sit, as thou wert taking
An inventory of parcels. I'll get up
Behind the curtain, on a stool, and hearken,
Sometime peep over, see how they do look,
With what degrees their blood doth leave their faces!
O, 'twill afford me a rare meal of laughter!

(5.2.69–87)

Volpone knows that the suitors will understand death not as a thing of
the body but only as a thing of the legal person, in which Volpone's will
preserves his intent to transfer his substance into his suitor, who turns
out to be his accomplice Mosca. Mosca's insistence on evoking the (tech-
nically nonexistent) stinking body is funny as a counter to the forgetfulness of the body and the ensuing decorporealization of identity that
Volpone counts on, though Mosca's account of the material body in its
sheer materiality also points forward to Volpone's own continuing life
after he has engineered his legal death, an animated bodily force haunting the streets of Venice.

After Volpone has declared himself to be dead, the suitors arrive and
are shocked as it dawns on them that Volpone has transferred his substance into Mosca. In response to their complaints Mosca affirms the continuing force of Volpone's disembodied will even after his (supposed)
biological death:

But I protest, sir, it [Volpone's wealth] was cast upon me,
And I could almost wish to be without it,
But that the will o' the dead must be observ'd.

(5.3.85–87)

Volpone has the delight of watching the shocked response of the suitors
as they scan the will to discover the reality of what has happened:

Be busy still. Now they begin to flutter:
They never think of me. Look, see, see, see!

How their swift eyes run over the long deed,
Unto the name, and to the legacies,
What is bequeathed them there—

(5.316–20)

The important point here is that for Volpone what is shocking about the new regime of legally defined personhood is that he himself, what he understands as his substance, essentially disappears: "They never think of me." Instead of looking upon him (either contemplating him or literally looking at him or what remains of him, his body), the suitors relate to Volpone only through the filter of legal frameworks and documents.

But despite his effort to hang onto his bodily life, by legally separating himself from his body Volpone is playing with fire, a fire that eventually consumes him. Volpone understands (and objects to the notion that) a will and a transfer of wealth is a transfer of himself, his most essential self, his "substance," into or onto another person. When he reveals himself at the end of the play it is precisely to block this transfer of himself into Mosca (who is already wearing Volpone's clothing but has not yet secured legal endorsement of the will that transfers the rest of Volpone's "substance," which he plans to use to marry into a powerful family in Venice): "My ruins shall not come alone; your match / I'll hinder sure; my substance shall not glue you, / Nor screw you, into a family" (5.12.86–88). In Volpone's reappearance, it is as if he is affirming one understanding of what his "substance" is (his body, his continuing bodily life) in order to block a different (and historically emergent) understanding of what constitutes Volpone's "substance" (his legally structured wealth).

But the state ultimately sides with Volpone's will, not his bodily life. The play concludes with the court separating Volpone's symbolic identity (as magnifico and as controlling agent for his wealth, or "substance") from the body. As the first of the Avocatori says:

Thou, Volpone,
By blood and rank a gentleman, canst not fall
Under like censure; but our judgment on thee
Is, that thy *substance* [italics added] all be straight confiscate
To the hospital of the Incurabili:
And since the most was gotten by imposture,
By feigning lame, gout, palsy, and such diseases,
Thou art to lie in prison, cramped with irons,
Till thou be'st sick and lame indeed. Remove him.

(5.12.116–24)

Here the state seizes upon the body and separates it from the "substance" that is now defined as legally entitled wealth. This is on the one hand an assertion of biopolitical power; the state affirms its right to seize and manage biological life by banishing Volpone to a prison where his body will in fact become "sick, and lame indeed." For critics interested in biopolitics this might seem like the most interesting moment in the play because of the way it homes in on the body and life itself as the ultimate objects of state power. And indeed Jonson's conservatism is typically aligned with a defense of state power and the institutions through which it is vectored.[24] A lot of left-leaning critique informed by Agamben's biopolitics has tried to seize on moments in which the body shows up as the object of state power as having a kind of deconstructive force that is framed as a critical political force. In other words, critics seeking a politics out of the Agamben model of pervasive sovereign power (also associated, of course, with Carl Schmitt) sometimes represent a utopianism of the disenfranchised that seeks to identify some transcendental subjectivity precisely in subject positions that are most radically disenfranchised or disempowered by the structural exercise of sovereign power. We can see this move, for example, in the efforts to develop a politics around the radical kind of disenfranchisement and abandonment that Agamben terms "bare life." This theoretical approach has the weird tendency to seek a utopian impulse within the most horrifying conditions of exclusion, including in refugee and concentration camps.[25]

But in thinking about the conclusion of the play it is more appropriate to see it teaching the lesson that if Volpone's body is identified as the subject of essentially biopolitical attention by the state, then this is presented as the counterpart of the rising state-mediated legal personhood that triumphs at the end (making the play, from Jonson's point of view, a tragedy). Ultimately even Mosca and Volpone must accept the regime of disembodied, legal personhood mediated by the state and its legal apparatus. The lesson of the play is that the biopolitical seizure of the body amounts to an endorsement of a very different kind of immortality, namely, the immortality of the legally entailed wealth and the legal person who is its carrier. This divorce is marked already during the trial scene when the lawyer speaks for Volpone: "may it please the court, / In the meantime, he may be heard in me" (4.5.24–25). The person who counts is not the one who is a body but the one who is a set of legal interests that can be legally represented before the court by a lawyer.

At the end of the legal state process, the separation of body and legal person is confirmed when Volpone's body is reduced to the object of biopolitical control in the same gesture whereby his substance (his wealth) is redirected to benefit the Hospital of the Incurabili. That institution now becomes the inheritor that the suitors had hoped to be, a point that illustrates the extent to which legal personhood has been divorced from the human body, for the Hospital of the Incurabili, like modern corporations, is defined as a legal person. It is worth noting that shortly before the initial production of *Volpone* King James granted a charter of rights and obligations to the East India Company in 1600 and then again the Virginia Company shortly thereafter, important markers in the history of corporate personhood.

What we catch sight of in *Volpone*, then, is a massive historical transition in the structure of identity, a transition leading to the ultimate triumph of a fully secularized version of the disembodied soul capable of full life even after the death of the body. *Volpone* shows how, at the dawn of the capitalist era, this particular version of resurrection thought is transformed into the notion of a legally structured personhood defined by its possession of legally entitled "substance" and that can survive the death of the body. It is a transition away from the strange, mysterious call to identify with the body as the basis of personhood that I have uncovered in the avant-garde poetry of the age. Instead of a monist-materialist vision of the person, body and identity are finally severed. Where body once was substance, now only legally entitled wealth is substance, with the body demoted to an extra thing, an appendage without the status of self. Henceforth, the self that counts will be the essentially disembodied legal person and its hypothetical will.

But if *Volpone* points to the future we have come to inhabit, then it also suggests that the body haunts this disembodied and virtualized selfhood, in the person of Volpone and his unruly desires and in his raw body after he transfers his legal "substance" to Mosca. I want to end this book by looking at the notion that in the midst of an increasingly disembodied understanding of selfhood, the body nevertheless persists as a haunting force, the repressed that always threatens to return, and for which the arts (including Jonson's own poems of praise) are a preferred vehicle for enacting this return. In our contemporary culture, it is the realm of TV, films, and videogames in which the body haunts us, for these media are at once maximally disembodied as pure digital images yet also the scenes of a sustained engagement with the body as it exists beyond the limits of death in the form of the zombie, the "returned," and the "undead," which increasingly populate the collective fantasy life of secular modernity and look back at centuries of official theology about the resurrection of the dead. It is to contemporary zombie culture that I turn in the Epilogue.

Epilogue: Resurrection and Zombies

I have argued that seventeenth-century avant-garde poetry should be seen as housing a form of critical theory based on a secularized version of the most materialistic and immanent understanding of resurrection as essentially a thing of the body and as already happening now, in this life. I have argued that poets value this idea for the kinds of thinking and imagining it makes possible. This view of resurrection opens the door to a vision of the self as containing within itself a strange, thing-like, material power that is never fully aligned with the socialized sense of self and identity that the person may achieve within a particular historical social and linguistic world. I have suggested that the autochthonous "theory work" performed by these poets is indexed to the particular place they occupy in the history of secularization, in which ancient monist resurrection beliefs are split into a soul/body dualism that foregrounds the soul as the scene of identity and postmortem life. I have argued that this focus on a disembodied soul separate from a mere body becomes something close to common sense within both a rationalized Christian discourse and various non-Christian discourses of selfhood and identity. But I have argued that the body and its fate after death is left free to act as a kind of critical lever that forces renewed attention to the critical force of the body itself, endowed with a vibrant and thing-like power (to use some of the key terms of the "new materialism" to which I have compared this discourse).

Because the theoretical power of the immanent materialist resurrectionism I have examined here is so strongly indexed to the particular phase of secularization that I have been tracking, it appears to be a historical phenomenon, and the notion of a resurrection of the flesh would seem to have been consigned to the dustbin of history, and from the perspective of many secular readers rightly so. But if the idea of the body being raised from death to new life and the possibility of catching sight of this apocalyptic future in the reality of the living body here and now are things of the past, are they not also things of the present, at least in the current pop-culture fascination with the undead body in TV shows, films, novels, and video games about zombies and other kinds of "undead" or "postdead?" I want to end this book by examining the possibility that the particular kind of thinking that the idea of the pop-culture zombie enables is a version of the same "critical theory" rooted in centuries of official theology about resurrection whose emergence at the dawn of secular modernity I have been examining.

Many times over the course of this book we have encountered images and ideas that seem to look forward to the "modern" zombie, beginning with Donne's gruesome depictions of his own body in a paradoxical state of putrefied animation in the *Devotions* and many of his sermons, including his famous final sermon, "Death's Duel." Something like the zombie also appears in Donne's erotic poems, including "The Relique," in which Donne imagines himself buried and putrefied with "A bracelet of bright haire about the bone" (6), so that at the day of resurrection his beloved's reanimated corpse will have to return to Donne's grave to seek him out to get her hair back. The image of the bone with the bright hair twined around it achieves a luminous intensity that only a few of Donne's lyric images do, and it highlights the reality of the arm bones in the grave and invites us to imagine it as reanimated with an unearthly, decayed life on the last day, when he and his beloved will become weirdly vibrant, zombie-like bodies haunting the earth with a strange hunger for all their parts. For Herbert's part, in "Longing" he imagines his "dust" animated with a strange, creeping vitality:

> Behold, thy dust doth stirre,
> It moves, it creeps, it aims at thee:
>   Wilt thou deferre
>   To succour me,
> Thy pile of dust, wherein each crumme
>   Sayes, Come?

("Longing," 37–42)

Herbert imagines his decomposed body as the scene of an animated force in which individual body parts (now become half dust) each exhibit their own decentralized agency (each whispers "come"), just as in "Dooms-day"

Herbert yearns for the day of resurrection, which means imagining himself at the moment where God reanimates precisely that decayed material:

> Come away,
>   Make no delay.
> Summon all the dust to rise,
> Till it stirre, and rubbe the eyes;
> While this member jogs the other,
> Each one whispring, *Live you brother*?

("Dooms-day," 1–6)

Here again the postdeath body is imagined to have a strange kind of decentralized agency—each limb whispers to the other limbs as it is reassembled. As we have seen, images of the undead body endowed with strange and deranging life play a role also in the poetry of Vaughan and Jonson.

In such images, seventeenth-century poetry seems to point forward to the "zombie" of contemporary culture, an often gruesomely physical body that is animated by a deranging vibrancy that seems to go beyond conventional ways of understanding agency and personhood. The contemporary zombie begins with George Romero, the Pittsburgh-based filmmaker, who brought together friends and volunteers and a small number of professional actors to create *Night of the Living Dead*, which he completed in 1967 and which was released in 1968. In the 2013 documentary *Birth of the Living Dead*, Romero cited a few resolutely nonreligious influences upon him, notably including the 1943 horror film *I Walked with a Zombie*, which loosely retells *Jane Eyre* in the context of a sugar plantation in the Caribbean. In that film, the "zombie" derives from voodoo practices and is a semicatatonic character whose will is captured by another person. Romero also cited the influence of the 1954 Richard Matheson science-fiction horror novel *I Am Legend*, which tracks the life of a lone survivor of a global pandemic who is besieged by undead vampires. Romero was also influenced by images from the political tumult and violence and mass protests of the 1960s, including around the Vietnam War and the TV imagery of that war and the civil rights movement. A connection between *Night of the Living Dead* and the civil rights movement is certainly suggested by Romero's decision to cast the African American actor Duane Jones as the (nonzombie) lead. Indeed, Romero suggested that to some extent the film was an expression of the overdetermined political moment of the 1960s, and he suggests that one way to look at *Night of the Living Dead* is that it is what happens when, as he puts it, "the revolution fails."[1]

But Romero's willingness to discuss various influences on his imagination notwithstanding, he is notably content to leave the basic premise of the film—the fact that the dead are returning in zombie form and that they seek to eat human flesh—as *sheer fact*, the irruption of something utterly different and unexpected into conventional life, and Romero sometimes reaches for religious language to account for this quality, saying that perhaps "God changed the rules" and there was "no more room in hell." It seems quite plausible to say that Romero's zombies do spring from an imagination schooled by the Catholicism of his childhood. In an interview with the British film website eyeforfilm.co.uk Romero describes his response to the death of his grandmother: "My grandmother died, and everybody said, 'Well she's in heaven now,' and I said, 'Maybe not!' My uncles and my father kicked my ass all over the street, at the age of seven. That makes you re-examine things."[2] In this story, Romero expresses doubt about the highly secularized and rationalized notion of a disembodied afterlife in which the essence of his grandmother lives on without her body. I want to suggest that in some sense the zombie occupies precisely the space of doubt about the forgetfulness, as it were, of the body that is represented by the notion that his grandmother is "in heaven now." In that sense, Romero's zombies represent a glance back to centuries of official theology about the resurrection of the flesh, and even if zombie bodies are in some very obvious way not the perfected bodies hoped for in resurrection, they are nevertheless quite insistent in pointing to the persistence of the life of the flesh, just as the decommissioned theology of the resurrection of the flesh does in the seventeenth-century poetry I have examined in this book. In the face of any comforting dualism, the zombie forces attention to the body as possessed of a strange animated power that goes beyond the subjectivity and agency of the person.

The subterranean connection between the zombie and the ancient religious hope for the resurrection of the flesh is made clearer by one of the most interesting torsions within zombie culture, namely, the subgenre of the "returned," in which dead characters come back to life but without the obvious physical and mental derangement of Romero's zombies. The subgenre of the returned has its roots in the French reception of *Night of the Living Dead*, which was especially acclaimed in that country—the journal *Positif* called it "enriching, extraordinary . . . a miracle"—and it inspired a burst of creative responses culminating in a 2012 French-language television series called *Les revenants*.[3]

The highly regarded French writer, filmmaker, and intellectual Emmanuel Carrère was initially instrumental in developing this 2012 TV series (together with Fabrice Gobert), before a disagreement with the financial backers of the series led him to pull out of the project. Carrère tells the story of his involvement in the project in his well-received 2014 *The Kingdom*, which combines a personal account of his own very surprising, brief, but intense conversion to Catholicism woven together with an imaginative re-creation of the life of the evangelist Luke. The first words of Carrère's book are:

> That spring, I collaborated on a script of a TV series. The logline ran like this: One night, in a small mountain town, some of the dead come back to life. No one knows why, nor why these dead and not others. They themselves don't even know they're dead. They discover it in the horror-stricken faces of their loved ones, next to whom they'd like to resume their natural place. They're not zombies, they're not ghosts, they're not vampires. It's not a fantasy film, but reality. . . . I stopped writing fiction long ago, but I can recognize a powerful fictional device when I see it. And this was by far the most powerful one I'd been offered in my career as a screenwriter. For four months, I worked with the director Fabrice Gobert every day, morning to night, in a blend of enthusiasm and, often, a state of shock at the situations we created, the feelings we manipulated.
>
> (3)

Carrère goes on to describe how, several months after he had quit the show, he had a dinner party with Gobert and Patrick Blossier, the director of photography for *Les revenants*, at which Carrère framed the book he was then working on, *The Kingdom* itself, as way of continuing to explore the "powerful fictional device" of *Les revenants* by other means. "But that night," he writes, "no doubt to vent my sour grapes and show that I, too, was doing something interesting, I told Fabrice and Patrick about the book on the first Christians I'd been working on for several years. I'd put it aside to work on *Les revenants*, and had just picked it up again. I gave them the story the way you pitch a series" (4).

The story he then pitches, and which he does indeed tell in *The Kingdom*, is that of Paul, who sets up shop in Corinth and starts preaching about Jesus. He "says that this prophet came back from the dead and that his coming back from the dead is the portent of something enormous, a mutation of humanity, both radical and invisible. The contagion comes about. The strange belief radiates out from Paul in the seedy parts of Corinth, and its followers soon come to see themselves as mutants disguised as friends and neighbors: undetectable" (5). Carrère concludes that "this story of the early days of Christianity is also the story of *Les revenants*. What we tell in *Les revenants* is the last days that Paul's followers were sure they would experience, when the dead come back to life and the judgment of the world is consummated. It's the community of outcasts and chosen ones that forms around this shocking event: a resurrection. It's the story of something impossible that nevertheless takes place" (4).

But if *Les revenants* is the genetic kernel and *The Kingdom* the continuation by other means, then *The Kingdom* (or at least the story of Carrère's conversion to Catholicism that it tells) is also presented as the genetic kernel and *Les revenants* as *its* continuation by other means. For Carrère describes how, at the dinner party, "out of the blue" as it were, Patrick Blossier remarks that "It is strange, when you think about it, that normal, intelligent people can believe something as unreasonable as the Christian religion, something exactly like Greek mythology or fairy tales" (5). And this reminds Carrère of something that he had evidently repressed completely, namely, the strange but intense period in his earlier life in which he was radically and unexpectedly converted to Catholicism, went to Mass daily, and committed himself to reading the Gospel of John and filling twenty notebooks on his thoughts about the gospel, which he now finds embarrassing and even shocking. Here we learn the (repressed) truth that what lay behind *Les revenants* was precisely the (doubly repressed) belief in resurrection that will now become the explicit focus of *The Kingdom*.

It is worth thinking through Patrick Blossier's objection: How or in what way can the idea of the resurrection be taken seriously? I want to suggest that it can be taken seriously precisely in the way that Carrère himself does, namely, as a powerful premise or pitch or logline ("a powerful fictional device . . . by far the most powerful one I'd been offered in my career as a screenwriter"), one capable of producing "shocking" emotional effects and experiences. In short, the answer to Blossier's objection is that even if resurrection is a crazy idea (as crazy as the stories about Zeus), then it is nevertheless a good idea to think with. And if zombie/returned culture is in some sense mere entertainment, then part of its appeal is nonetheless the particular incitement to thinking that it represents.

In the case of *Les revenants* and zombie culture more generally, as in the poetry I have examined, the idea of resurrection of the flesh is valuable as a kind of theoretical lever; the idea creates critical effects and insights comparable to the experience of falling under the grip of a theorist or a school of critical theory, say, psychoanalysis or Marxism. Taking resurrection seriously makes the world—including selfhood, agency, and symbolic identity—look and feel different in a way that for many people is precisely the effect of theoretical lenses. If it is uncommon to have the strange experience that Carrère had of being suddenly and inexplicably interpolated into Christianity, many people have nevertheless experienced the particular incitement to thought represented by the zombie and "returned" characters.

Intellectuals and academics have certainly experienced the zombie as an incitement to thought, at least judging from the fact that a search of the MLA bibliography for the word "zombie" turns up eight hundred results. Critics have used the figure of the zombie to reflect on the body and selfhood, race, gender, Buddhist mindfulness, disability, and, in view of the roots of modern zombies in Caribbean voodoo practices, colonialism.[4] To some extent, this plethora of critical responses reflects the fact that the zombie/returned is overdetermined. As we have seen, starting right from the outset with Romero, the zombie represented the crystallization of many influences, and from his work forward the zombie has been pregnant with a multiplicity of meanings. It seems that the critical work of making sense of or even just contextualizing zombies is never finished.

But at the risk of reducing this complex and multifaceted body of criticism, I want to suggest that there is a common theme running through all of it, a theme provoked by the basic facts of a fictional device that violates the border between the living and the dead and that, at the same time, undermines the mind/body dualism that, I have argued, is one of the pillars of secular modernity. The commonality of the critical thought that zombies and other undead inspire concerns the inescapability but also the strangeness and even otherness of the body and its life to the conventionally socialized lives we lead within fixed social coordinates of identity. Zombies, for all their otherness, nevertheless provoke in viewers an engagement with how we, too, are zombies, with how we, too, are defined by a bodily life that ultimately escapes from our own intentions and the symbolic identities that define us.[5] This is most evident in the way zombie culture invites or even demands that viewers identify with the zombie, see the zombie within themselves, reimagine themselves as a zombie or a potential zombie.[6] Thus, in their influential article "A Zombie Manifesto," Sarah Juliet Lauro and Karen Embry argue that

> The lumbering, decaying specter of the zombie affirms the inherent disability of human embodiment—our mortality. Thus, in some sense, we are all already zombies . . . for they represent the inanimate end to which each of us is destined. Yet the zombie is intriguing not only for the future it foretells but also for what it says about humanity's experience of lived frailty and the history of civilization, which

grapples with mortality in its structures as well as in its stories. Humanity defines itself by its individual consciousness and its personal agency: to be a body without a mind is to be subhuman, animal; to be a human without agency is to be a prisoner, a slave. The zombie(i)/e is both of these, and the zombie(i)/e (fore)tells our past, present, and future.[7]

Lauro and Embry argue that in foregrounding the dead body among the living, the zombie also collapses the subject/object distinction because the zombie is neither pure object (which would be passive in the face of physical forces) nor pure subject (in which case their agency would be interchangeable with the agency of nonzombie persons). This basic perspective suggests how seeing the self in light of the zombie can open a new sense of the person or the self as both enabled and constrained or disempowered by the life of the human body, a vision fascinating and empowering and at the same time deeply unsettling.

I have argued that in the case of Donne, Herbert, Vaughan, and Jonson, the critical theory of resurrection manifests as an impulse toward formal experimentation, and something very similar appears to be the case with zombie culture, for the zombie premise seems to inspire artists to develop distinctive technical and formal approaches that push past simple representation. This formal experimentalism is evident in zombie films from *Night of the Living Dead* onward. One of the noteworthy formal effects of Romero's film is its self-consciously theatrical staginess and fakeness, something very much heightened by Romero's decision (driven by financial necessity) of using many nonprofessional actors in the film.[8] In his 1968 review of *Night of the Living Dead*, the *New York Times* film critic Vincent Canby picked up on this antimimetic artificiality of the film, writing that it is "a grainy little movie acted by what appear to be non-professional actors who are besieged in a farmhouse by some other non-professional actors, who stagger around, stiff-legged, pretending to be flesh-eating ghouls."[9] But while the film's departure from mimetic realism opens it to Canby's contempt, self-consciousness about its own theatricality is in fact part of the aesthetic of the film and part of why self-consciously avant-garde audiences embraced the film, a tendency heightened by the very disgust and contempt that the film triggered among aesthetically conservative viewers. Indeed, the avant-garde quality of the filming and the acting, including its seemingly unsophisticated, unpretentious, do-it-yourself black-and-white cinematography, is part of what accounts for the cult appeal of the film, and this avant-garde self-reflexiveness is surely part of what explains MoMA's decision to include the film in its permanent collection.

As in seventeenth-century poetry so too in contemporary film culture: The zombie demands avant-gardist attacks on conventional canons of mimetic (and beautiful) art. Moreover, the push to formal experimentation evident in the film medium is also evident in the other media in which the zombie has appeared, including in literary treatments. Thus, the formal inventiveness that the zombie demands can be seen in Max Brooks's career writing about zombies, which traverses media boundaries, including a fake "survival guide" with some limited illustrations (*The Zombie Survival Guide* [2003]), a full-blown graphical novel in which images are central to the experience but in which narrative is suppressed almost to zero (*The Zombie Survival Guide: Recorded Attacks* [2009]), and a fully textual treatment in *World War Z: An Oral History of the Zombie War* (2006), which does not contain any images but which uses a distinctive retrospective mode of narration and which was made into a 2013 film (and accompanying video game), both of which were striking for the innovative, computer-assisted representations of the zombie "horde." The pressure for formal experimentation and avant-garde technique here echoes the pressure for formal experimentation in, for example, Donne's sermons, in which the driving rhythms and shocking departures from decorum force his listeners to reimagine their own personhood in light of decaying bodies, or in Herbert's poems, in which the attack and sound of the poetry transport the apocalyptic future in which the body will be reendowed with a zombie-like life and zombie-like speech into the here and now of readers forced to identify with an alien, decentering life at their own cores.

The rise of zombies in contemporary pop culture is in some sense a "return of the repressed," in which dim echoes of centuries of official theology about the resurrection of the body are reanimated as a reaction against the modern fantasy that the self is, in its essence, disembodied and therefore reducible to information, data, and code, a vision that makes it possible to imagine a cybernetic afterlife that might take the form of entering into the disembodied life of the digital world.[10] In the midst of this dream of disembodied and virtualized selfhood, the zombies and the other undead of contemporary culture, much like the poetry I have studied in this book, are a reminder of the body's abiding vulnerabilities, limitations, and also potentials for transcendence. In the love of zombies that drives so much of our popular culture today I detect a yearning for transcendence, but not "up" into some hypothetically spiritual realm not touched with materiality (like pure information housed on a computer server somewhere). Rather, I detect a yearning for a transcendence "down" into what we all truly are, bodies that link with one another and with the natural world in profound ways. And in cultivating this vision, the ancient discourses of resurrection are not our enemy, the foolish remains of an unenlightened world; rather these discourses are friends, structures of thought that found hope in the body long before we came to understand—perhaps at the last moment—that it is upon this hope that our future depends.

Acknowledgments

While writing this book I have benefitted from the help of many people who provided everything from critical feedback and publishing opportunities to simple encouragement. I would particularly like to thank the following: Helge Alsleben, Sam Arnold, Sara Arnold, Catherine Bates, Laura Bovilski, Joseph Campana, Patrick Cheney, Barbara Correll, Mark Dennis, Frances Dickey, Katherine Eggert, Cora Fox, Alan Gallay, David Glimp, John Guillory, Graham Hammill, Elizabeth Harvey, Alex Hidalgo, Rick Keyser, San-Ky Kim, Julie Kimmel, Aaron Kunin, James Kuzner, Rebecca Lemon, Julia Reinhard Lupton, Jason Manriquez, Bill Meyer, Karen Newman, Curtis Perry, Michael Schoenfeldt, Richard Strier, Peter Szok, Brian Warren, and Scott Williams. Joe Darda provided encouragement when it was truly needed. At the Mary Couts Burnett Library I want to thank June Koelker for providing me with office space and Ammie E. Harrison for maintaining a great collection in early modern studies. I owe a special debt of gratitude to James O. Duke and Warren Carter, both at Brite Divinity School, for their willingness to help me fill in some gaps in my knowledge of the intellectual history of Christianity. At Fordham, the two anonymous readers for the book manuscript provided extraordinarily detailed and insightful responses, and this book is far better because of their input. My editor, Thomas Lay, offered invaluable guidance; for that and for his belief in my project I will be forever grateful. At Fordham I also want to thank John Garza, Rob Fellman, and Margaret Noonan for their expert help through production. Anne Frey is my chief interlocutor eternal. Madeleine Gil and Elena Gil are the joys of my life. Finally, Jonathan Goldberg gave me the intellectual world that

I love. I cannot thank him enough for all he has done for me over the years. Flawed though it is, this book is dedicated to him.

An earlier version of Chapter 3 was published as "The Resurrection of the Body and the Life of the Flesh in Henry Vaughan's Religious Verse," *ELH: English Literary History* 82, no. 1 (Spring 2015): 59–86; and an earlier version of Chapter 4 was published as "What It Feels Like to Be a Body: Humoralism, Cognitivism, and the Sociological Horizon of Early Modern Religion," in *This Distracted Globe: Worldmaking in Early Modern Literature*, ed. Marcie Frank, Jonathan Goldberg, and Karen Newman (New York: Fordham University Press, 2016). These materials are republished by permission.

Notes

Preface: Christianity as Critical Theory

1. Or, to put it another way, I see secularization as a process of "repetition with variation," a view obviously heavily indebted to Dominick LaCapra. I have vectored this understanding of secularization through Charles Taylor's attacks on "subtractive theories" of secularization, in which secularity is simply less religion. See Charles Taylor, *A Secular Age* (Cambridge, MA: Harvard University Press, 2007). I have also relied upon Marcel Gauchet's argument that secularity is prefigured in the theology of Christianity. See *The Disenchantment of the World*, trans. Oscar Burge (Princeton, NJ: Princeton University Press, 1999).

2. As Brian B. Cummings writes, "In one direction, the key change of emphasis implied in the idea of radical secularity is the absence of a concept of the afterlife." See *Mortal Thoughts: Religion, Secularity, and Identity in Shakespeare and Early Modern Culture* (New York: Oxford UP, 2018), 17.

3. Notably, Jane Bennett, *Vibrant Matter: A Political Ecology of Things* (Durham, NC: Duke University Press, 2010).

4. See Giorgio Agamben, *Homo Sacer: Sovereign Power and Bare Life*, trans. Daniel Heller-Roazen (Stanford, CA: Stanford University Press, 1998). For my own earlier effort to capture the critical force of something like "bare life" as "flesh" in early modern culture, see my *Shakespeare's Anti-Politics: Sovereign Power and the Life of the Flesh* (New York: Palgrave-Macmillan, 2013).

5. In making this claim I am drawing on Raymond Geuss's classic account of the distinctive methodology and goals of "critical theory," especially as practiced by members of the Frankfurt School. Raymond Geuss, *The Idea of a Critical Theory: Habermas and the Frankfurt School* (New York: Cambridge University Press, 1981). As Geuss discusses it, critical theory is a form of knowledge that is not merely reflective (something he associates with positivistic natural sciences) but that is instead oriented toward social critique and even transformation, "enlightenment," and emancipation.

6. Jean-Luc Nancy, *Noli me tangere: On the Raising of the Body*, trans. Sarah Clift, Pascale-Anne Brault, and Michael Naas (New York: Fordham University Press, 2008).

7. Alain Badiou, *Saint Paul: The Foundation of Universalism*, trans. Ray Brassier (Stanford, CA: Stanford University Press, 2003).

8. Eric L. Santner, *On the Psychotheology of Everyday Life* (Chicago: University of Chicago Press, 2001).

9. Slavoj Žižek, "Series Foreword," in *The Puppet and the Dwarf: The Perverse Core of Christianity* (Cambridge, MA: MIT Press, 2003).

10. By taking the risk of taking seriously the discourse of the resurrection of the flesh as that discourse is touched and transformed by the first wave of secularization in the seventeenth century, and by tracking the ways this discourse animates and drives avant-garde literary projects, I am also engaging with the notion of "postsecularity." See the discussion in Jürgen Habermas et al., *An Awareness of What Is Missing: Faith and Reason in a Post-Secular Age* (New York: Polity, 2014).

Introduction: Secularization and the Resurrection of the Flesh

1. In treating early modern ideas as containing philosophical and critical resources that are relevant to us today, my approach is similar to recent work that has explored strands of ancient ethics in early modern Europe, including skepticism and Lucretian epicureanism, as in James Kuzner, *Shakespeare as a Way of Life: Skeptical Practice and the Politics of Weakness* (New York: Fordham University Press, 2016); and Jonathan Goldberg, *The Seeds of Things: Theorizing Sexuality and Materiality in Renaissance Representations* (New York: Fordham University Press, 2009). I apply the methodology of taking early modern ideas and culture seriously for their critical effects on the religious discourses that are surely among the "master discourses" of early modern culture but that often seem strangest and most easily dismissible to our modern secular ears. In doing this I am aligned with other scholars who treat early modern religious discourse as a discourse that demands from us complex acts of imagination and that potentially contains critical potentials for thinking through problems within secular modernity. Examples include Julia Reinhard Lupton's work on how early modern religious discourses both support and trouble a modern framework defined (for her) by exclusionary national and religious identity formations, as in her *Citizen-Saints: Shakespeare and Political Theology* (Chicago: University of Chicago Press, 2005). Similarly, Graham Hammill, *The Mosaic Constitution: Political Theology and Imagination from Machiavelli to Milton* (Chicago: University of Chicago Press, 2012), argues that early modern religious discourse remains at the heart of political frameworks at the cusp of modernity. See also Ryan Netzley, *Lyric Apocalypse: Milton, Marvell, and the Nature of Events* (New York: Fordham University Press, 2015); Ken Jackson, *Shakespeare and Abraham* (Notre Dame, IN: University of Notre Dame Press, 2015); and Joseph Campana, *The Pain of Reformation: Spenser, Vulnerability, and the Ethics of Masculinity* (New York: Fordham University Press, 2012). Feisal Mohammed, *Milton and the Post-Secular Present* (Stanford, CA: Stanford University Press, 2011), advances important arguments about the continuing relevance of early modern theopolitical debates to contemporary issues and develops the important concept of "postsecularism" in ways that have influenced my work.

2. I see Gordon Teskey's wonderful *Delirious Milton* (Cambridge, MA: Harvard University Press, 2006) as making a similar argument in claiming that Milton anticipates the distinctive role of the artist in the modern world.

3. See Alain Badiou, *Saint Paul: The Foundation of Universalism*, trans. Ray Brassier (Stanford, CA: Stanford University Press, 2003); Judith Butler, *Gender Trouble: Feminism and the Subversion of Identity* (New York: Routledge, 2015); Pierre Bourdieu, *Distinction: A Social Critique of the Judgment of Taste*, trans. Richard Nice (Cambridge, MA: Harvard University Press, 1984); Jean-Luc Nancy, *The Inoperative Community*, ed. Peter Connor, ed. and trans. Peter Connor, Lisa Garbus, Michael Holland, and Simon Sawhney (Minneapolis: University of Minnesota Press, 1991); Jean-Luc Nancy, *Noli me tangere: On the Raising of the Body*, trans. Sarah Clift, Pascale-Anne Brault, and Michael Naas (New York: Fordham University Press, 2008); and Roberto Esposito, *Communitas: The Origin and Destiny of Community*, trans. Timothy C. Campbell (Stanford, CA: Stanford University Press, 2009). On "bare life," see Giorgio Agamben, *Homo Sacer: Sovereign Power and Bare Life*, trans. Daniel Heller-Roazen (Stanford, CA: Stanford University Press, 1998), and for an effort to connect the idea of bare life to the aesthetic enjoyment of watching decommissioned characters on the stage, see my *Shakespeare's Anti-Politics: Sovereign Power and the Life of the Flesh* (New York: Palgrave Macmillan, 2013).

4. See Ian Bogost, *Alien Phenomenology, or What It's Like to Be a Thing* (Minneapolis: University of Minnesota Press, 2012); Graham Harman, *Object-Oriented Ontology: A New Theory of Everything* (New York: Penguin, 2018); Timothy Morton, *Hyperobjects: Philosophy and Ecology after the End of the World* (Minneapolis: University of Minnesota Press, 2013); and Jane Bennett, *Vibrant Matter: A Political Ecology of Things* (Durham, NC: Duke University Press, 2010).

5. See Gilles Deleuze and Félix Guattari, *A Thousand Plateaus: Capitalism and Schizophrenia*, trans. Brian Massumi (Minneapolis: University of Minnesota Press, 1987). Bennett tries to reimagine agency in a less human-centric way, as the effect of many objects and systems interacting with one another, of which humans are only one. In this she is participating in the project of object-oriented ontology promoted by Graham Harman and Bruno Latour, who situate human agency within large, complex interacting systems and objects pulling in different directions. As Latour writes, this perspective is meant to honor the phenomenological insight that "there are events. I never *act*; I am always slightly surprised by what I do. That which acts through me is also surprised by what I do, by the chance to mutate, to change, and to bifurcate." Bruno Latour, *Pandora's Hope: Essays on the Reality of Science Studies* (Cambridge, MA: Harvard University Press, 1999), 281.

6. See Charles Taylor, *A Secular Age* (Cambridge, MA: Harvard University Press, 2007); Taylor's arguments are presumed throughout this book. See also José Casanova, "The Secular, Secularizations, Secularisms," in *Rethinking Secularism*, ed. Craig Calhoun, Mark Juergensmeyer, and Jonathan VanAntwerpen (New York: Oxford University Press, 2011), 55–74. For a skepticism about the applicability of contemporary models of secularization on early modern material I have consulted Brian Cummings's valuable and far-ranging *Mortal Thoughts: Religion, Secularity, and Identity in Shakespeare and Early Modern Culture* (New York: Oxford University Press, 2013).

7. See Caroline Walker Bynum, *The Resurrection of the Body in Western Christianity, 200–1336* (New York: Columbia University Press, 1995); Fernando Vidal, *The*

Sciences of the Soul: The Early Modern Origins of Psychology, trans. Saskia Brown (Chicago: University of Chicago Press, 2011); and N. T. Wright, *The Resurrection of the Son of God* (Minneapolis, MN: Augsburg Fortress Press, 2003). As Bynam sketches it, the early church was almost defined by its commitment to bodily resurrection, despite persistent attacks on this view by the implicit and explicit philosophical/metaphysical view of the Hellenistic world. This tension led to many fascinating treatises in which early Christian writers attempted to work out the specifics of bodily resurrection. N. T. Wright makes clear that for early Christians, the idea of a "soul" as separate from the body, when it occurred at all, seemed like a Greek falsification of their fundamental understanding of Christ's resurrection. For some of the unintended consequences of the newly canonical dualism in early modern culture see Paul Cefalu, Gary Kuchar and Bryan Reynolds, eds., *The Return of Theory in Early Modern English Studies* (Basingstoke: Palgrave Macmillan, 2014).

8. For a discussion of the intellectual issues in play at this stage in Christian intellectual history, see Katharina Greschat, "'Fremdkoerper' (alien body) or *caro salutis est cardo*? On the Precise Nature of Christ's Body in Tertullian and his Adversaries," in *Bodies in Question: Gender, Religion, Text*, ed. Darlene Bird and Yvonne Sherwood (Burlington, VT: Ashgate, 2005), 187–98.

9. For one recent summation of gnosticism, see Elaine Pagels, *The Gnostic Gospels* (New York: Random House, 2004).

10. On Augustine, see Virginia Burrus and Karmen MacKendrick, "Bodies without Wholes: Apophatic Excess and Fragmentation in Augustine's City of God," in *Apophatic Bodies: Negative Theology, Incarnation, and Relationality*, ed. Chris Boessel and Catherine Keller (New York: Fordham University Press, 2010), 79–93. The same collection also features an article by John D. Caputo, in which he writes, "transcendence is not foreign to the materiality of the body but is a modality of the body, a dimension of bodily life that demands everything of us, or takes everything out of us." "Bodies Still Unrisen, Events Still Unsaid: A Hermeneutic of Bodies Without Flesh," 94–116. For the implications for poetics, see Karmen MacKendrick, "Eternal Flesh: The Resurrection of the Body," *Discourse* 27, no. 1 (Winter 2005): 67–83.

11. Adam G. Cooper emphasizes how Aquinas actively refuses a wholesale body/soul distinction that he sees as tantamount to gnosticism. See *Life in the Flesh: An Anti-Gnostic Spiritual Philosophy* (New York: Oxford University Press, 2008).

12. Concilium Lateranense IV, Cap. 1, *De fide catholica*: DS 801, http://www.vatican.va/archive/catechism_lt/p123a11_lt.htm.

13. While Dante represents the cutting edge of dualism, there is a countertradition within literature that does not fit into my model insofar as it simply accepts embodied selfhood as the condition of human life. Thus Richard Strier argues that Petrarch accepts the unity of soul and body and the "slantendess" of his will and accepts the consequences. See his *The Unrepentant Renaissance: From Petrarch to Shakespeare to Milton* (Chicago: University of Chicago Press, 2011). Ramie Targoff, *Posthumous Love: Eros and the Afterlife in Renaissance England* (Chicago: University of Chicago Press, 2014) also offers a powerful argument that early modern culture, starting with Dante and continuing through Shakespeare, contains an impulse to reverse the drive toward an afterlife by emphasizing the mortal experience of human love. For a more dualist account of the way Shakespeare's plays represent the possibilities of an afterlife, see Donovan Sherman, *Second Death: Theatricalities of*

the Soul in Shakespeare's Drama (Edinburgh: Edinburgh University Press, 2016). He argues that souls are not representable but are performable.

14. Quoted in Nelson H. Minnich, *Decrees of the Fifth Lateran Council (1512–17): Their Legitimacy, Origins, Contents, and Implementation* (New York: Routledge, 2016).

15. See Philippe Ariès, *Western Attitudes toward Death: From the Middle Ages to the Present*, trans. Patricia Ranum (Baltimore, MD: Johns Hopkins University Press, 1975).

16. See Gergely M. Juhász, *Translating Resurrection: The Debate between William Tyndale and George Joye in Its Historical Context* (Leiden: Brill, 2014).

17. This is noted by Kimberley Anne Coles, "The Matter of Belief in John Donne's Holy Sonnets," *Renaissance Quarterly* 68 (2015): 889–931. According to Coles, Melanchthon thought that the soul could only be known through the body and therefore that a complete description of the whole body was necessary to know the soul, a position shared by Luther, who assumed the whole human being, body and soul, to be the subject of grace. Melanchthon saw the body as a map for the soul. Calvinists had a serious soteriological problem with this, since it led to the worry that the body's organic character might resist grace. Similarly, Michael Edwards describes the influence of Melanchthon's interest in joining the sciences of the soul with anatomy to create a study of human nature. Edwards sees this approach as a protestant revision of traditional Catholic hylomorphism. Michael Edwards, "Body, Soul, and Anatomy in Late Aristotelian Psychology," in *Matter and Form in Early Modern Science and Philosophy*, ed. Gideon Manning (Leiden: Brill, 2012), 33–76.

18. The basic distinction between the so-called magisterial Reformation and the radical Reformation, characterized by an exaggerated degree of individualism, is developed at length in Brad S. Gregory, *The Unintended Reformation: How a Religious Revolution Secularized Society* (Cambridge, MA: Harvard University Press, 2012).

19. Also see Stephen McKnight, *The Religious Foundations of Francis Bacon's Thought* (Columbia: University of Missouri Press, 2006), which tracks the ways that Bacon's *New Atlantis* is grounded in religious convictions including the fundamental notion of "instauration," an apocalyptic concept that refers to the restoration of humanity to its prelapsarian condition.

20. Thus, see Athanasius Kircher's notion of the "universal sperm," described by John Glassie, *A Man of Misconceptions: The Life of an Eccentric in an Age of Change* (New York: Riverhead, 2012). Glassie writes that Kircher believed that "seeds of a vegetative and sentient nature" are "scattered everywhere among the elemental bodies." For Glassie, Kircher was making a larger, more fundamental argument against the new mechanistic, material philosophy of Descartes and others, based on which even animals and plants were nothing but elaborate machines. In a sense, Kircher refused to concede that the physical world was *merely* physical. Similarly, on the religious roots of the distinctive alchemical understanding of matter, including in Robert Fludd and Robert Boyle, see Michael Thomson Walton, *Genesis and the Chemical Philosophy: True Christian Science in the Sixteenth and Seventeenth Centuries* (Brooklyn: AMS, 2011). Though her book is focused on Thomas Brown, Claire Preston offers a fascinating account of early modern England as caught between two intellectual eras, the one Christian with its ideal of Resurrection and

the other scientific with its ideal of (in Preston's phrasing) "regeneration" or (in Brown's phrasing) "verdancy." Claire Preston, *Thomas Browne and the Writing of Early Modern Science* (New York: Cambridge University Press, 2009).

21. As Vidal discusses it, in early modern science there is a strong move on the part of Christian practitioners to square science with resurrection by discovering physical causal mechanisms that would allow the body to live again at the Resurrection. This movement eventually gives rise to "germ theory" and embryology (that is, an effort to find the lowest common material denominator of the physical person that would allow the whole person to be regenerated). Indeed, almost all the major scientists of the early modern period wrestled with how to make resurrection compatible with the emerging, empiricist discipline, and early modern science resisted the move toward dualism at various registers before the "mature" science emerged founded on an absolute distinction between what is merely material and therefore subject to analysis in terms of the laws of nature and what is purely spiritual or conscious or soul-like and therefore ruled out of bounds for empirical science. For a useful sketch of efforts by early modern philosophers to produce an exclusively corporeal account of the Resurrection, see Lloyd Strickland, "The Doctrine of 'the Resurrection of the Same Body' in Early Modern Thought," *Religious Studies* 46 (2010): 163–83. Strickland examines the early modern interest in the question of what defines the identity of the person in a reassembled body. Stuart Brown notes that under the influence of alchemical views, Leibniz was drawn to the view that humans have a material kernel that survives even apparent dissolution and can be used to regenerate them, and he thought of the ashes that remain after a fire as a model for this. He developed the notion that there must be some tiny physical point that would survive at least in the case of humans; this is the basis for the later notion of the stamen. Stuart Brown, "Soul, Body, and Natural Immortality," *The Monist* 81, no. 4 (October 1998): 573–90.

22. Justin E. H. Smith, "'Spirit Is a Stomach': The Iatrochemical Roots of Leibniz's Theory of Corporeal Substance," in *Matter and Form in Early Modern Science and Philosophy*, ed. Gideon Manning (Leiden, Brill, 2012), 203–24.

23. Thus, in the *Essay Concerning Human Understanding*, Locke famously separated identity from substance altogether not because he thought identity was unstable across time but because he saw it as created only through telling stories about the self. John Locke, *Essay Concerning Human Understanding*, ed. Kenneth P. Winkler (New York: Hackett, 1996).

24. See Gary Hatfield, "Mechanizing the Sensitive Soul," in *Matter and Form in Early Modern Science and Philosophy*, ed. Gideon Manning (Leiden, Brill, 2012), 151–86.

25. George Makari, *Soul Machine: The Invention of the Modern Mind* (New York: Norton, 2015). Also see A. C. Grayling, *The Age of Genius: The Seventeenth Century and the Birth of the Modern Mind* (NY: Bloomsbury USA, 2016).

26. See Raymond Martin and John Barresi, *The Rise and Fall of Soul and Self* (New York: Columbia University Press, 2006). They also argue that as the status and importance of this underlying Christian framework dwindles within an increasingly disenchanted modernity, the stability and autonomy of the self also dwindles. With the rise of atomism and critique of Aristotelianism, visible properties are no longer accidents, manifestations of underlying substance characterized by potentiality; rather they became features of basic particles.

27. See Thomas Nagel, *Mind and Cosmos: Why the Materialist Neo-Darwinian Conception of Nature Is Almost Certainly False* (New York: Oxford University Press, 2012).

28. See Diane Kelsey McColley, *Poetry and Ecology in the Age of Milton and Marvell* (Aldershot: Ashgate, 2007).

29. In a useful aside, Vidal states that in the early modern period resurrection discourses became differentiated. He says that poetry and visual arts emphasized the carnal elements, theology expounded doctrine, and alchemists and natural philosophers tried to explain processes by which resurrection might take place.

30. Indeed, Constance M. Furey sees the issue of the ways the body inhabits social and symbolic systems of meaning as very much at the heart of religious practices, and therefore she argues that it ought to be at the heart of the scholarly study of religion. Constance M. Furey, "Body, Society, and Subjectivity in Religious Studies," *Journal of the American Academy of Religion* 80, no. 1 (March 2012): 7–33.

31. In his classic discussion, Louis Martz argues that the Catholic meditative tradition was imported into England and created the basis for the poetry of Herbert, Donne, Vaughan, and Crashaw. Louis Martz, *The Poetry of Meditation: A Study in English Religious Literature of the Seventeenth Century* (New Haven, CT: Yale University Press, 1954).

32. See Renato Poggioli, *The Theory of the Avant-Garde*, trans. Gerald Fitzgerald (Cambridge, MA: Harvard University Press, 1968), 38. Moreover, Poggioli writes, "the American literary criticism that calls itself New Criticism and is, basically, an avant-garde criticism, in its struggles against the commonplaces of traditional aesthetics, does not restrict itself to refuting them simply as errors but condemns them as fallacies and seals them as heresies" (33). Adorno's views are developed throughout his writings on music, but an influential statement of his views on lyric poetry are to be found in "On Lyric Poetry and Society," in *Notes to Literature*, ed. Rolf Tiedemann, trans. Shierry Weber (New York: Columbia University Press, 1991), 37–55. For a representative selection of Russian formalist accounts, including Shklovksy's "Art as Technique," see Lee T. Lemon and Marion J. Reis, eds. *Russian Formalist Criticism: Four Essays*, intro. Gary Saul Morson (Lincoln: University of Nebraska Press, 2014).

33. As Adorno and other members of the Frankfurt School see it, in the context of social domination and reification, autonomous art can hold out the ideal of a full humanity and a richer individualism—both in the image of the artist as a creator and in the reader or listener or viewer's experience of response and interpretation. This critical-utopian dimension of autonomous art is also brought out by Herbert Marcuse, *Eros and Civilization: A Philosophical Inquiry into Freud* (Boston: Beacon, 1955), notably in chap. 7, "Phantasy and Utopia."

34. T. S. Eliot, *Selected Essays* (New York: Harcourt, Brace, 1950), 250.

35. The years since the September 11 terrorist attacks and the ensuing "war on terrorism" have seen a remarkable growth of sophisticated interdisciplinary work about the nature of secular society, the historical processes that have shaped it, and the role of religion within modernity. Major contributors to this body of scholarship include Charles Taylor, Talal Asad, José Casanova, Olivier Roy, and William T. Cavanaugh.

36. For Marcel Gauchet, disenchantment is the effect of a specific theological tendency within Christianity, which he sees as marked by waves of reform in which

the divine is, again and again, concentrated and purified, leaving ever larger areas of life to be merely profane and subject to human intervention and mastery (Gauchet calls Christianity "the religion of the end of religion"). Marcel Gauchet, *The Disenchantment of the World: A Political History of Religion*, trans. Oscar Burge (Princeton, NJ: Princeton University Press, 1997). An important much earlier statement of continuity theory is Carl L. Becker, *The Heavenly City of the Eighteenth-Century Philosophers* (1932; New Haven, CT: Yale University Press, 2003), which argues that eighteenth-century intellectuals were indebted to the Christian tradition far more than they would have acknowledged.

37. See Stephen Gaukroger, *The Emergence of a Scientific Culture: Science and the Shaping of Modernity, 1210–1685* (Oxford: Oxford University Press, 2006); and Hans Küng, "God: The Last Taboo? Science, God, and the University," in *Theology and the University: Essays in Honor of John B. Cobb Jr.*, ed. David Ray Griffin and Joseph C. Hough Jr. (Albany: State University of New York Press, 1991), 51–66. See also Küng's account of the role of Christian theology in the Hegelian dialectic in *The Incarnation of God: An Introduction to Hegel's Theological Thought as a Prolegomena to a Future Christology*, trans. J. R. Stephenson (New York: Crossroad, 1987), originally published in German in 1970. In *Seven Types of Atheism* (New York: FSG, 2018), John Gray has also argued for the difficulty of consistently transcending a theistic perspective even by self-avowed atheists.

38. See the account of his Geneva years in F. Bruce Gordon, *Calvin* (New Haven, CT: Yale University Press, 2011).

39. What Dominick LaCapra, deploying a Freudian vocabulary, calls "repetition with variation." For one brilliant statement among many see his *History and Criticism* (Ithaca, NY: Cornell University Press, 1985).

40. See Jane Bennett, *Unthinking Faith and Enlightenment: Nature and the State in a Post-Hegelian Era* (New York: New York University Press, 1987).

41. See Olivier Roy, *Holy Ignorance: When Religion and Culture Part Ways*, trans. Ros Schwartz (New York: Oxford University Press, 2014).

42. The word "countersecularization" appears in Peter L. Berger, *A Rumor of Angels: Modern Society and the Rediscovery of the Supernatural*, exp. ed. (New York: Anchor, 1990), 137, though the concept is not very developed.

43. See Simon During, "Completing Secularism: The Mundane in the Neoliberal Era," in *Varieties of Secularism in a Secular Age*, ed. Michael Warner, Jonathan VanAntwerpen and Craig Calhoun (Cambridge, MA: Harvard University Press, 2013), 105–25.

44. See Piero Boitani, *The Gospel According to Shakespeare*, trans. Vittorio Montemaggi and Rachel Jacoff (Notre Dame, IL: University of Notre Dame Press, 2013), 85. This "use" of the discourse of material resurrection might be fruitfully connected to Katherine Eggert's notion of a general turn toward "disknowledge," by which she means discourses (including alchemy) whose literal truth is less important than the way they function as a set of enabling metaphors. Katherine Eggert, *Disknowledge: Literature, Alchemy, and the End of Humanism in Renaissance England* (Philadelphia: University of Pennsylvania Press, 2015).

45. See Hugh Chandler, "Wittgenstein on the Resurrection," *Philosophical Investigations* 33, no. 4 (October 2010): 321–38.

46. Some of these modern fantasies and their religious background are explored in Michel Houellebecq, *The Possibility of an Island*, trans. Gavin Bowd (New York: Vintage, 2007); and Don DeLillo, *Zero K: A Novel* (New York: Scribner, 2016).

47. See Bernard E. Harcourt, *Exposed: Desire and Disobedience in the Digital Age* (Cambridge, MA: Harvard University Press). In his review essay in the *New York Review of Books*, November 26, 2015, Edward Mendelson notes that "this seems accurate about common feelings, but overestimates the likelihood of digital immortality; in fact vast Web-based communities, with all their history, have been swept away with a click."

48. See "Digital Bodies and the Transformation of the Flesh," in *Toward a Theology of Eros: Transfiguring Passion at the Limits of Discipline*, ed. Virginia Burrus and Catherine Keller (New York: Fordham University Press, 2006), 153–66.

49. A view central to Bersani's project across many books but whose canonical statement is perhaps *The Freudian Body* (New York: Columbia University Press, 1986).

1 / Secularization, Countersecularization, and the Fate of the Flesh in Donne

1. *De veritate*, from Peter Gay, ed., *Deism: An Anthology* (Princeton, NJ: Van Nostrand, 1968), 39. Subsequent citations are given internally.

2. Charles Taylor, *A Secular Age* (Cambridge, MA: Harvard University Press, 2007).

3. See William T. Cavanaugh, "The Invention of the Religious-Secular Distinction," in *At the Limits of the Secular: Reflections on Faith and Public Life*, ed. William A. Barbieri Jr. (Grand Rapids, MI: Eerdmans, 2014), 105–28.

4. Similarly, in Locke's *Essay Concerning Human Understanding* (1690) he says that revelation is reason "extended" but that if revelation controverts reason then it is not revelation but deception. That said, in Herbert's autobiography he describes his decision to publish *De veritate* as the result of receiving a divine sign.

5. *De veritate*, 45–46.

6. The disembodied mentalistic selfhood that Herbert champions ultimately culminates in fantasies that the self is capable of living in a virtual form separate from bodily life, including the related fantasy that the self, in its essence, is merely information that can persist in other media after the death of the body. These fantasies appear already in Edward Herbert's own famous autobiographical project, which was not published until 1764 by another icon of secularization, Horace Walpole, through his Strawberry Hill Press.

7. Ramie Targoff, *John Donne, Body and Soul* (Chicago: University of Chicago Press, 2008)

8. All quotations from Donne's poetry are from Charles M. Coffin, ed., *The Complete Poetry and Selected Prose of John Donne*, intro. Denis Donoghue (New York: Modern Library, 2001).

9. See "A Sermon Preached at White-hall, April 21, 1616," in *The Sermons of John Donne*, ed. George R. Potter and Evelyn M. Simpson (Berkeley: California, 1953), 1:169. Unless otherwise noted, all sermons I discuss in this chapter are quoted from this edition.

10. M. Thomas Hester, ed., *Letters to Several Persons of Honour* (1651; New York: Scholars' Facsimile and Reprints, 1977), 43. For an account of Donne's struggle to articulate the reasons for his own conversion see Brooke Conti, *Confessions of Faith in Early Modern England* (Philadelphia, PA: University of Philadelphia Press, 2014). See also John G. Demaray, "Donne's Three Steps to Death," *Personalist* 46 (1965): 366–81.

11. James Kuzner argues that in *Biathanatos* Donne presents a case that public reasoning about suicide (or any other matter of importance) is destined to be flawed and to end in failure. The way Donne thinks about the public sphere and the inevitable weakness of public argumentation is, in fact, a mark of his strong effort to secularize the very idea of truth and, especially, religious truth. James Kuzner, "Donne's *Biathanatos* and the Public Sphere's Vexing Freedom," *ELH* 81, no. 1 (Spring 2014): 61–81. The shift from theology (as a discourse that authorizes violence) to philosophy as an irenic counterdiscourse is a central concern of John Guillory, "Marlowe, Ramus, and the Reformation of Philosophy," *ELH* 81, no. 3 (Fall 2014): 693–732.

12. Katrin Ettenhuber, *Donne's Augustine: Renaissance Cultures of Interpretation* (Oxford: Oxford University Press, 2011), 54.

13. Alison Shell and Arnold Hunt, "Donne's Religious World," in *The Cambridge Companion to John Donne*, ed. Achsah Guibbory (New York: Cambridge University Press, 2006), 65–82. For another effort to reconstruct Donne's theology, see Mark S. Sweetnam, *John Donne and Religious Authority in a Reformed Church* (Dublin: Four Courts, 2014).

14. For an account of Donne's efforts to create a space for conscience where disagreements cannot be settled by means of logical syllogisms, see Ceri Sullivan, *The Rhetoric of the Conscience in Donne, Herbert, and Vaughan* (Oxford: Oxford University Press, 2008).

15. See Robert Whalen, *The Poetry of Immanence: Sacrament in Donne and Herbert* (Toronto: Toronto University Press, 2002). See also Eleanor McNeese, "John Donne and the Anglican Doctrine of the Eucharist," *TSLL* 29, no. 1 (Spring 1987): 94–114, esp. 100–1. See also Margret Fetzer, *John Donne's Performances: Sermons, Poems, Letters and Devotions* (Manchester: Manchester University Press, 2010). Regina Schwartz argues that in light of the Protestant insistence that the Eucharist is mere remembrance and not transubstantiation, poets like Donne seek to use poetry to create an alternative space in which the divine is present, an argument she extends to the erotic lyrics in which a "communion of the flesh" amounts to a sacramental union of the material and the transcendental. Regina Schwartz, *Sacramental Poetics and the Dawn of Secularism: When God Left the World* (Stanford, CA: Stanford University Press, 2008).

16. Jonathan Goldberg, *James I and the Politics of Literature* (Baltimore, MD: Johns Hopkins University Press, 1983).

17. For a whiggish account of the advance brought by the rejection of final causes, see Craig Martin, *Renaissance Meteorology: Pompanozzi to Descartes* (Baltimore, MD: Johns Hopkins University Press, 2011).

18. For an important exploration of these issues, see Elizabeth D. Harvey and Timothy M. Harrison, "Embodied Resonances: Early Modern Science and Tropologies of Connection in Donne's Anniversaries," *ELH* 80, no. 4 (Winter 2013): 981–1008. Donne was especially concerned about the protoscience of alchemy. See Don Cameron Allen, "John Donne's Knowledge of Renaissance Medicine," *Journal of English and Germanic Philology* 42, no. 3 (July 1943): 322–42. For a more recent account, see Mary E. Zimmer, "'In whom love wrought new Alchimie': The Inversion of Christian-Alchemical Resurrection in John Donne's 'A Nocturnal upon S. Lucie's day,'" *Christianity and Literature* 51, no. 4 (2002): 553–68. For Donne's relationship to anatomy and knowledge about the human body, see Richard Sugg, *Murder after*

Death: Literature and Anatomy in Early Modern England (Ithaca, NY: Cornell University Press, 2007).

19. John Donne, *Devotions upon Emergent Occasions*, ed. Anthony Raspa (Montreal: McGill-Queen's University Press, 1975).

20. Terry G. Sherwood tracks the ways the notion of "a calling" applies to Donne in *The Self in Early Modern Literature: For the Common Good* (Pittsburgh, PA: Duquesne University Press, 2007).

21. John Donne, sermon preached May 8, 1625, in John Carey, ed., *The Major Works* (New York: Oxford University Press, 2009), 360.

22. Kimberley Anne Coles, "The Matter of Belief in John Donne's Holy Sonnets," *Renaissance Quarterly* 68 (2015): 889–931; and David A. Hedrich Hirsch, "Donne's Atomies and Anatomies: Deconstructed Bodies and the Resurrection of Atomic Theory," *SEL* 31, no. 1 (1991): 69–94.

23. Douglas Trevor, "John Donne and Scholarly Melancholy," *SEL* 40, no. 1 (2000): 81–102.

24. See Nancy Gail Selleck, "Donne's Body," *SEL* 41, no. 1 (2001): 149–74. Michael Schoenfeldt has countered this tendency by arguing that humoral conceptions of the self open the door to stoical management techniques whose very aim is to arrive at a controlled and managed body with defined borders. See *Bodies and Selves in Early Modern England: Physiology and Inwardness in Spenser, Shakespeare, Herbert, and Milton* (New York: Cambridge University Press, 1999).

25. For a strong discussion of this sermon and others, see Blaine Greteman, "'All this seed pearl': John Donne and Bodily Presence," *College Literature* 37, no. 3 (Summer 2010): 26–42. Greteman notes that though Donne sometimes does privilege the soul, he often works on the strange union of soul and body, where it becomes a kind of hybrid substance, like beaten airy gold or a liquid.

26. See Suzanne Smith, "The Enfranchisement of the 'In-Mate Soule': Self-Knowledge and Death in Donne's *Anniversaries*," *Literature and Theology* 24, no. 4 (December 2010): 313–30.

27. Quoted in Smith, "The Enfranchisement of the 'In-Mate Soule,'" 320.

28. This picture of decay and putrefaction, in turn, leads to the question of why Christ alone was exempt from this vermiculation, and the answer is a strong statement of Barthian neo-orthodoxy: "We look no further for causes or reasons in the mysteries of religion, but to the will and pleasure of God: Christ himself limited his inquisition in that *ita est, even so Father, for it seemeth good in thy sight*. Christ's body did not see corruption therefore because God had decreed it should not."

29. See Achsah Guibbory, "Figuring Things Out: Donne's Devotions upon Emergent Occasions," in *Returning to John Donne* (Farnham: Ashgate, 2015), 7–15. Stephen Penders also discusses how Donne understands God's purpose to be written on his body in disease. Stephen Penders, "Essaying the Body: Donne, Affliction, and Medicine," in *John Donne's Professional Lives*, ed. David Colclough (New York: Brewer, 2003), 215–48, esp. 220. For a discussion of Donne's will to self-destruction, see Ross B. Lerner, "Donne's Annihilation," *JMEMS* 44, no. 2 (Spring 2014): 407–27.

30. See Rebecca Ann Cach, "(Re)placing Johns Donne and the History of Sexuality," *ELH* 72, no. 1 (Spring 2005): 259–89. Also see Achsah Guibbory, "Depersonalization, Disappointment, and Disillusion," in *Returning to John Donne* (Farnham: Ashgate, 2015).

31. See Drew Daniel, "A Political Necrology of God," *JEMCS* 13, no. 3 (Summer 2013): 105–25, esp. 120.

32. Stanley Fish, "Masculine Persuasive Force: Donne and Verbal Power," repr. in *John Donne*, ed. Andrew Mousley (New York: Macmillan, 1999), 157–81. For an account that casts important light on the question of the body and masochism, albeit in a different interpretive context, see Melissa E. Sanchez, "The Politics of Masochism in Mary Wroth's *Urania*," *ELH* 74, no. 2 (2007): 449–78.

33. When consummation does happen, other mechanisms of masochism take over from nonconsummation. In "The Canonization" consummation only serves as an opportunity to highlight Donne's failings in the historical world, as with the invitation to his friend to "chide my palsy, or my gout;/ My five gray hairs, or ruin'd fortune flout." If love here (and in its sister poem, "The Sun Rising") is a compensation for loss in the real world, then it is also an opportunity to highlight that loss, often by foregrounding the body as the scene of vulnerability and unfulfilled desire.

34. Ben Saunders notes that Donne only writes sonnets in relation to men and God, an observation that comes in the midst of a discussion of eighteenth-century complaints about the irregularity of Donne's meter as a screen for complaining about his "sexual irregularity." Ben Saunders, *Desiring Donne: Poetry, Sexuality, Interpretation* (Cambridge, MA: Harvard University Press, 2006).

35. In a powerful discussion of poetry by Herbert, Vaughan, and especially Donne, James Kuzner, "Metaphysical Freedom," *MLQ* 74, no. 4 (2013): 465–92, argues that the holy sonnets plunge readers into a form of freedom defined by an almost freakish passivity and detachment.

36. Kimberly Johnson, *Made Flesh: Sacrament and Poetics in Post-Reformation England* (Philadelphia: University of Pennsylvania Press, 2014).

37. Judith Scherer, "Reading and Rereading Donne's Poetry," in *The Cambridge Companion to John Donne*, ed. Achsah Guibbory (New York: Cambridge University Press, 2006), 106.

38. See his introduction to *The Complete English Poems of John Donne*, ed. C. A. Patrides (London: Dent & Sons, 1990). Herz writes that Donne's poems "baffle provocatively and usefully any attempt to fix their meanings, directing our attention to the words, their figuration, shape, and patterns, often more than to the ideas." Judith Scherer Herz, "Reading and Rereading Donne's Poetry," in *The Cambridge Companion to John Donne*, ed. Achsah Guibbory (New York: Cambridge University Press, 2006), 106.

39. See *Russian Formalist Criticism: Four Essays*, trans. and intro. Lee T. Lemon and Marion J. Reis (Lincoln: University of Nebraska Press, 1965).

40. See Stephen Bann and John E. Bowlt, eds., *Russian Formalism: A Collection of Articles and Texts in Translation* (New York: Barnes & Noble, 1973), 41–47.

41. The poetry and especially the formal experimentation (including in Donne's prose work) is always designed to make you aware of the historical conditions of actual language and thus to make you think about what is outside of it. *That* issue is thematized, which is to say, it is represented inside the language itself, but there is a wish for the imagination to leap beyond language when the poem or prose gets too hard or breaks down in some way. Thus as you read Donne you become aware of the materiality of language, and that, in turn, makes you cease to look at language from inside your language community. That is not an end in itself; rather, it is an

invitation to touch things outside of the significances that are imputed to them within human language communities in time and to use poems to do so, or at least to begin to articulate the desire to do so.

42. For an account of poetry not as representation but as orientation in space, see Elizabeth Fowler, "Art and Orientation," *NLH* 44, no. 4 (2013): 595–616.

43. See Peter Bürger, *Theory of the Avant-Garde*, trans. Michael Shaw (Minneapolis: University of Minnesota Press, 1984).

44. T. S. Eliot, *Selected Essays* (New York: Harcourt, Brace, 1950), 243. Subsequent citations are given internally.

45. See Jane Bennett, *Vibrant Matter: A Political Ecology of Things* (Durham, NC: Duke University Press, 2010), 4.

46. Cited from T. S. Eliot, *The Complete Poems and Plays, 1909–1950* (New York: Houghton Mifflin Harcourt, 2014).

47. For a contextualization of Donne's *Songs and Sonnets* in earlier literary history, see Andrew Hadfield, "Literary Contexts: Predecessors and Contemporaries" in *The Cambridge Companion to John Donne*, ed. Achsah Guibbory (New York: Cambridge University Press, 2006), 49–64. For the ways Donne's poetry percolated through seventeenth-century culture and created communities of readers around itself, both during his lifetime and immediately after he died, see a series of notes by W. Milgate in *Notes and Queries* 195 (May 1950): 229–31, 246–47, 290–92, 381–83; *Notes and Queries* 198 (October 1953): 421–24.

2 / Wanting to Be Another Person: Resurrection and Avant-Garde Poetics in George Herbert

1. For a discussion of Herbert's "realized eschatology," see Paul Cefalu, "Johannine Poetics in George Herbert's Devotional Lyrics," *ELH* 82, no. 4 (2015): 1041–71.

2. All Herbert poems are quoted from C. A. Patrides, ed., *The English Poems of George Herbert* (London: Dent & Co., 1974).

3. See Richard Strier, *Love Known: Theology and Experience in George Herbert's Poetry* (Chicago: University of Chicago Press, 1986). The classic new historicist view is Michael C. Schoenfeldt, *Prayer and Power: George Herbert and Renaissance Courtship* (Chicago: University of Chicago Press, 1991). For Schoenfeldt, the relationship to God that Herbert tracks in his poems is ultimately informed by his social concerns with relating to or courting superiors, including the king. Schoenfeldt also connects Herbert's poems to civility handbooks that offer advice for how to manage social superiors. See also Cristina Malcolmson, *George Herbert: A Literary Life* (New York: Palgrave Macmillan, 2004), which I discuss in detail later in this chapter. Ilona Bell remarks that "scholars have placed Herbert at every point along the spectrum of English Protestantism, from ceremonial Anglo-Catholicism to radical puritanism." Ilona Bell, "Herbert's Valdésian Vision," *ELR* 17, no. 3 (1987): 303–28, 304.

4. For an account that roots Herbert's thinking about the body and its sounds to Augustine and that also treats the emphasis on the body as the basis for a potent affirmation of sexuality, see Warren M. Liew, "Reading the Erotic in George Herbert's Sacramental Poetics," *George Herbert Journal* 31, nos. 1–2 (2007/ 2008).

5. See Phillip J. Donnelly, "The Triune Heart of *The Temple*," *George Herbert Journal* 23, nos. 1–2 (Fall 1999/Spring2000): 35–54.

6. See Tom MacFaul, "George Herbert's Bravery," *Essays in Criticism* 65, no. 4 (2015): 383–400.

7. I think there is a plausible source for Herbert's "quotation" in the phrase "fair, kind and true," which Shakespeare repeats three times in Sonnet 105, a sonnet also marked by a (supposed) voluntary renunciation of poetic power.

8. See Stanley Fish, *Self-Consuming Artifacts: The Experience of Seventeenth-Century Literature* (Berkeley: University of California Press, 1972)

9. See Roberts W. French, "'My Stuffe Is Flesh': An Allusion to Job in George Herbert's 'The Pearl,'" *Notes and Queries* 27 (1980): 329–31.

10. Though he frames it in a less optimistic light, Richard Strier also discusses the notion of a forced or "unfree" voice in poetry in "Bondage and the Lyric: Philosophical and Formal, Renaissance and Modern," in *The Work of Form: Poetics and Materiality in Early Modern Culture*, ed. Ben Burton and Elizabeth Scott-Baumann (New York: Oxford University Press, 2014), 73–87.

11. Thus Malcolmson argues that "'The Posie' does not imply that Herbert gave up singing or reciting the lyrics before an audience" (176).

12. See Ramie Targoff, "The Poetics of Common Prayer: George Herbert and the Seventeenth-Century Devotional Lyric," *ELR* 29, no. 3 (1999): 468–90.

13. For a counterpoint, see Catherine Nicholson, *Uncommon Tongues: Eloquence and Eccentricity in the English Renaissance* (Philadelphia: University of Pennsylvania Press, 2014).

14. See Johanna Drucker, "Not Sound," in *The Sound of Poetry/The Poetry of Sound*, ed. Marjorie Perloff and Craig Dworkin (Chicago: University of Chicago Press, 2009), 237–48.

15. See Alison Knight, "'This Verse Marks That': George Herbert's *The Temple* and Scripture in Context," in *The Oxford Handbook of the Bible in Early Modern England, c. 1530–1700*, ed. Kevin Killeen, Helen Smith, and Rachel Willie (New York: Oxford University Press, 2015), 518–532, 525.

16. See Roman Jakobson, "Linguistics and Poetics," in *Style in Language*, ed. Thomas Sebeok (Cambridge, MA: MIT Press, 1960). "The Altar" also illustrates the formal estranging technique of subordinating Herbert's "own" voice to snippets of Bible language in a gesture that Alison Knight calls "self-effacement."

17. See Jonathan Culler, "Why Lyric?," *PMLA* 123, no. 1 (2008): 201–6. Culler argues that with the rise of the novel, a model of poetry based on representation has come to hold sway, and by contrast he calls for a return to the formal dimension of poetry as having a life of its own, especially rhythm and sound patterning as constitutive, intertextual relations, and what he calls the "characteristic extravagance" of lyric, which frequently engages in speech acts without a known real-world counterpart. For a countervailing view, see Shoshana Benjamin, "On the Distinctiveness of Poetic Language," *NLH* 43, no. 1 (2012): 89–111.

18. For a parallel view, see Hillary Kelleher "'Light thy Darkness is': George Herbert and Negative Theology," *George Herbert Journal* 28, no. 1 (2004/2005): 47–64.

19. See Renato Poggioli, *The Theory of the Avant-Garde*, trans. Gerald Fitzgerald (Cambridge, MA: Harvard University Press, 1981).

20. Peter Bürger, *Theory of the Avant-Garde*, trans. Michael Shaw (Minneapolis: University of Minnesota Press, 1984). In suggesting that Herbert might be placed in the deep genealogy of the avant-garde movements of the early twentieth century I

am also suggesting that avant-gardism might best be understood as an effect of the broad movement of secularization I have been exploring in this book, in which a set of religious ideas about the resurrection of the flesh that seemed to have been discredited and abandoned at the dawn of secular modernity in fact come to have a powerfully determining effect on subsequent literary history. Though not theorized in terms of the avant-garde, Louis Martz also intuits a connection between Herbert and distinctively modern aesthetic formations, including in the work of Proust and Giacometti. See Louis L. Martz, "Voices in the Void: The Action of Grief in Proust and Herbert," *George Herbert Journal* 18, nos. 1–2 (1994/1995): 91–104.

21. This narrative sees autonomous art emerging from fully religious or "auratic" art (to use Walter Benjamin's term) that is embedded in social worlds permeated by the sacred. In the West—so goes the narrative—the first move toward secular art comes at the great courts of Europe, including Henry VIII's, with art whose purpose is to represent aristocratic patrons in ways that reaffirm or shore up status or prestige, which is indeed the function of much art (including Holbein's famous images) and poetry at the court of Henry VIII.

Once art has carved out this autonomy it can represent historical processes of society from the outside, as it were, as in the tradition of great realist novels from Scott to Balzac. This autonomous, reflective art is well described by critics in the Marxist tradition, notably see György Lukács, *The Historical Novel*, trans. Hannah Mitchell and Stanley Mitchell (Lincoln: University of Nebraska Press, 1983).

22. Pierre Bourdieu, *The Field of Cultural Production: Essays on Art and Literature*, trans. Randal Johnson (New York: Columbia University Press, 1993).

23. Jonathan Goldberg, *Sodometries: Renaissance Texts, Modern Sexualities* (Stanford, CA: Stanford University Press, 1992), 249.

24. See Harry Berger Jr., *Revisionary Play: Studies in the Spenserian Dynamics* (Berkeley: University of California Press, 1988). Obviously the remains of the classical tradition also play a complex role in defining something like an autonomous sphere, an issue that I take up to some extent in the chapter on Jonson.

25. Izaak Walton, *Lives of Donne and Herbert*, ed. S. C. Roberts (New York: Cambridge University Press, 2014), 73.

26. Quoted in C.A. Patrides, ed., *George Herbert: The Critical Heritage* (Boston: Routledge & Kegan Paul, 1983), 78.

27. Jenna Townend applies quantitative methods to track the influence of Herbert on English and American culture. See her "Quantitative and Qualitative Approaches to Early-Modern Networks: The Case of George Herbert (1593–1633) and His Imitators," *Literature Compass* 14, no. 3 (2017).

28. Quoted in Patrides, ed., *George Herbert*, 20.

29. Joshua Poole, *The English Parnassus, or, A help to English poesie containing a collection of all the rhyming monosyllables, the choicest epithets and phrases: with some general forms upon all occasions, subjects, and theams, alphabeticaly digested together with a short institution to English poesie, by way of preface*. London: Printed for Henry Brome, Thomas Bassett, and John Wright, 1677. EEBO.

30. Both of these examples are discussed by Robert H. Ray, "Two Seventeenth-Century Adapters of George Herbert," *Notes & Queries* 27 (1980): 331–32.

31. Indeed, in her entry on Herbert in the *Oxford National Dictionary of Biography*, Helen Wilcox speculates that the rise of sequences of religious poems in

the seventeenth century on both sides of the Atlantic may be attributed to the pattern of *The Temple*.

32. See Daniel W. Doerksen, *Picturing Religious Experience: George Herbert, Calvin, and the Scriptures* (Newark: University of Delaware Press, 2011), 37.

33. See Paul Valéry, *The Art of Poetry*, trans. Denise Folliot (New York: Pantheon, 1958), 256.

34. On differentiating God-infused emotional impulses from merely human ones in Jonathan Edwards, see Timothy H. Robinson, "Jonathan Edwards: On Religious Affections," in *Christian Spirituality: The Classics*, ed. Arthur Holder (New York: Routledge, 2010).

35. Quoted in Patrides, ed., *George Herbert*, 29.

36. Michael C. Schoenfeldt, "George Herbert's Consuming Subject," *George Herbert Journal* 18, nos. 1–2 (1994/1995): 105–32. There has been extensive work on the intersection between religious and literary culture in early modern England, much of it focused on differing views of the Eucharist correlated with the use of metaphors in poetry. For a critical review of such work, see Ryan Netzley, "'Take and Taste': Sacramental Physiology, Eucharistic Experience, and George Herbert's *The Temple*," in *Varieties of Devotion in the Middle Ages and Renaissance*, ed. Susan C. Karat-Nunn (Turnhout: Brepolis, 2003), 179–206.

37. Margaret R. Miles, *Practicing Christianity: Critical Perspectives for an Embodied Spirituality* (New York: Crossroad, 1988).

38. Michael Schoenfeldt, *Prayer and Power: George Herbert and Renaissance Courtship* (Chicago: University of Chicago Press, 1991), 15.

39. For a related account that sees early modern poets valuing religious sorrow for its power to move people out of a this-worldly perspective and toward an encounter with the radial alienness of God, see Gary Kuchar, *The Poetry of Religious Sorrow in Early Modern England* (Cambridge: Cambridge University Press, 2008).

40. I see important parallels in Deborah Kuller Shuger, *Habits of Thought in the English Renaissance: Religion, Politics, and the Dominant Culture* (Berkeley: University of California Press, 1990), 105.

41. Moreover, the poems also function as a technology that operates at the level of representation but also rhythm and sound to effect a mood transfer between poem and readers, and this accounts for the powerful effects the poems have upon readers.

42. Jonathan Flatley, "How a Revolutionary Counter-Mood Is Made," *NLH* 43, no. 3 (2012): 503–25. See also Stephan Strasser, *Phenomenology of Feeling*, trans. and intro. Robert E. Wood (Pittsburgh, PA: Duquesne University Press, 1977), 190.

43. Qtd. from Henry Vaughan, *The Complete Poems*, ed. Alan Rudrum (New Haven, CT: Yale University Press, 1976).

3 / Luminous Stuff: The Resurrection of the Flesh in Vaughan's Religious Verse

1. Though my approach is quite different, Thomas O. Calhoun also argues that resurrection is the primary framework in Vaughan's verse. See his *Henry Vaughan: The Achievement of Silex Scintillans* (Newark: University of Delaware Press, 1981), 131–85.

2. I am influenced by Andrea Nightingale, *Once out of Nature: Augustine on Time and the Body* (Chicago: University of Chicago Press, 2011), and her idea of the

resurrected person as "trans-human." For a philosophical account of immanent resurrection, including some discussion of implications of this theory for an understanding of poetic language, see Karmen MacKendrick, "Eternal Flesh: The Resurrection of the Body," *Discourse* 27, no. 1 (2005): 67–83.

3. See also Ryan Netzley, *Lyric Apocalypse: Milton, Marvell, and the Nature of Events* (New York: Fordham University Press, 2015).

4. All Vaughan quotations are taken from Alan Rudrum, ed., *Henry Vaughan: The Complete Poems* (New Haven, CT: Yale University Press, 1976).

5. Jane Bennett, *Vibrant Matter: A Political Ecology of Things* (Durham, NC: Duke University Press, 2010).

6. In noting Vaughan's interest in a vitally animated material body I am broaching the debate on the role of hermetic thought in Vaughan's poetry and prose. It is worth saying that I deemphasize hermeticism in favor of attention to the determinative role of Vaughan's theory of resurrection. See A. W. Rudrum, "'The Night': Some Hermetic Notes," *Modern Language Review* 64, no. 1 (1969): 11–19; and E. C. Pettet, *Of Paradise and Light: A Study of Vaughan's Silex Scintillans* (New York: Cambridge, 2011), 70–75. For a contextualization of Vaughan's ideas in early modern ecoconsciousness, see Diane Kelsey McColley, *Poetry and Ecology in the Age of Milton and Marvell* (New York: Ashgate, 2007). One of McColley's larger aims is to identify a Christian vitalist perspective that sees life as a property that is inherent in matter, a perspective I fold into my account of immanent eschatology of the body.

7. See F. E. Hutchinson, *Henry Vaughan: A Life and Interpretation* (Oxford: Oxford University Press, 1947). For Vaughan's Welsh identity and its influence on his English-language poetry, see 157–59.

8. The metaphor of death as sleep is an important part of medieval folk Christianity even as it is increasingly opposed by official theology and practice, as described in Philippe Ariès, *The Hour of Our Death: The Classic History of Western Attitudes toward Death over the Last One Thousand Years*, trans. Helen Weaver (New York: Vintage, 1982). See also Garrett A. Sullivan Jr., *Sleep, Romance, and Human Embodiment: Vitality from Spenser to Milton* (New York: Cambridge University Press, 2012).

9. All italics in quotations are by Vaughan. Vaughan's use of italics is sometimes puzzling.

10. Caroline Walker Bynum, *The Resurrection of the Body in Western Christianity, 200–1336* (New York: Columbia University Press, 1995), 72.

11. Though Vaughan here seems to devalue his body as a "cell / of clay, and frailty," the thing within him that he feels budding is nevertheless as material as clay, but a clay infused with life, a material, organic, growing thing that is not under Vaughan's control, that is, in other words, separate from Vaughan's conventional self. To grow this second biological life within his biologically living body, Vaughan invites Christ to infuse his blood into Vaughan, thereby causing the (physical) seed of resurrection to grow.

12. Vaughan's theory is quite different from Leibniz's theory of a "flower of substance" that is a physical thing inside the body that defines its essential identity over time and that can swell back into a fully articulated body at the general resurrection. See Gottfried W. Leibniz, "On the Resurrection of Bodies," in *Sämtliche schriften und briefe*, ed. Akademie der Wissenschaften, multiple volumes in 8 series (Berlin: Akademie Verlag, 1923–), series II, 1:183–89. By contrast, Vaughan's (implicit)

theory sees the resurrection body and the historical body that is destined to die as so intertwined that it is impossible to catch sight of the resurrection body except by looking *through* the historical body. On Leibniz, see Lloyd Strickland, "Leibniz, the 'Flower of Resurrection,' and the Resurrection of the Same Body," *Philosophical Forum* 40, no. 3 (Fall 2009): 391–410.

13. See David Glimp, "Figuring Belief: George Herbert's Devotional Creatures," in *Go Figure: Energies, Forms, and Institutions in the Early Modern World*, ed. Judith H. Anderson and Joan Pong (New York: Fordham University Press, 2011). The issue of what Vaughan's perspective on the flesh implies for an understanding of sexuality (including the masochistic desire to step from personhood into objecthood) is a complex one. For an important treatment, see Richard Rambuss, *Closet Devotions* (Durham, NC: Duke University Press, 1998).

14. In a footnote to this poem, Rudrum understands Vaughan to be saying that "they have not got heaven to look forward to." Rudrum, ed., *Henry Vaughan*, 603.

15. See Jonathan F. S. Post, *Henry Vaughan: The Unfolding Vision* (Princeton, NJ: Princeton University Press, 1982), which offers an excellent account of Vaughan's verse in general.

16. Susan Stewart, *Poetry and the Fate of the Senses* (Chicago: University of Chicago Press, 2002). I am also drawing on the related model of poetic language and function articulated by Allen Grossman in conversation with Mark Halliday in *The Sighted Singer: Two Works on Poetry for Readers and Writers* (Baltimore, MD: Johns Hopkins University Press, 1991).

17. This is the point that Walter Benn Michaels and Steven Knapp made in an influential article in which they reflect on the phenomenological precondition of textual analysis. See "Against Theory," *Critical Inquiry* 8, no. 4 (1982): 723–42.

18. Roman Jakobson, and "Linguistics and Poetry" in *Language in Literature*, ed. Krystyna Pomorska and Stephen Rudy (Cambridge, MA: Harvard University Press, 1990), 62.

19. See Joshua Calhoun, "The Word Made Flax: Cheap Bibles, Textual Corruption, and the Poetics of Paper," *PMLA* 162, no. 2 (2011): 327–44. Calhoun describes how early modern paper often bears embedded traces of the raw materials of which it is manufactured—for example, traces of clothing, fiber, or physical contaminants such as feathers. He emphasizes early modern worries that the meaning of texts (especially of the Bible) might be corrupted by imperfections in physical component materials of paper and ink. Calhoun's article makes it seem quite plausible that the spark for Vaughan's brilliant poem may have come from his noting a physical trace of constituent material in his personal Bible. Margreta de Grazia also discusses the tensions between reading for meaning and paying attention to the "thinglike" quality of texts. See her "Words as Things," *Shakespeare Studies* 28 (2000): 231–35.

20. By its nature, the immanent perspective on resurrection breaks with conventionally linear understandings of time, and in that sense it connects with the perspective that Jonathan Gil Harris offers in *Untimely Matter in the Time of Shakespeare* (Philadelphia: University of Pennsylvania Press, 2009).

21. Florian Ebeling notes that the Hermetic tradition regarded hieroglyphs as natural signs that stood in an immediate relationship to the world, and, for these traditions, the world was a cosmos of signs and a system of relationships in which each thing was imprinted with the "signature" of its meaning. Florian Ebeling, *The*

Secret History of Hermes Trismegistus: Hermeticism from Ancient to Modern Times, trans. David Lorton (Ithaca, NY: Cornell University Press, 2007).

4 / The Feeling of Being a Body: Resurrection and Habitus in Vaughan's Medical Writings

1. For their early feedback on this chapter I want to thank Cora Fox, Curtis Perry, and Aaron Kunin.

2. The major works that defined the paradigm include Gail Kern Paster, *Humoring the Body: Emotions and the Shakespearean Stage* (Chicago: University of Chicago Press, 2004); Michael C. Schoenfeldt, *Bodies and Selves in Early Modern England: Physiology and Inwardness in Spenser, Shakespeare, Herbert, and Milton* (New York: Cambridge University Press, 1999); Bruce R. Smith, *The Key of Green: Passion and Perception in Renaissance Culture* (Chicago: University of Chicago Press, 2008); and Mary Floyd-Wilson, *English Ethnicity and Race in Early Modern Drama* (New York: Cambridge University Press, 2003). These groundbreaking scholarly accounts of humoral thought in early modern England were often quite nuanced, whereas second-generation accounts are characterized by increasing simplification of the basic model—something we might term "vulgar humoralism" on an analogy to "vulgar Marxism." My polemic about the absence of a sociological perspective in scholarship on the humors notwithstanding, it is important to note that attention to the sociological significance of the theory of the humors does play a role in the best humoral criticism as a second-order effect of humors. For instance, both Paster and Floyd-Wilson bring the social world into their highly nuanced discussions, but implicitly they ask: Given early modern beliefs about somatic and emotional life as fundamentally mechanical, how did early moderns coassemble humoral beliefs with social commitments they already had—for example, that women and the lower classes are undisciplined?

3. See, among others, Mary Thomas Crane, *Shakespeare's Brain: Reading with Cognitive Theory* (Princeton, NJ: Princeton University Press, 2000); Arthur F. Kinney, *Shakespeare's Web: Networks of Meaning in Renaissance Drama* (New York: Routledge, 2004); Amy Cook, *Shakespearean Neuroplay: Reinvigorating the Study of Dramatic Texts and Performance through Cognitive Science* (New York: Palgrave Macmillan, 2010); Evelyn Tribble, *Cognition in the Globe: Attention and Memory in Shakespeare's Theatre* (New York: Palgrave Macmillan, 2011); Lina Perkins Wilder, *Shakespeare's Memory Theatre: Recollection, Properties, and Character* (New York: Cambridge University Press, 2010); Raphael Lyne, *Shakespeare, Rhetoric, and Cognition* (New York: Cambridge University Press, 2011); Sophie Read, "Shakespeare and the Arts of Cognition," in *The Oxford Handbook of Shakespeare's Poetry*, ed. Jonathan Post (Oxford: Oxford University Press, 2013), 62–76.

4. For another quite powerful effort to break with the cognitivist/humoralist bifurcation, see Drew Daniel, *The Melancholy Assemblage: Affect and Epistemology in the English Renaissance* (New York: Fordham University Press, 2013), which reads melancholy as a network that assembles things and people.

5. Jane Bennett, *Thoreau's Nature: Ethics, Politics, and the Wild* (Thousand Oaks, CA: Sage, 1994). Page citations given internally.

6. Jane Bennett, *Unthinking Faith and Enlightenment: Nature and the State in a Post-Hegelian Era* (New York: New York University Press, 1987), 75.

7. I am relying on Bourdieu's *Distinction: A Social Critique of the Judgment of Taste*, trans. Richard Nice (Cambridge, MA: Harvard University Press, 1984). I tend to inflect Bourdieu's model in a Heideggerian direction because I find useful the notion that emotions (especially background emotions) are the way a world comes to light to a person. For the connection between Heidegger and Bourdieu, see Hubert L. Dreyfus, *Being-in-the-World: A Commentary on Heidegger's Being and Time, Division I* (Cambridge, MA: MIT Press, 1991). For a set of useful articles on the Heideggerian framework for analyzing emotional life, see the Summer 2012 special volume of *New Literary History* edited by Rita Felski and Susan Fraiman, which contains several essays focused on mood as something that discloses a world, an idea I assume throughout this discussion.

8. A scholarly program of applying Bourdieuvian cultural sociology to the problem of emotional life in early modern England could also take the *discourse* of early modern humoralism as an object of sociological analysis and explore the ways this discourse is a symptom of the dynamics of early modern culture. This would certainly be an interesting research program, but it would not reveal an answer to the second question I posed earlier, the question of how real people in early modern England really experienced their emotional life.

9. For an account of Vaughan's effort to distinguish himself from Puritan critics by means of a distinctive theory of resurrection, see Jonathan F. S. Post, *Henry Vaughan: The Unfolding Vision* (Princeton, NJ: Princeton, 1982), 122–26.

10. Quoted from Alan Rudrum, ed., *Henry Vaughan: The Complete Poems* (New Haven, CT: Yale University Press, 1976).

11. Though what I term the immanent eschatology of the body is easy to locate in Paul's letters, I certainly do not mean for my claims here to address the voluminous body of work on Paul's own understanding of the body and the flesh. It is noteworthy, however, that the new life Paul describes in his letters is not understood as a positive place to stand but only as a characteristic displacement from Jewish and Greco-Roman ways of life. It is a nonfoundational foundation, and recognizing this is what is so important about Badiou's account of Paul's thought. See Alain Badiou, *Saint Paul: The Foundation of Universalism*, trans. Ray Brassier (Stanford, CA: Stanford University Press, 2003). The implications of Badiou's account for early modern English culture are powerfully examined by Jonathan Goldberg, *The Seeds of Things: Theorizing Sexuality and Materiality in Renaissance Representations* (New York: Fordham University Press, 2009), 20–25. My interest in reasoning with and through early modern religious discourse rather than subjecting it to a kind of sociological debunking is methodologically if not thematically indebted to the work on political theology by both Lupton and Hammill. See Julia Reinhardt Lupton, *Citizen-Saints: Shakespeare and Political Theology* (Chicago: University of Chicago Press, 2005); and Graham Hammill, *The Mosaic Constitution: Political Theology and Imagination from Machiavelli to Milton* (Chicago: University of Chicago Press, 2012).

12. I am quoting from *Flores Solitudinis* (London, 1654), EEBO.

13. In Jane Bennett's writing on Thoreau she conceptualizes something similar, writing that "one uncanny effect of the experience of profound entanglement with Nature [i.e., through Thoreau's writing] is that the self becomes more awake, more attentive to that in oneself that differs from oneself as an ordered, organized They-self" (52). A different conceptual apparatus for grasping the same experience is Alain Badiou's notion of the "Christ-event." For Badiou the Christ-event is

interesting precisely because it wrenches those who have undergone it from the conventional (in the Greco-Roman world) ways of associating—primarily in the political arena, via a relationship to Caesar, and in the ethnic domain, via a sense of identification with others based on a supposed shared history or culture or indeed a shared cultic practice, though Badiou also, importantly, believes that the Christ-event separates selves from gender and gender-based roles. In short, Badiou thinks that the "Christ-event"—which I am recasting as first and foremost an experience of resurrection unfolding now and in yourself—separates you from an "identity" defined by occupying social roles within the political order or cultural system. Badiou sees the "Christ-event" as an analogue for a radical politics that emphasizes the "break" with the present social order and the modes of social organizing delivered by the present world. In short, Badiou sees the Christ-event as the model for a new politics.

14. See Lloyd Strickland, "The Doctrine of 'the Resurrection of the Same Body' in Early Modern Thought," *Religious Studies* 46 (2010): 163–83.

15. See Diane Kelsey McColley, *Poetry and Ecology in the Age of Milton and Marvell* (Aldershot: Ashgate, 2007). For accounts that highlight the influence of hermeticism on Vaughan, see A. W. Rudrum, "'The Night': Some Hermetic Notes," *Modern Language Review* 64, no. 1 (1969): 11–19; E. C. Pettet, *Of Paradise and Light: A Study of Vaughan's Silex Scintillans* (New York: Cambridge University Press, 2011), 70–75. In his introduction to Florian Ebeling, *The Secret History of Hermes Trismegistus: Hermeticism from Ancient to Modern Times*, trans. David Lorton (Ithaca, NY: Cornell University Press, 2007), Jan Assmann traces hermeticism from Egypt through the Greeks to Europe into the twentieth century. He argues that there are two somewhat different traditions, one that comes from Ficino's translations of Plato and the other more properly alchemical and that is evident in the work of Paracelsus and his imitators.

16. All citations are from Heinrich Nolle, *Hermetical physick: or, The right way to preserve, and to restore health. By that famous and faithfull chymist, Henry Nollius. Englished by Henry Uaughan, Gent.* (London, 1655), EEBO.

17. Vaughan's additions to the original are revealed when we compare the translation Vaughan published in 1655 with the original Latin published by Nolle in Hanover in 1617 as "Theoria philosophiae hermeticae." This text is available in the microfiche series History of Science Landmarks. My thanks to the library of the University of Oklahoma for making a copy of this microfiche available to me.

18. Strange but not altogether atypical in early modern literature. I see one possible analogue of this experience in *King Lear* when Edgar reports that his father died because "his flaw'd heart, / Alack, too weak the conflict to support! / 'Twixt two extremes of passion, joy and grief, / Burst smilingly" (5.3.189–92). Quoted from *William Shakespeare: The Complete Works*, ed. Stephen Orgel and A. R. Braunmuller (New York: Penguin, 2002).

19. I thank Brian Warren for his help with this translation.

20. In making this suggestion I am drawing on Margaret R. Miles's discussion of Augustine's postresurrection sexuality, which is defined by transcending the mere use of genitals. See "Sex and the City (of God): Is Sex Forfeited or Fulfilled in Augustine's Resurrection of Body?" *Journal of the American Academy of Religion* 73, no. 2 (June 2005): 307–27.

21. See Leo Bersani, "Is the Rectum a Grave?" *October* 43 (1987): 197–222. This article is reprinted in Jonathan Goldberg, ed., *Queering the Renaissance* (Durham, NC: Duke University Press, 1993). See also Leo Bersani's seminal *The Freudian Body: Psychoanalysis and Art* (New York: Columbia University Press, 1986).

5 / Resurrection, Dualism, and Legal Personhood: Bodily Presence in Ben Jonson

1. Jonson's religious commitments are hard to pin down and are discussed in many of the major biographies, including David Riggs, *Ben Jonson: A Life* (Cambridge, MA: Harvard University Press, 1989). See also Marshelle Woodward, "Ben Jonson's Sacramental Poetics: Manners as Mystery in His Poetry and Drama," *Ben Jonson Journal* 22, no. 1 (2015): 41–61.

2. This commitment to formal patterning as a way of transcending the fleetingness of everyday speech in poetry might have been part of what motivated Jonson's famous comment that "Done for not keeping of accent deserved hanging." See "Ben Jonson's Conversations with William Drummond of Hawthornden," in *The Collected Works of Ben Jonson*, ed. C. H. Herford, Percy Simpson, and Evelyn Simpson (Oxford: Clarendon, 1925–1952), 1:128–78, ll. 48–49.

3. All poems are quoted from Ben Jonson, *The Complete Poems*, ed. George Parfitt (New York: Penguin, 1975).

4. Sara van den Berg quotes a dream vision in which Jonson says he saw his son as "he shall be at the resurrection." Sara van den Berg, "True Relation: The Life and Career of Ben Jonson," in *The Cambridge Companion to Ben Jonson*, ed. Richard Harp and Stanley Stewart (New York: Cambridge University Press, 2000), 7.

5. For a discussion of the role of Jonson's body in figuring his authorship, see Joseph Loewenstein, "The Jonsonian Corpulence, or the Poet as Mouthpiece," *ELH* 53, no. 3 (1986): 491–518.

6. Stanley Fish, "Authors-Readers: Jonson's Community of the Same," *Representations* 7 (1984): 26–58.

7. Ian Donaldson, "Jonson's Poetry," in *The Cambridge Companion to Ben Jonson*, ed. Richard Harp and Stanley Stewart (New York: Cambridge University Press, 2000), 119–39, 124.

8. For a discussion of the use of the name as a stand-in for the person, see Joshua Scodel, *The English Poetic Epitaph: Commemoration and Conflict from Jonson to Wordsworth* (Ithaca, NY: Cornell University Press, 1991).

9. Jonathan P. Lamb argues that earlier publishing ventures to mourn the death of Prince Henry influenced the effort to create a material presence in the Folio. Jonathan P. Lamb, "Ben Jonson's Dead Body: Henry, Prince of Wales, and the 1616 Folio," *Huntington Library Quarterly* 79, no. 1 (2016): 63–92.

10. For an account of how the very fragmentation of ancient culture was recognized as the key to its survival and thus as the key to any possibility for contemporary writers achieving near immortality, see Andrew Hui, *The Poetics of Ruins in Renaissance Literature* (New York: Fordham University Press, 2016).

11. Brian Sheerin, for example, situates the play in terms of an emerging credit economy, and his basic argument is that credit requires and creates a culture-wide readiness to believe and to trust that also applies in the theater, where people are quite ready to see one thing for another. Brian Sheerin, "The Substance of Shadows:

Imagination and Credit Culture in *Volpone*," *Journal of Medieval and Early Modern Studies* 43, no. 2 (Spring 2013): 369–91. The play can also be situated within the economic "world-systems" approach of Fernand Braudel and others, in which the financial speculation that constitutes the essence of capitalism invades, colonizes, and disrupts more socially embedded market mechanisms and forms of social life, as also described by Karl Polanyi, *The Great Transformation: The Political and Economic Origins of Our Time* (Boston: Beacon, 2001). The dupes that Volpone makes fun of are first and foremost speculators who are not only willing to turn away from various natural forms of relationship for money but who are willing actively to use and abuse natural relationships for money. Sir Politic-Would-Be represents something similar but in the key of farce; he has various economic schemes that are not involved in production but in exploiting information and disrupting traditional trade routes.

12. Though his main argument is that any sense of a separable self, whether legally or psychologically codified, is deviant in the ancient context and remains so until well into the seventeenth century, Timothy J. Reiss nonetheless reviews some of the legal basis of (and limits to) personhood in the context of Roman law. Timothy J. Reiss, *Mirages of the Selfe: Patterns of Personhood in Ancient and Early Modern Europe* (Stanford, CA: Stanford University Press, 2003).

13. For a good discussion of the legal specifics of common law and the percentages of various subpopulations that used wills, as well as for the way this background legal situation is refracted in plays, see Michelle M. Dowd, *The Dynamics of Inheritance on the Shakespearean Stage* (Cambridge: Cambridge University Press, 2015). Dowd notes that common law does provide constraints upon the transfer of wealth but that it only covered real property and not movables, giving much flexibility. She notes that by the mid–seventeenth century, up to 30 percent of the population did have wills (36n14). See also Gary Watt, *Shakespeare's Acts of Will: Law, Testament, and Properties of Performance* (London: Bloomsbury Arden Shakespeare, 2016). Watt notes the "epochal shift" caused by Henry VIII's Statute of Wills (1540) because it allowed landed gentry to have testamentary control over their property estates, as opposed to the tradition of lineal descent or inheritance by bloodline, allowing for the transfer of property through free will.

14. Indeed, the two go together in the sense that two of the main functions of early modern wills are (1) to provide specific information about the disposal of the physical body in a tomb (sometimes with very specific instructions about location in relation to other bodies and for the design of the funerary sculpture) and (2) to settle debts and disagreements in this world and engage in final charitable distributions to help to bring about the health of the soul in the afterlife. Thus, to some extent, the way wills and last testaments functioned in the early modern world represents a kind of secularized hangover of purgatorial thinking.

15. Maggie Vinter sees the play as staging an inverted form of the "the good death," in which the community gathers around the dying person and reaffirms shared values. Maggie Vinter, "'This Is Called Mortifying of a Fox': Volpone and How to Get Rich Quick by Dying Slowly," *Shakespeare Quarterly* 65, no. 2 (Summer 2014): 140–63, expanded in *Last Acts: The Art of Dying on the Early Modern Stage* (New York: Fordham University Press, 2019).

16. All quotations from *Volpone* are taken from Robert Watson's edition (New York: Methuen, 2014).

17. Nonetheless, by discursively articulating a distinction between the form and the substance, Thomist theory does open the door to a dualism whose very possibility was initially recognized as a challenge to Christian orthodoxy. Indeed, as I have noted before, Thomist teaching on resurrection was initially condemned by the Catholic Church precisely for being excessively dualist before being ruled orthodox at the fifth Lateran council in 1512–1517. But the conceptual wedge between soul and body to which Thomist discourse opened the door ultimately represents a powerful impulse in a dualist direction.

18. This transformation of a set of religious ideas about resurrection into a secularized understanding of the essence of the person as the legally entitled wealth that will live on after the person has died is at least suggested by the way the words "wealth" and "substance" track each other in a Google ngram search. The words are noncorrelated, with the use of the word "substance" peaking in the early 1650s, probably reflecting debates within the nascent scientific community about the fundamental nature of matter, but starting in the 1650s the words "wealth" and "substance" start to track each other more and more closely until they appear with virtually identical frequency from 1750 onward.

19. To emphasize that dualism is the object of their derision, Jonson gives Nano and Androgyno a poetic performance (written by Mosca) that is a mock-Pythagorean progress of the soul through various human and animal bodies, ending in that "very strange beast," the Puritan, described here as "a precise, pure, illuminate brother." As I suggested in my Introduction, in the context of England, the Puritans are very much the source of the most fully developed dualism, especially in consideration of the afterlife, so that a mock performance that derives from classical body/soul dualism ends by landing, so to speak, on the source of contemporary Christian body/soul dualism.

20. A similar account of sex as an effort to make the other into a body as contextualized in Christian theology about the body is offered in Adam G. Cooper, *Life in the Flesh: An Anti-Gnostic Spiritual Philosophy* (New York: Oxford University Press, 2008), esp. chap. 7, "Mind and Body." Cooper also refers to Roger Scruton's interest in limit experiences that foreground the corporeality of the body, as "In smiling, blushing, laughing and crying, it is precisely my loss of control over my body, and its gain of control over me, that create the immediate experience of an incarnate person. The body ceases, at these moments, to be an *instrument*, and reasserts its natural rights as a person. In such expressions the face does not function merely as a bodily part, but as the whole person: the self is spread across its surface, and there 'made flesh.'" Roger Scruton, *Sexual Desire: A Philosophical Investigation* (New York: Continuum, 2006), 70.

21. Somewhat paradoxically, Celia is on the side of Volpone in the attack on legal personhood; she affirms her embodiment and especially her view of sex as a noncommodifiable experience of the body. She asks, "Is that [i.e., sex], which ever was a cause of life, / Now placed beneath the basest circumstance, / And modesty an exile made, for money?" That is the same point that Volpone is making, even if in a somewhat different key. Celia frames sex as the (reproductive) cause of life—which it doesn't seem to be in the case of her relationship with Corvino, given his announced preference for pleasures that are "backward." But the claim that sex is associated with life is also the claim that sex is essentially by and for the body and therefore should not be reduced to a commodity with a price.

22. Michael O'Connell, *The Idolatrous Eye: Iconoclasm and Theater in Early Modern England* (New York: Oxford University Press, 2000), 9.

23. See Brandon S. Centerwall, "'Tell Me Who Can When a Player Dies': Ben Jonson's Epigram on Richard Burbage and How It Was Lost to the Canon," *Ben Jonson Journal* 4 (1997): 27–34.

24. In some sense this celebration of state power is aligned with his interest in an emerging critical sphere. Rather than buying into the liberal Habermasian idea that the public sphere is external to the state and capable of criticizing it from the outside, Jonson's play may reveal that the critical public sphere is in fact a product of state power. And it is perhaps true to say that encountering the sheer fact of the body (decommissioned from its social identity as a magnifico) has a certain critical-deconstructive force.

25. One example is Donald E. Pease, "From the Camp to the Commons: Biopolitical Alter-Geographies in Douglass and Melville," *Arizona Quarterly* 72, no. 3 (Autumn 2016): 1–23. As Pease writes, "I intend the phrase 'from the Camp to the Commons' to index the emergence of the Commons as a transformative biopolitical geography" (7). To some extent I would now include my own *Shakespeare's Anti-Politics* as engaging in this kind of deconstructive politics centered on the bodily life of those most radically exposed to sovereign power. For a fuller discussion of the political implications of sovereigntycentric approaches, see my "Sovereignty, Communitarianism, and the Shakespeare Option," *SEL* 58, no. 1 (Winter 2018): 77–94.

Epilogue: Resurrection and Zombies

1. Unless otherwise noted, quotations are taken from the documentary *Birth of the Living Dead*, dir. Rob Kuhns (First Run Features, 2013).

2. "Romero: Master of the Macabre," *Eye for Film*, https://www.eyeforfilm.co.uk /feature/2015-07-08-george-a-romero-talks-zombies-religion-and-genocide -in-karlovy-vary-feature-story-by-richard-mowe.

3. The French TV series was remade into the American series *The Returned*, which appeared on A&E in 2014. Around the same time, the American author Jason Mott explored the same idea but on a global scale in his novel *The Returned*, which was itself made into a 2014 ABC TV series entitled *Resurrection*.

4. See Christopher M. Moreman, "Dharma of the Living Dead: A Meditation on the Meaning of the Hollywood Zombie," *Studies in Religion/Sciences Religieuses* 39, no. 2 (2010): 263–81. See also Elizabeth McAlister, "Slaves, Cannibals, and Infected Hyper-Whites: The Race and Religion of Zombies," *Anthropological Quarterly* 85, no. 2 (2012): 457–86, which argues that the explosion of zombies in contemporary culture represents an effort to come to terms with increasing cross-cultural contact under conditions of globalized modernity. McAlister traces the origin of the "zombie" in Haitian folklore and sees it as a way of thematizing colonial domination and enslavement, and she therefore argues that race is and remains central to the cultural insecurities that zombies activate. See also Thomas Kette, "Haitian Zombie, Myth, and Modern Identity," *Comparative Literature and Culture* 12, no. 2 (2010): 12–30, which frames the zombie as a challenge to the notion that humans have an invulnerable, continuous, self-possessed subjectivity and places this argument in the context of its origin in a "third world" that tries to resist being objectified by Western knowledge production.

5. Similarly, other critics have connected the zombie to psychoanalytic notions of the self as riven by forces that cannot be contained by subjectivity, including the death drive. As Cohen puts it, zombies are "difference made flesh," and they are therefore "excluded from personhood and agency as in every way different, monstrous." Jeffrey Jerome Cohen, "Monster Culture: Seven Theses," in *Monster Theory: Reading Culture* (Minneapolis: University of Minnesota Press, 1996). See also the influential essays collected in Sarah Juliet Embro, ed., *Zombie Theory: A Reader* (Minneapolis: University of Minnesota Press, 2017).

6. This tendency is thematized in the "returned" subgenre insofar as the ability of the undead to "pass" as living leads characters to wonder whether, unbeknownst to themselves, they too are "returned," and some characters find precisely that this is true.

7. S. Lauro and K. Embry, "A Zombie Manifesto: The Nonhuman Condition in the Era of Advanced Capitalism," *Boundary* 2 35, no. 1: 85–108, 90. This essay is reprinted in Embro, ed., *Zombie Theory*.

8. Sometimes the staginess and fakeness of the work flips, as it were, into hyperrealism, especially of the gore of the film, as with Romero's bemused account of how one of the nonprofessional actors in the film, Ross Harris, who was a meatpacker, brought cow intestines and livers to the shoot to represent the humans that the zombies feast on. What the hyperrealism in the gore and the hypertheatricality of the acting have in common is a certain vitiation of a simple mimetic/realistic aesthetic in which art feigns reality.

9. Vincent Canby, "Night of the Living Dead," *New York Times*, December 5, 1968.

10. For a somewhat unsympathetic survey of the topos of the "return of the repressed" in the criticism and commentary on zombies, see James McFarland, "Philosophy of the Living Dead: At the Origin of the Zombie-Image," *Cultural Critique* 90 (2015): 22–63.

Index

Perkins, William, 8
Persius, 164
personhood: and "buffered self," viii, 4, 10, 22, 40–41, 48, 54, 99, 102, 125, 148, 166; corporate, 179; as legally entitled wealth, 149–150, 165–166; and state power, 178–179
Petrarchan tradition, 55, 88–89, 196n13
Pettet, E. C., 209n6, 213n15
phenomenology, of emotions, ix, 23, 98–100, 124–127, 133–136
pietism, 93
Pliny, 160, 164
poetic language, 12–13, 57–63, 75, 81, 84–85; in Jonathan Culler, 206n17; in Donne 57–61, 204n41; in Herbert, 89–91; as hieroglyphs, 123; in Jonson, 26, 152–166; and poetic function, 119–120; in Susan Stewart, 118–119; in Vaughan,101–102, 114–116, 122–123
poetry: and courtliness, 75–81, 86–90; doing the work of resurrection, 11, 26, 152, 165–166; and emotions, 93–100; as "happening," 15–16, 63, 89–90, 92; and language community, 60, 74, 204n41; as therapy, 99. *See also* avant-garde; poetic language
Poggioli, Renato, 13, 86, 199n32, 206n19
Polanyi, Karl, 214n11
Poole, Joshua, 91, 207n29
Porphyry, 5
Post, Jonathan F. S., 210n15, 212n9
post-secularity, 194n10, 194n1
pregnancy, as metaphor for resurrection body, 11–13, 73, 107, 187
Preston, Claire, 197n20
Proust, Marcel, 206n20
public sphere, 16, 155, 202n11, 217n24
purgatory, 6–7, 215n14
puritanism, 8, 102, 174, 197n17, 216n19
Pythagoras, on transmigration, 216n19

race: inscribed on the body, 3, 11, 187; and zombies, 217n4
Rambuss, Richard, 210n13
Ray, Robert H., 207n30
Read, Sophie, 211n3
Reformation: and dualism, 4–10; magisterial vs radical, 8–10, 197n18; and secular politics, 16; and soul sleep, 7–8
Reiss, Timothy J., 215n12
resurrection body, ix, 2, 12, 23–24, 29, 34, 100, 101–102, 107, 109, 112–113, 124, 135–139, 143, 209n12

Returned, The, 217n3
Revenants, Les, 184–185
Reynolds, Brian, 195n7
Riggs, David, 214n1
Robinson, Timothy H., 208n34
Romanticism, 24, 101, 104
Romero, George, 20, 183–184
Rosenzweig, Franz, x
Roy, Olivier, 18, 199n35, 200n41
Rudrum, A. W., 209n6, 210n14, 213n15
Russian formalism, 14, 58, 199n32, 204nn39,40

saints, veneration of, 60
Sanchez, Melissa E., 204n32
Santner, Eric L., x, 194n8
Saunders, Ben, 204n34
Scarry, Elaine, 57–58
Scherer, Judith, 57, 204n37
Schmitt, Carl, 178
Schoenfeldt, Michael, 80, 94, 125, 203n24, 205n3, 208nn36,38, 211n2
scholasticism: substance in, 169, 216n17; theory of resurrection in, 6
Schwartz, Regina, 202n15
science, vii–ix, 4–5, 9–10, 16, 21–22, 38–39, 41, 44–45, 129, 139, 193n5, 197n20, 198n21, 202n18
Scodel, Joshua, 214n8
Scrutton, Roger, 216n20
secularization: applicability to early modern culture, 30–34, 195n6; and avant-garde art, 13, 206n20; and "comparative religions," 31–34; dialectic of, 17–19, 200n37; and dualism, 9–10; as intrinsic to Christianity, 199n36; and optionality, 31–32; and September 11, 199n35; subtraction theories of, 193n1; theory of, vii, 16–19, 86–91, 195n6
seeds, discourse of, ix, 11–12, 24, 44–46, 106–108, 124, 126, 135–136, 143. *See also* Paul
self-consuming artifact, 114
Selleck, Nancy Gail, 42, 203n24
Seneca, 164
sexuality, 3, 22, 25, 44, 125, 145–147; and Augustine, 213n20; in Donne, 48–57; as effort to make person into body, 171, 216n20; and transcendence of self, 146–147; in *Volpone,* 171–173. *See also* masochism
Shakespeare, 19, 200n44; *King Lear,* 213n18; *Sonnets,* 206n7; *The Tempest,* 88, 174

Daniel Juan Gil is the author of *Shakespeare's Anti-Politics: Sovereign Power and the Life of the Flesh* (Palgrave, 2013), *Before Intimacy: Asocial Sexuality in Early Modern England* (Minnesota, 2006), and many articles on topics including sexuality, the body, sovereign power, communitarianism, literary autonomy, and the sociology of religion. His work has appeared in *Shakespeare Quarterly, Common Knowledge, ELH, SEL, Borrowers and Lenders, Literature and Theology*, and a variety of edited collections.

Lightning Source UK Ltd.
Milton Keynes UK
UKHW010810101120
373129UK00007B/296